SHORT
SUNDERLAND

SUNDERLAND

SHORT SUNDERLAND

THE 'FLYING PORCUPINES' IN THE SECOND WORLD WAR

BY
ANDREW HENDRIE

Pen & Sword
AVIATION

First published in Great Britain in 1994 by
Airlife Publishing Ltd.

Reprinted in this format in 2012 by
PEN & SWORD AVIATION
An imprint of
Pen & Sword Books Ltd
47 Church Street
Barnsley
South Yorkshire
S70 2AS

ISBN 978 1 84884 779 8

Printed and bound in England
By CPI Group (UK) Ltd, Croydon, CR0 4YY

Pen & Sword Books Ltd incorporates the Imprints of Pen & Sword Aviation,
Pen & Sword Family History, Pen & Sword Maritime, Pen & Sword Military,
Pen & Sword Discovery, Wharncliffe Local History, Wharncliffe True Crime,
Wharncliffe Transport, Pen & Sword Select, Pen & Sword Military Classics,
Leo Cooper, The Praetorian Press, Remember When,
Seaforth Publishing and Frontline Publishing

For a complete list of Pen & Sword titles please contact
PEN & SWORD BOOKS LIMITED
47 Church Street, Barnsley, South Yorkshire, S70 2AS, England
E-mail: enquiries@pen-and-sword.co.uk
Website: www.pen-and-sword.co.uk

Contents

For this edition, I would like to extend my thanks to the following individuals: Martin Mace, John Grehan and Sara Mitchell for their assistance in preparing the manuscript; John Evans and David Pring of The Pembroke Dock Sunderland Trust for their help in sourcing many of the images. Following Andrew's death in 2004, his collection of Sunderland photographs was presented to the Trust's archive. For more information on this organisation, visit: www.sunderlandtrust.org.uk

Evelyn Hendrie, Storrington, 2011.

Introduction

In 1933 the Air Ministry gave a specification for a general purpose, four-engined flying boat able to operate from the outposts of the Empire. Such was achieved by Short Bros with the Sunderland designed and built parallel with the Empire flying boat.

At the outbreak of war in 1939, four RAF squadrons were equipped with Sunderlands, one in the Far East, one at Malta, and two in the United Kingdom. These were the only long endurance aircraft available to Coastal Command. Their initial task was long range reconnaissance against possible breakout of German naval forces. Disadvantages for aircrews with early Sunderlands were a limited armament of seven ·303-inch guns, overstretched engines and non-feathering propellers.

During the Norwegian campaign, Sunderlands co-operated with both Naval and Army forces, taking commanders such as General Carton de Wiart, VC. At the time of the *Bismarck* breakout, a Sunderland co-operated with the shadowing cruisers HMS *Norfolk* and *Suffolk*.

In 1939 the Sunderland squadron at Malta was promptly recalled to the United Kingdom, and following the collapse of France and the hostility of Italy, No. 230 Sqdn was withdrawn from the Far East to operate in the Eastern Mediterranean with No. 228 Sqdn. Over the eastern Mediterranean, the Sunderlands became Admiral Cunningham's 'cruisers' exemplified by the vital sighting and shadowing prior to the battle of Cape Matapan. Despite hostile fighters, they made a number of attacks on enemy submarines.

During the evacuation of Greece, Crete and Yugoslavia, Sunderlands transported many from Princes and Princesses to – a parrot. The largest number of passengers recorded for a single aircraft being seventy-two.

The transport of VIPs is acknowledged in some autobiographies by such as the Rt. Hon. Anthony Eden who flew Sunderland when the weather was too rough for a destroyer.

The rescue of the whole crew of the ss *Kensington Court* by Sunderlands gained much publicity, but many open sea rescues were to follow.

Post-war, Sunderlands, with their crews, proved their adaptability in what became known as the 'Berlin Airlift', transporting supplies into Berlin and flying out both people and goods. For the Greenland Expeditions in the early fifties, Sunderlands gave support as far as Britannia Lake.

'The Battle of the Atlantic was the dominating factor all through the war' wrote Winston Churchill; it was in that battle the Sunderland may be best remembered. The collapse of France provided Biscay ports for U-boats and bases for enemy fighters. 'The Bay' became 'Tiger Country' for lone Sunderland crews to battle against the cannon on both U-boats and enemy fighters which always out-ranged them. By June 1944, some Sunderlands were armed with 18 guns, justifying the term 'Flying Porcupine', but the odds against them over the Bay remained no less high.

In this project I have endeavoured to cover all successful attacks on German and Italian submarines involving Sunderlands, but am aware that some may appear controversial. For these, I've referred to operational records, official published lists, and have gained advice from aircrew who were directly concerned. Such attacks appear in the text and are listed in the appendices. Representative air-to-air combats appear in the text.

Andrew Hendrie
Storrington

Chapter 1
The Machine

SHORT BROS became interested in heavier-than-air flying machines in 1908 and, following contact with the Wright Bros, were by 1909 manufacturing biplanes on the Isle of Sheppey. In 1912 Shorts built their first monoplane, influenced by Blériot's design.

In 1913, Shorts moved their factory from Eastchurch, Isle of Sheppey to Rochester on the River Medway which provided sheltered water for their first seaplanes.

From 1918, Shorts were building Felixstowe F3 and F5 flying boats under licence, and in 1921 constructed of wood the 'Cromarty' flying boat, a biplane but with a wingspan about the same as a Sunderland.

Their first all-metal hull flying boat was produced in 1924, their own version of the F5 with a stressed skin duralumin hull which first flew in January 1925.

Between 1926 and 1937 further designs were the civil flying boats 'Calcutta' – and 'Kent' with a military version of the 'Calcutta' – the 'Rangoon' – also the military 'Singapore' Marks I, II and III. A six-engined variation of the Singapore II was the 'Sarafand' which did not go into general service.

Of flying boats produced by Shorts, the 'Singapore' III served as the predecessor of the Sunderland at the outbreak of WW2.

The Air Ministry's specification R2/33 in 1933 was for a long range, general purpose flying boat, either biplane or monoplane, powered by four engines. While considering a tender for the R2/33, Shorts received an order from Imperial Airways for two aircraft to replace their 'Kent' flying boats resulting from the development of the Empire Air Mail scheme.

Oswald Short with designer Arthur Gouge had already produced a twin-engined high wing monoplane – 'Scion' – followed by four-engined and seaplane versions which served as half-scale models for what followed as the 'Empire' flying boat and the Sunderland.

The first of the Empire flying boats *Canopus*, a four-engined high wing monoplane with a span of 114 ft and wing area 1,500 sq ft with an all up weight 40,500 lb, flew on 3 July 1936.

The Air Ministry had received tenders for the R2/33 specification from both Shorts and Saunders-Roe, and ordered prototypes from those companies allocating serial No.K4774 to Shorts design S.25.

The original Sunderland design allowed for a 37 mm cannon in the nose and a single ·303-inch gun FN11 turret in the tail. This was changed to a single ·303-in FN11 nose turret and a four ·303-in gun FN13 tail turret. There were two open single gun dorsal positions, thus initially, a total of seven ·303-in machine-guns. The shift in the centre of gravity which resulted, was compensated for by a 4¼ degree sweep back of the wings and modifications to the hull with a move back and change of depth to the main step.

The first flight of the prototype K4774 then fitted with 950 horsepower Bristol Pegasus X engines and with unswept wings, was made on 16 October 1937. It was tested again on 7 March 1938 after the wings had been swept back and Pegasus XXII 1010 hp engines had been installed.

Sunderland Marks
The first batch of eleven Mark I Sunderlands with serial numbers L2158 to L2168 produced at Rochester were fitted with three-bladed DH Hamilton propellers. The propellers were non-feathering with only coarse and fine pitch

A Short Singapore at Calshot c. 1940 used on the flying boat course.

and r.p.m. controlled by the throttle. By June 1938 they were being flown by 210 Sqdn and 230 Sqdn.

In Mark II Sunderlands Pegasus XVIIIs with two-speed superchargers replaced Pegasus XXII engines and with DH rack type constant speed propellers but still with no feathering facility. A FN7 2-gun turret replaced the two open gun positions and a FN4a 4-gun turret succeeded the FN13 in the tail but with 1000 rounds per gun instead of 500.

The Mark IIs were being equipped with ASV having Yagi aerials under the wings and dipoles on the hull. Short & Harland at Belfast came to producing Mark IIs as also Blackburns at Dumbarton.

A converted Mark I became the Mark III first flown on 28 June 1941. It differed from the Mark II by a faired main step which reduced aerodynamic drag by about 10% but the hull was prone to porpoising on the water. With a de Havilland constant speed propeller, there was still no fully-feathering facility. With the Mark III, the maximum take-off weight was increased to 58,000 lb.

The Short S.45 Sunderland Mark IV with four Bristol Hercules 130 engines was built of heavier gauge metal permitting an all up weight of 75,000 lb. It had four-bladed propellers which were fully feathering, the wing span remained the same but the length of the hull was increased by 39 inches. The tailplane area was increased by 20% and was with a 5° dihedral. In the Seaford, as it came to be named, a 33-inch higher tail fin was given a dorsal fairing. Of the two prototypes, MZ269 and MZ271, MZ269 first flew on 30 August 1944. Only eight (NJ200–NJ207) of the initial production order for 30 were delivered. In 1946 they were allocated to No. 201 Sqdn but with NJ201 to Transport Command. They were later converted to a civil version – the Solent.

It was a suggestion from No. 10 Sqdn RAAF at Mount Batten that Pratt & Whitney Twin Wasp engines should replace Bristol engines on the Sunderland. ML839 was so converted at No. 10's base in May 1944. This initiative resulted in the Mark V Sunderland with P&W Twin Wasp R1830 engines of 1,200 hp being built at Rochester and Belfast and with further conversions from Mark IIIs to Mark Vs at Dumbarton.

Capt Vic Hodgkinson was one of the original Sunderland pilots with No. 10 Sqdn RAAF in 1939; he later served in the South Pacific on Catalinas. My thanks are due to him for the following notes on Sunderlands:

'Flying boats were similar to their landplane counterparts when airborne. It was contact with the water which introduced radical differences and similar to a sailing boat when once the mooring was slipped. The only way one could proceed was forwards with no means of stopping, reversing and limited control over direction which was by the combination of rudder, ailerons and engines. The tendency was to weathercock into wind. Added to these were the variations of wind, currents, the surface of the water from a glassy calm to a swell, restricted

The mid-gunners' position in a Sunderland Mk 1 looking forward.

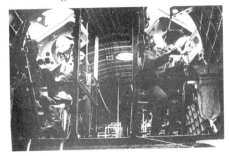

operating areas, (contrary to general belief), in the form of shallows, channels, obstacles (other marine craft stationary and moving), buoys, markers, debris etc. Night operations posed further problems of short flarepaths, barrage balloons, unlit shipping and of course, hills etc on approach and landing.

Flying boats had their individual peculiarities. The Catalina was more difficult to turn and taxy downwind as the engines were close inboard; the Sunderland with the outers farther outboard, gave greater purchase. The Catalina hull lay lower in the water and was prone to spray covering the windscreen – from the bow wave and being whipped up by the props. The Sunderland with its higher profile hull was considerably more free of spray over this area and seldom shipped water over the bow although occasionally it was whipped up by the inners in a rough sea.

'Operation from the Pilot's point of view. On approaching the aircraft at moorings it was prudent to observe the position and lay of the aircraft relative to the current, wind and surrounding obstacles, both moving and stationary and consider the path to be taken on slipping the moorings.

The aircraft would have been placed on short slip by the rigger, all drogues stowed, pitot head cover off, hatches closed – except for the retractable nose turret (open to allow the rigger to attend to moorings), and watertight doors between cabins in the closed positions.

'On the flight deck the flying control-lock would be removed, stowed and the flying controls checked for movement. Throttle, mixture and pitch control exactors were primed and set and main fuel/oil hydraulic flight-deck cocks moved forward to ON. The first course was set on both compasses (P4, P8) and altimeters set to zero and not reset throughout the flight as base weather and altimeter settings were not transmitted to the aircraft. If weather deteriorated at base then the aircraft was recalled or diverted. If no signal was received, it was assumed that weather at base was above limits.

'In reasonable conditions the flying controls would be set to bring the mooring buoy to port side, in view of the skipper, to keep it in view during start-up and slipping. This was to prevent the aircraft overriding the buoy causing damage to the hull.

'The order to start engines was given to the flight engineer who would prime engines, normally outers followed by inners, beginning with the port outer. With engines running at 'Idle' sufficient to ease the strain on the short slip, the rigger was signalled to slip moorings. He would stow the bollard, close the bow turret and secure it. At night he would remain in the bow with the Aldis lamp sweeping ahead to ensure it was clear of obstructions, until instructed to close the turret. The inners were started after the buoy was passed to prevent the port prop fouling the buoy.

'The APU was located between the starboard inner and the hull aft of the leading edge and not accessible in flight. In addition to generating 24 volts it could serve to bilge the hull and floats and pump fuel, although refuelling barges at RAF bases carried their own pumps.

'For taxying, the outer engines were normally used for controlling direction in conjunction with rudder and ailerons.

The engineer's position in a Mk 1 Sunderland.

The bow turret position in a Mk IB Sunderland of No. 40 Sqdn RAAF.

'On approaching the selected take-off position the engines were run-up and ignition checked for mag. drop (100 r.p.m. max) and pitch control moved from 'fine' to 'coarse' and back to 'fine' to exercise the prop system.

'If a mag. drop was greater than 100 r.p.m. then selecting 'Lean' on the mixture control and running the engine at take-off r.p.m. for a couple of minutes might clear oiled plugs.

'With the aircraft into wind, the flaps were run out one-third, elevator to 2° nose up, Rich mixture set, and with the flight engineer's checks confirmed, the ailerons were set to raise the downwind float out of the water as soon as aileron control became effective – to reduce drag by that float, which might cause the aircraft to turn in that direction. Control column fully back – to assist the hull onto the step and also to assist the bow wave to move back past the inboard props – so that the inners could

be opened at the earliest opportunity. The rudder was set in conjunction with the downwind outer engine to control the direction of take-off. The engines were opened up with the up-wind engine throttle leading and the downwind engine being advanced in co-ordination with the rudder to maintain sufficient directional control. Much like trimming the sails of a boat to give optimum control with the rudder.

'The throttle lever on the downwind engine could be anywhere between Idle and near Full power, depending on the strength of the cross-wind. It was desirable to wait until the bow wave had passed the inboard props before opening them up to prevent damage to the props. As speed increased and so greater control by the rudder, the downwind throttle was gradually opened up to full power. During this time the aircraft should be rising onto the step and the elevators progressively eased to the centre to maintain a slightly nose up attitude. Nose down could result in loss of directional control ending up with a water loop. This could also happen on landing if the nose were allowed to plough in.

'Another problem was "porpoising" when the aircraft would "rock" in the fore and aft plane. It could be caused by an excessive C. of G. aft and/or the state of the sea. In these circumstances, if it

Looking towards the tail turret in a Mk I Sunderland.

The wireless operator's position equipped with a Marconi transmitter and receiver (TR1154/1155).

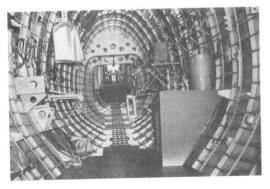

was not corrected immediately, these gyrations would increase with the aircraft diving into the sea. The procedure for correcting this was to ease the control column back and hold it there until the porpoising ceased and then allow the control to return to attain the original planing position. In severe porpoising it was necessary to hold the column hard back to correct it. If the porpoising continued and didn't reduce then it was a case of throttling back and starting again.

'At around 90 knots one would expect the aircraft to become "unstuck" but this varied according to weight, state of the sea, temperature, wind direction and the handling by the pilot. Glassy calm or swell conditions were the worst. In glassy conditions the drag and suction on the planing surface was considerable and in swell conditions one could be thrown into the air well below take-off speed to thump back onto the water and have this repeated several times – if one survived.

'In these circumstances, if one had reasonable flying control, it was essential to ensure on each touchdown that the aircraft was level laterally in the landing attitude, anticipating each arrival at the surface and, if possible, prevent it repeating the process by holding it onto the water. Lobbing into a trough meant slamming into the next wave – and curtains!'

'After "unsticking" the aircraft was levelled out to gain climb speed and at 200 ft the flaps were retracted and climb power set. At cruising altitude around 1000 ft, the power was reduced to a maximum of 0 lb/sq in. and 2,250 r.p.m., 120 knots I.A.S. and as fuel was used, the r.p.m. reduced to maintain that speed (on Marks I–III).

'On approaching the alighting area for landing, the exactors were primed, mixture control to "Rich", 2300 r.p.m., flaps one-third and speed reduced to 115 knots. On final approach in daylight, 2/3rds to full flap and glide the aircraft at 100 knots. At night a power-assisted final approach and landing was made. Glassy calm-day conditions when the surface was difficult to judge, required night procedure. The aircraft would touch down at 75 knots approx., the aim being to touch down on the step with the nose slightly up. Nose too far down could induce a waterloop, and too far up in a rough sea would cause the aircraft to become airborne if a large wave was encountered. As speed reduced, the control column was gradually eased back until it was fully back as the hull came off the step. At this point the outers were opened up to prevent water from the step damaging the elevators.

'After the landing run, flaps were retracted, fine pitch on the props, and head for the moorings. An engine test similar to before take-off, was followed before mooring up.

'Variations of wind to tide required modifications to the ideal of wind and tide moving in the same direction on final approach to mooring. In these ideal conditions the inners would be stopped and the props trimmed – one blade up, two down – to give maximum clearance for boats passing under the mainplane and engines. Outers could be trimmed to take the way off the aircraft and flaps could be lowered to provide further drag and with the drogues streamed. The rigger would have retracted the nose turret and secured the retractable bollard before climbing a ladder with the free end of the short slip to pass through the harness of the buoy, catch it as it passed through, climb the ladder and secure it round the bollard. He would then have signalled the skipper, making sure he wasn't trapped between the short slip rope and the bow.

'Outers were stopped, props trimmed, flaps retracted, drogues recovered, controls locked, and switches off etc. Rudder and ailerons were locked in neutral position but with the elevator down when moored to reduce pitching in a rough sea, although on land the elevators were locked in neutral.

The galley in a Sunderland with (apparently) eggs and beans being cooked.

Racks from the bomb bay loaded with 250lb bombs; they could be wound out electrically or manually.

Landing lights were never used for landing as under glassy conditions the surface would not be seen and could be struck in a nose down position. They were seldom used for take-off.

'Meals were prepared by one of the crew on a double Primus stove in the galley amidships. They were substantial and well-presented in the circumstances. The flight deck crew were served in the wardroom and other crew members in the cabin aft of the bomb bay. Tables were laid with cloth and accessories all "borrowed" "for the duration".

'Navigation. It was mostly DR navigation using a drift recorder and three course winds. In daytime, sea markers were dropped and the drift taken by the tail gunner who would line up his sight on the marker (a flame float at night), and read from a scale on the turret giving the degree of drift to port or starboard. In the early 1940s marine sextants were issued but were not suitable for air navigation. The early ASV, although unreliable, did give an indication of distance from land. Later in the war, the Mark 9 (bubble) sextant improved navigation – when heavenly bodies were visible.

'After 12 hours over the Atlantic or around the Bay, day and night in all conditions, constantly altering course to conform to pre-arranged search patterns, the navigator's ultimate problem was to make a reasonable landfall. With blackout in force, at night

one was searching for the three float-supported paraffin flares which made up the flare path. Communication was by Aldis lamp – Green to land, Red – not to land. At Plymouth in particular, one had to contend with a crowded harbour of unlit shipping, barrage balloons short-hauled at 100 ft. Complete confidence in the Flarepath officer, (one of the pilots), and the local knowledge of the marine craft crews was essential.

'Sunderland Features. The obsolescent Pegasus engine, considering its age and being "stretched" from around 600 hp in the 1930s to 1050 hp prior to the war, was "fairly" reliable but took a thrashing in some military aircraft. Its major weakness was that the valves were not lubricated, i.e. ran dry, sometimes seizing, sometimes breaking off and dropping into the cylinder, with perhaps then, the cylinder parting from its casing. Propellers were also shed as a

The 1st and 2nd pilots' positions in a Mk V Sunderland.

result, but sometimes the shaft broke due to fatigue.

'The exactor system was a primitive hydraulic arrangement with pistons connected to the throttles, mixture and pitch control levers which operated through hydraulic lines on pistons at the engine ends of the relevant controls. They worked reasonably well when new, but with wear, air entered the system with the throttles more prone and it was necessary to continually advance these to maintain boost settings.

'The auto-pilot proved unreliable. It had a nasty habit of shoving the control column fully forward without prior warning. It had a disengagement clutch for such emergencies but the clutch could not be re-engaged in the air. Direction was controlled by a lever – forward to turn right, aft for left, and the aircraft performed flat turns. For more than a few degrees, it was disengaged and the turn made manually.

'Self-sealing fuel lines were of three-ply with the inner and outer surfaces of petrol-resistant material. The layer between would expand in contact with petrol and if a leak developed at joints, would result in fuel supply to the engine being cut off.

'Propeller synchronisation was achieved by selecting an inner as the "master engine" to set the cruise r.p.m. The other inner was then adjusted to minimise "beat". The two outers were

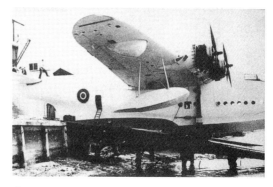

The prototype Mk IV Sunderland which was developed into the Seaford.

then adjusted to stabilise the stroboscopic effect, (in the form of a shadow). This would require fairly constant adjustment for they rarely remained in synchronisation for long. At night the Aldis lamp was used to see the "shadow".

'The flaps were driven electrically and an "In", "Stop", and "Out" selector switch controlled them. A group of lights indicated "Flap one-third out" etc. To the right of these was the position-of-flap indicator. Once in the air, the aircraft was very stable and responsive to controls, which were light to handle, the rudder being the heaviest.

'Floats were the weakest part of the structure. The rigging would not tolerate side loads and once one of the four bracing wires broke another usually followed leaving the float dangling from the two struts. The immediate action was to turn the aircraft to bring the damaged float side up-wind and to deploy crew on the opposite wing.

'*Bomb Load.* In the early part of the war the load was four Naval 450 lb depth charges. They were attached to the bomb trolleys located in the bomb bay and run out under the mainplane when airborne and retracted for landing. Doors on the sides of the hull needed to be first lowered and closed after the load had been run out or retracted. Later, 250 lb A/S bombs proved "friendlier" and eight were carried on the racks with two as spares for re-loading. Subsequently,

Sunderland assembly lines at Shorts, Belfast.

A Seaford still with RAF markings and serial No. NJ203 when possibly on the river Medway c. Oct. 1946. It is now in the USA.

eight 250 lb Torpex-filled DCs comprised the load. Later also, a release lever next to the captain was fitted. This released the bomb doors and triggered a switch to run out the DCs. This allowed the load to be kept within the hull until the target was to be attacked, thus reduced drag in flight. The port bomb door was a large removable cut-out which could be unbolted to enable such as spare engines to be slung into the bomb compartment.'

A Sunderland with fuel tanks removed from within the wings.

Chapter 2
Prelude to War – *Early Sunderland Deliveries*

O N 16 MAY 1938 two crews with four pilots from 210 Sqdn then based at Pembroke Dock were on detachment to Felixstowe for Sunderland experience. Four days later, 210's CO – W/Cmdr W.N. Plenderleith, with F/Lt Hughes, flew L2159 from Felixstowe to Pembroke Dock in connection with Empire Air Day scheduled for 28 May

L2159 was captained by F/Lt Hughes on 9 June when he flew to Gibraltar en route for Singapore. This delivery flight intended for 230 Sqdn was via Malta, Alexandria, Habbaniya, Bahrein, Karachi, Gwalior, Calcutta, Rangoon, and Mergui to Seletar where Hughes arrived on 22 June.

Meanwhile L2160 and L2161 were received by 210 Sqdn and they, captained by F/Lts Watts-Reade and Ainslie, were ferried out to 230 Sqdn arriving at Seletar in July.

On 24 June all 210's Singapore flying boats were due for major inspections and the next two Sunderlands from Shorts at Rochester – L2161 and L2163, were allotted to 210 Sqdn and in July, flown to Invergordon for the Navy's Home Fleet exercises. In August, 210 Sqdn took delivery of three more Sunderlands to go on to the squadron's strength – L2165, L2167 and L2168 and by September some pilots were attempting night landings. On 20 September L2162 captained by S/Ldr Watts-Reade, broke up on touch-down at Pembroke Dock and two of the crew were lost with others severely injured.

At Seletar, 230 Sqdn had by then received two more Sunderlands flown out by 209 Sqdn crews – L2164 and L2166 and during September, 230's Sunderlands were employed on close convoy patrol to HMS *Medway*, *Diana*, and *Westcott*.

In the second half of September 1938 the German-Czechoslovak crisis resulted in an emergency being declared: 230 Sqdn stopped training exercises and 210 Sqdn personnel were recalled from leave for the unit to move to Newport, its war station. At Newport the Sunderlands were prepared for war and practice was carried out with turrets and guns.

In the Far East, christening ceremonies were arranged for three of 230's Sunderlands beginning on 30 September with L2166 named *Perak* by the Sultan of Perak. This was followed in October by L2160 and L2164 respectively dubbed *Selangor* and *Pehang* by the Sultans of those States.

A long-distance record attempt by three RAF Wellesley aircraft from Ismalia to Australia in November was given security cover by 230's L2160 operating from Kuching and captained by F/Lt D.C. Oliver.

On 15 November W/Cmdr G.M. Bryer arrived at Seletar with Sunderland L5801 to assume command of 230 Sqdn. He was later present at Port Dickson when L2161 was christened *Negri-Sembilan*

A Colonial Development Cruise was flown by three Sunderlands from 230 Sqdn in December covering Trincomalee, Colombo and Galle as potential bases. On 12 December a search was made for an Italian cruiser reported heading for Singapore with one of the search aircraft being L2160. A true prelude to war as that same aircraft was tracking Italian cruisers in the eastern Mediterranean on 12 October 1940 when the *Artigliere* was sunk.[1]

While on the search for the Italian cruiser, L2160 suffered seizure of its port outer engine, the propeller sheared off and touched the port inner which also was lost. Captained by W/Cmdr Bryer with F/Lt Alington, course was set for the Nicobar islands but a touch-down was made at

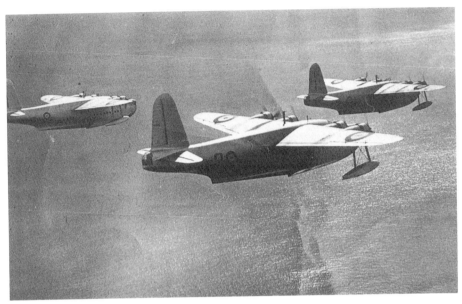

A Flight of 228 Sqdn Sunderlands including L5806 off the Sussex coast 1939.

Sunderland H/210 at Woodhaven on the River Tay, Scotland 2.10.38.

A 230 Sqdn Sunderland over Seletar 21.3.39. 230 Sqdn was recalled to the U.K. on the outbreak of war.

Nancowry. S/Ldr Francis in L5801 landed there to assist, returning later to Seletar. Until the arrival of the Mark Vs in later years, with the P&W Wasp engines, seizure of engines and loss of props was to be a recurring hazard for Sunderland crews.

In the United Kingdom, 210 Sqdn was equally active at the end of 1938. A trip was made to Lerwick to consider it as a possible base, but ultimately Sullom Voe was selected for flying boats in the Shetlands. By December 1938, nineteen of 210's pilots had converted to Sunderlands for day flying, and twelve for night flying.

Of the eight Sunderlands despatched to 230 Sqdn at Seletar, four were flown by 210 Sqdn pilots. On 22 December, with the arrival of L5804 ferried by F/O Newman,

230 Sqdn was considered completely re-equipped with eight Sunderlands. No. 210 Sqdn had been allotted at least six Sunderlands and the unit's Singapore flying boats were delivered to Nos 209 and 240 Sqdns.

Number 228 Sqdn based at Pembroke Dock was informed on 20 November that it would be re-equipped with Sunderlands to replace its Stranraer flying boats. The first was collected from Shorts the following day – L5805 and on 10 December, S/Ldr Paddon took delivery of L5806. Three pilots who had just completed a conversion course at Calshot – P/Os McKinley, Ellsworth and Farries, were posted to 228 Sqdn on the sixteenth.

In January 1939 No. 228 Sqdn was still re-equipping with Sunderlands and remained based at Pembroke Dock with 210 Sqdn. On 28 March, W/Cmdr Daddo-Langlois, 210's CO, with P/O Skey flew the first Sunderland to Guernsey where new dinghy trials were undertaken in the harbour.

In April a signal was received from No. 16 Group that 202 Sqdn in Malta was to re-equip with Sunderlands from 228 Sqdn which would be re-equipped later. Sunderlands L5807 and N6135 captained by P/Os T.M.W. Smith and David McKinley left Pembroke Dock for Malta. L5807 force-landed at Berre with the port outer seized, but N6135 with McKinley reached Malta.

No. 230 Sqdn at Singapore in 1938. It was during 1938 that 230 Sqdn converted to Sunderlands.

A Flypast at Calshot in honour of either H.M. The King or the French President.

Number 228 Sqdn was warned by 16 Group that the unit was to operate from Alexandria to augment RAF forces in the Near East. On 9 May, 228's ground party with S/Ldr Menzies embarked on HMT *Dumana* at King George V dock, London. That same day, P/Os Skey, Ware, Craven, Bevan-John, Fitzpatrick and Sgt Briggs were posted from 210 to 228 Sqdn.

On 10 May, 228 received a signal from Air Ministry that the unit's strength was to be six aircraft. They were to be based on HMT

L5083 of 210 Sqdn on the slipway at Pembroke Dock.

Dumana and *Pass of Balmaha* under No. 86 Wing, Alexandria the departure date was postponed until 29 May.

There was a further forced-landing with L5806 touching down at Athens and a new engine which it required was flown out by F/O Brooks in L5805. Number 228 Squadron's record for 7 June gives F/Lt Case of 202 Sqdn leaving Alexandria with the C.-in-C. Mediterranean Sir Dudley Pound in Sunderland N6135 for England. Sir Dudley was to become Admiral of the Fleet, First Sea Lord, and Chief of Naval Staff, five days later.[2]

On 16 June 210 Sqdn at Pembroke Dock commenced Sunderland training of personnel from 204 Sqdn. In the Far East, Sunderlands of 230 Sqdn were taking part in exercises with the China Sea Fleet and were involved with setting up D/F stations for use in war. On 5 June L5801 captained by F/O W.W. Campbell crashed in the

Sunderland L2167 of 210 Sqdn at Pembroke Dock. This aircraft was lost over Oslo fjord on 9.4.40 at the time Norway was invaded.

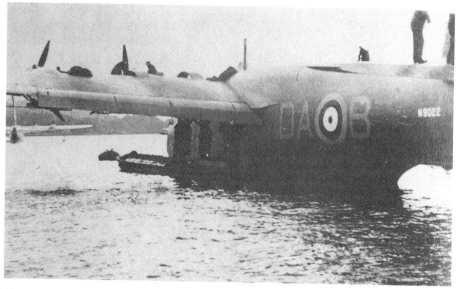

N9022 coded DA-B for 210 Sqdn; it crashed at Oban 27.12.40.

Johore Straits; two of the crew were drowned and a third died in hospital. The aircraft was a write-off and the following month was replaced by N9029 which was camouflaged and had a modified bomb-aimer's hatch.

When Nos 11 and 39 Sqdns were moved from India to reinforce Singapore in August, Sunderlands of 230 Sqdn were deployed to set up W/T stations, give met. reports and act as 'safety boats' to cover the move.

There had been some rivalry between Nos 205 and 230 Sqdns but on 25 August they were officially co-operating on all general reconnaissance tasks and three days later, one aircraft from each (Singapore and Sunderland), were at 60 minutes notice on standby.

On 1 September four Sunderlands from 230 Sqdn searched for HMAS *Sydney* and four destroyers. They were captained by Alan Lywood, 'Pop' Alington, Geoffrey Francis and A/F/Lt Garside. All four pilots later served with distinction in the eastern Mediterranean.

All 228 Sqdn's Sunderlands had been bombed up and refuelled on 27 August and when war was declared on 3 September against Germany, they had eight aircraft serviceable, five at Alexandria and three in Malta.

References
[1] GF p. 214 (Vol IV) & letter from G/Capt G. Francis
[2] SWRI I frontispiece

Chapter 3
Maritime Patrols from the United Kingdom

THE AIR Ministry had directed in 1937 that Coastal Command's prime role in war would be to co-operate with the Royal Navy in protecting trade routes[1] and in April 1941, it officially came under the Admiralty's operational control. Long before that date however, Sunderlands of 228 and 230 Sqdns became 'the eyes of the Fleet' in the eastern Mediterranean.[2]

At the outbreak of war, Biscay ports were still under French control and the extensive Norwegian coastline was 'neutral'. The Admiralty's prime consideration was to counter the breakout of German raiders north-westwards. Two raiders, the pocket battleships *Graf Spee* and *Deutschland* had however, sailed on 21 and 24 August respectively.

Reconnaissance aircraft then available to Coastal Command for covering those northern routes were Sunderlands of 12 hours duration and Hudsons of six hours, but both aircraft with inadequate offensive and defensive armament.

By 1 April 1939 it had been estimated that 194 aircraft would be available for convoy escort and reconnaissance duties although a total of 339 were specified as being required.[3]

Although in the early stages of the war U-boats were not considered such a great threat as surface raiders, anti-submarine operations were to become a major part of the duties for Sunderlands.

The first three squadrons to operate Sunderlands from the United Kingdom in September 1939 were 204, 210 and 228. Number 204 Sqdn was based at Mount Batten and by the following January was equipped with seven aircraft. Number 210 Sqdn based at Pembroke Dock was to have detachments on the river Tay, Cromarty Firth, Loch Ryan and Oban. Number 228 Sqdn was moved from Malta and Aboukir to Pembroke Dock with three aircraft from Malta arriving on 11 September and with most having returned by the twenty-second. Number 228 Sqdn came also to have a detachment on the Cromarty Firth.

A fourth Sunderland squadron in the early part of the war was No. 10 Sqdn RAAF which took delivery of N9048 on 11 September, the intention initially being for Sunderlands to be flown to Australia. Instead, No. 10 Sqdn RAAF remained in the UK operating under Coastal Command control but retaining some Australian freedom of action.

One of the first encounters with the enemy was by No. 210 Sqdn on the ninth when F/Lt Ainslie in L2165, after leaving a convoy which included *Empress of Australia* attacked a U-boat which had just submerged.

In the second half of September, four of the pilots from No. 10 Sqdn – Charles Pearce, 'Dick' Cohen, Ivan Podger and Hugh Birch – were loaned to 210 and 228

The rescue of the *Kensington Court* crew on 18.9.39 by A/F/Lt Smith in N9025 Z/228 in position 5031N 0826W.

Squadrons. Number 10's CO – W/Cmdr Leon Lachal – was informed on 8 October that his unit would remain in the UK and their first trip was taken on the tenth when N9049 was flown by F/Lt Garing to Bizerta with a spare engine for a 228 Sqdn aircraft.

The lessons learned in WW1 were not being applied in September 1939. Many ships were sailing independently and of the forty-six vessels sunk in that month, only three are listed with a surface vessel escort.[4] For possible attacks against U-boats, the Sunderland armament included just one forward-firing gun and DCs designed to be released from the air were still awaited.

Of those ships torpedoed in September which 'hit the headlines' were the *Athenia*, a liner sunk without warning by U-30 on the third; the *Kensington Court* a tramp steamer; and the carrier HMS *Courageous*.

On the 14th at 1106 hrs the merchant vessel *Vancouver City* was torpedoed in position 5123N 0703W by U-28. At 1200 hrs L2167 captained by S/Ldr Pearce of 210 Sqdn was airborne from Pembroke Dock to search for the enemy. At 1310 hrs the Sunderland crew sighted a surfaced U-boat six miles away. S/Ldr Pearce made an attack with two bombs on the last observed position of the U-boat but no evidence of damage was recorded.

The *Kensington Court* came into the news due to an exceptionally successful operation undertaken by Sunderlands of Nos 204 and 228 Squadrons. At about 1235 hrs on 18 September the ship was torpedoed by U-32 seventy miles west of the Scillies (5031N 0827W). Accounts vary, but airborne at that time were Sunderlands from 204 and 228 with the war diary of the latter stating that signals from *Kensington Court* were received by three out of four of their aircraft. A/F/Lt Thurston-Smith with co-pilot P/O Bevan-John was airborne from Pembroke Dock at 0630 hrs in N9025 and S/Ldr Menzies in L5805 at 1115 hrs. Two other captains of 228 who were airborne at that time – A/F/Lt Brooks and P/O McKinley – reported patrols 'without incident'.

G/Capt Bevan-John recalls:

'I was co-pilot to A/F/Lt Thurston-Smith on the 18th and we were returning from an A/S patrol in the SW approaches 9 hrs 50 mins duration when we picked up an SSS as it was then. On plotting it I found it was not far from our position, so we altered course and very soon came upon the *Kensington Court* which was well down by the bow and all her crew were in one lifeboat. Having searched for the sub without success we decided to try a landing. It was a lovely day and the sea seemed like a millpond. A/F/Lt Smith made an excellent landing on what turned out to be quite a swell. The lifeboat, which seemed very full came towards us during its passage. Another Sunderland captained by Jackie Barrett appeared overhead. He signalled by Aldis lamp asking if we wished him to land. We replied that it was up to him as we considered it a risky business. He decided he would – and did. By the time we had picked up the captain and 19 of his crew, we were prepared to take the whole lot had it been necessary but were quite happy that the load was to be shared.

'The take-off was somewhat hairy but again Smithy did a good job. We found that we had landed with our bombs on . . . we had to jettison them before take-off and to cap it all, two hung up and had to be pushed off with a boat hook.'

From a report in the *News Chronicle* the master of the ship was Capt. Schofield who searched for one of his crew who had gone overboard but was recovered after an hour. F/O J. Barrett of 204 Sqdn picked up the remaining fourteen survivors from the ship, while another Sunderland from 228, captained by S/Ldr Menzies, remained on guard overhead before attacking later what was believed to have been the U-boat which sank *Kensington Court*. Both Barrett and Smith received the DFC; Smith was awarded his by HM the King at Wyton – the first for 228 Sqdn in WW2.

Six days later, 228 Sqdn Sunderlands were again involved in the rescue of survivors from a ship – the *Hazelside* which had been

Hazelside after being torpedoed by U-31 on 24.9.39 and here sighted by Sunderland X/228 in position 5118N 0922W.

The *Empress of Britain* on fire after bombing by the Luftwaffe. Sunderland P9622, captained by F/L Craven directed destroyers to the scene, 26.10.40.

sunk by U-31 SW of Ireland. Two Sunderlands, N9023 and N9020 captained by A/F/Lts Brooks and Skey respectively, proceeded to its aid and, according to Don Purcell, an engineer in Brooks' crew, *Hazelside* was found sinking by the stern as the U-boat was submerging. Brooks bombed along the visible wake of the U-boat but without obvious result. The Sunderland kept in touch with survivors but made a search for rescue vessels. Darkness was falling and both wind and sea rising when a small open vessel flying the Irish flag came out from the coast; its delay had been due to waiting for a suitable tide. Very lights were fired from the Sunderland to guide the vessel to survivors.

Mark I Sunderlands were listed as having an endurance of 12 hours[5] but N9025 captained by P/O McKinley on 25 October flew an anti-submarine patrol which lasted 14 hrs 10 mins. Two other pilots with him were P/O Bevan-John and one of the original RAAF to serve with No. 10 – P/O Ivan Podger. On 2 November, P/O L.L. Jones in Sunderland N9025 of 228 Sqdn sighted the American ship ss *City of Flint* flying a German flag but in Norwegian territorial waters. *City of Flint* had earlier been captured by the pocket battleship *Deutschland* and sailed with a prize crew to Murmansk, then ostensibly 'neutral', before attempting to reach Germany via Norway's neutral waters. The prize crew was interned.

In the latter part of 1939 and early 1940, the Australian No. 10 Squadron was receiving both Sunderland aircraft and personnel. By 21 December the unit had accepted ten aircraft and by 3 January was within No. 15 Group, Coastal Command. On 1 February No. 10 was considered operational and on the 6th F/Lt C. Pearce undertook the first operational sortie – as an escort to HMS *Repulse* with its attendant destroyers.

The Royal Navy had mined the Straits of Dover in September–October and effectively prevented U-boats using that route to break out into the Atlantic.[6] This resulted in the regular Coastal Command

Sunderland DQ-Y N9025 of 228 Sqdn at Invergordon on 28.4.40 after returning from Åndalsnes. It was shot down by Italian CR42s on 6.8.40.

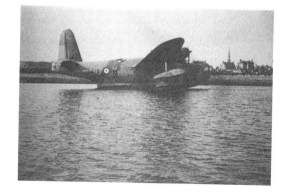

patrols over the North Sea, initially designed to thwart surface raiders, sighting U-boats. The Sunderlands and other aircraft, however, still lacked effective armament, and their crews had not yet gained expertise in anti-submarine operations.

By the middle of November 1939, U-boats were effectively waging unrestricted warfare against ships of France and Britain and on the 13th Coastal Command received a directive that A/S operations were to be considered of equal importance to their reconnaissance missions.[7]

In January 1940, No. 228 Sqdn was based at Pembroke Dock but with a detachment at Invergordon. It was a period when Coastal Command was still being armed with A/S bombs which, it had been found, were not lethal, although arrangements had been made for the development of depth charges suitable for release from the air.[8]

On 21 January KL Werner Heidel in U-55 had sunk a ship in position 5818N 0225W and on the 30th sank *Vaclite* and *Keramiai*, both in an outward bound convoy from the Thames through the English Channel (OA80G), about position 49°N 07°W. Acting F/Lt E.J. Brooks as captain of Sunderland N9025 was ordered out on a strike. At the time of the attack on the convoy, only the sloop HMS *Fowey* was on escort but two destroyers had been sent to its assistance in addition to the Sunderland.

Brooks located HMS *Fowey* and a French destroyer rescuing survivors from a torpedoed ship. He later saw two more escort vessels which must have been ordered to the scene. Half-an-hour later a surfaced U-boat was sighted and apparently unable to submerge. It was bombed and machine-gunned by the Sunderland before Brooks directed the escort vessels to the position. The U-boat crew scuttled their vessel in position 4837N 0746W; the survivors were picked up by HMS *Fowey*.

It was U-55 and the first U-boat 'kill' in which a Coastal Command aircraft shared the success. According to the Naval historian – Capt. Roskill – U-55 would probably have escaped but for the presence

of the Sunderland.[9] The Sunderland itself (N9025) was shot down the following August by Italian fighters in position 3219N 2342E when captained by A/F/Lt Thurston-Smith.

A very different mission was undertaken by another Sunderland from 228 while on detachment at Stranraer. This was by N6133 captained by F/Lt Craven on 2 February. Due to bad weather, Stranraer was virtually cut off from normal supplies. There was a shortage of bread, not due to lack of flour, but lack of yeast. F/Lt Craven gained permission to fly the aircraft to Belfast where 500 lb of yeast were taken on board N6133 before returning to Stranraer that afternoon.

A Diplomatic Mission to Rabat

The French had begun negotiations for an armistice with Germany on 17 June 1940 and it was signed on the 23rd by Petain's Government.[10] With British strategy based on having France as an ally and not an enemy, it was hoped that French colonies with units of the powerful French fleet would remain friendly and not become hostile.

When Churchill learned that some French politicians had reached Rabat he sent as envoys Mr Duff Cooper and Lord Gort. They were flown out by F/Lt 'Dick' Cohen in Sunderland P9602 G/10 RAAF with David Stewart as second pilot.

F/Lt Cohen flew from Calshot to touch down in Morocco on a narrow river as Rabat harbour was filled with vessels which had left French ports. He arrived at 1900 hrs on the 25th to find Rabat in mourning, flags were at half-mast and a cathedral service bewailed the fall of France.

Attempts were made to see the French Minister Georges Mandel but were obstructed by the Deputy Governor of Rabat – Morice, who followed the orders of the French C-in-C North Africa – General Noguès.

A radio message was received on the Sunderland for Lord Gort which Cohen was to take ashore. After two attempts were thwarted by police, Cohen ordered all lights on in the Sunderland to attract attention. When the police arrived Cohen and Stewart had revolvers ready and demanded to be put ashore.

There was further obstruction by the French when Cohen reached the British Consulate with the threat of an armed guard being placed on the Sunderland. Cohen pretended that Stewart was in charge and by this subterfuge was allowed to go, ostensibly to purchase rations but in fact he met Consular officials, with one of them taking Cohen by car to near the Bollima Hotel where the message was delivered.

Lord Gort was prevented from completing his mission; even at the hotel the French police attempted to restrain Cohen who again used his revolver and in an exchange of shots, made his escape. Eventually the whole of Lord Gort's party was airborne at dawn on the 26th from Rabat with enough fuel to reach Gibraltar.

F/Lt 'Dick' Cohen, now writing in retrospect as G/Capt Sir Richard Kingsland recalls:

'During and after my mission, I was briefed never to reveal the degrading difficulties Lord Gort and I had with the French Authorities, after the female British consular official dropped me a block away from the hotel and when Viscount Gort and I were, to put it nicely, "restrained".'

Lady de L'Isle, the daughter of Lord Gort, when writing a biography of her father, contacted Sir Richard requesting details of the episode but diplomatically, he declined.

The French treated their former Ministers as escaped prisoners and they were taken back to France in the auxiliary cruiser *Massilia*. Churchill attempted to arrange their rescue but without success. His wish to set up a strong French Government in London or Africa was thwarted.[11]

Coastal Command's Second Anti-Submarine Success

Sunderland P9603 H/10 was airborne at 0200 hrs on 1 July 1940 from Mount Batten

with the captain, F/Lt W.N. 'Hoot' Gibson, RAAF, detailed for an A/S patrol. Shortly after take-off he was ordered to position 4803N 1111W where a ship in convoy OA175 had been torpedoed.

As one of the Sunderland crew – Bill Vout – recalls:

'We arrived on the scene at dawn. The ship ss *Zarian* was down by the stern and had obviously taken a torpedo there. A lifeboat with some of the crew aboard was alongside and a corvette was standing by.'

Gibson began a search for the U-boat and the second pilot – Geoffrey Havyatt – sighted a disturbance ahead, apparently the U-boat. Four A/S bombs were released and Gibson circled the area. Vout continues:

'Suddenly the bow of the submarine broke surface at a very steep angle before levelling off. Hoot released a second salvo which fell about forty yards from the sub's midships. I saw the U-boat's crew pouring out of the conning tower and it looked as if each was placing his hand on the next's shoulders when suddenly they all jumped overboard and swam clear. The U-boat began to settle by the stern, slowly at first but then gathering momentum, it tipped up the bows and slid under the sea at the same steep angle as it had risen.'

The U-boat had earlier been attacked by HMS *Gladiolus* with depth charges which had caused serious damage.

It had been sighted by HMS *Rochester* and also by the Sunderland, after surfacing in an attempt to escape at high speed on the surface. Its commander, KK Heinz Scheringer, gave the order to abandon U-26 which was scuttled in position 4803N 1130W. Forty-one survivors were picked up.

Of U-boats damaged by Coastal Command aircraft, a Sunderland again opened hostilities. By August 1940, U-boats were using French ports effectively extending their range to 25° west[12] and had sunk 56 ships in the North Sea / Atlantic Ocean areas.[13] By then depth charges in addition to A/S bombs were becoming available to Coastal Command.

F/O Baker captained H/210 Sunderland P9624 on the 16th for a patrol and to escort convoy OA198. He was airborne at 0624 hrs and on reaching the convoy two hours later, was asked to search for a Norwegian vessel 20 miles astern. It was not sighted but the Sunderland was asked to report that another ship MV *Empire Merchant* had been torpedoed and sunk in position 5521N 1340W.[14]

A search must have been undertaken by Baker for at 1415 hrs his second pilot – P/O Bowie – sighted the deck and conning tower of a submarine. The 210 Sqdn record gives one DC dropping 20 feet ahead of the conning tower and a second DC exploding 10 feet from it. Four A/S bombs were then released 30 yards ahead of the wash. A gush of oil 30 feet in diameter was followed by a large air bubble. The second DC had blown the U-boat right out of the water, and just under an hour later, the oil patch had spread to 30 yards diameter. It was believed that the U-boat had sunk but post-war records give these attacks as being on U-51 which was seriously damaged needing it to return to port.

The following year, on 6 January, F/Lt Baker of 210 Sqdn, and in that same aircraft P9624, made another attack on a submarine. After being airborne from Oban at 0943 hrs, a U-boat was sighted on the surface. DCs were released, with one falling 20 yards and another, 60 yards ahead of the swirl. Oil covered the sea for about a mile. American and British lists credit 210 Sqdn with sinking the Italian submarine *Marcello* on 6 January 1941 in position 5838N 1151W or 'West of the Hebrides'. From the official Italian history however, *Marcello* left Verdon, Bordeaux on 11 January and arrived back at Pauillac, Bordeaux on the 24th.[15]

The Liner *Empress of Britain*

The Canadian Pacific liner of 42,348 tons *Empress of Britain* was returning from the Middle East on 26 October 1940. When about 70 miles north-west of Donegal Bay, the liner was bombed by German aircraft and set on fire.[16] Sunderland P9622 captained by F/Lt Craven of 228 Sqdn, then on detachment to Oban, was airborne at 1057 hrs to escort and assist the ship. Visibility was good with 7/10ths cloud at 2000 feet and the burning liner was located near position 5505N 1045W. F/Lt Craven circled the area and located survivors and a capsized lifeboat. A dinghy was dropped from the Sunderland and destroyers were directed to the scene by firing Very cartridges.

A 204 Sqdn Sunderland being serviced at Sullom Voe, Shetland Isles in February 1941.

T9047 RB-L of No. 10 Sqdn RAAF rescuing a Hudson crew 9.7.41. Both Hudson and Sunderland crews were picked up by HMS *Brocklesby*.

Officers of No. 201 Sqdn with Sunderland 'S' W6014 c. 1942.

Empress of Britain was taken in tow but on the 28th, when in position 5516N 0950W, was sunk by U-32 captained by KL Hans Jenisch who fired two torpedoes.[17] U-32 was herself sunk two days later by escorts HMS *Harvester* and *Highlander*. Of this incident, F/Lt Craven's co-pilot, the Canadian P/O L.L. 'Slim' Jones, recorded in his log: '*Empress of Britain* on fire 14°West, 1000 people on board – 2 destroyers, 3 trawlers carried out the rescue.'

References

1   SWR I p. 30

2   Ibid.
3   SWR I p. 35
4   SWR I p. 106 gives 114 Allied MVs sunk Sep–Dec 1939, only 12 of those in convoy
5   DR I p. 412
6   SWR I p. 96
7   SWR I 105 & DR I p. 60
8   DR I p. 61
9   SWR I p. 129
10   WSC II p. 194
11   WSC II p. 194
12   SWR I p. 349
13   SWR I p. 350 and JR pp. 25–7
14   This was by U-100 (JR p. 25)
15   UMU XII p. 144
16   SWR I p. 351
17   JR p. 35

A 'routine' sight for many Coastal Command aircrew in WW2. 'Boring' for some; exciting for others.

Chapter 4
Norway

NORWAY'S COASTLINE extending from the Skagerrak to North Cape was of great strategic importance in World Two. With ports such as Stavanger, Bergen, Trondheim and Narvik, protected anchorage could be provided for U-boats and battleships. Covering the northern route from Germany to the North Atlantic and for a potential sea route to Russia, a battleship in a Norwegian fjord would provide much more than a 'vague menace'.

Two-thirds of Germany's supply of high grade iron ore came from Sweden via Lulea or Narvik, and when Lulea became ice-bound, Narvik and its sea route through the leads of the Norwegian coast became vital.

Both Churchill as First Sea Lord of the Admiralty and Hitler's Chief of Naval Staff were aware of these aspects. Churchill referred to them in memos as early as 19 September 1939[1] while Admiral Raeder on 3 October proposed to Hitler[2] that bases in Norway should be taken.

On 14 December Raeder introduced the Norwegian traitor – Quisling – to Hitler who then gave the order to prepare for the invasion of Norway.[3] Hitler on 1 March 1940 ordered the occupation of Denmark and Norway, and on 2 April ordered the attacks for the 9th.[4]

Landings in Norway were to be made at Narvik, Trondheim, Bergen, Egersund, Kristiansand, Arendal and Oslo. German sailings began on sixth and on the eighth a Polish submarine sank ss *Rio de Janeiro* taking German troops. Survivors were picked up by Norwegian ships giving, effectively, the final warning of their homeland being invaded.[5]

The Royal Navy's deployment was still geared to preventing a break-out of surface raiders although on the eighth their destroyers had mined the channel leading to Narvik. Norway protested to Britain but that same night German warships approached Oslo. Denmark was overrun. Norway and Denmark had lost their neutrality.

From the outset in WW2, Coastal Command had laid on patrols to the Norwegian coast, then undertaken by Hudsons and Sunderlands but with the Sunderlands flying the more northerly trips due to their greater range.

In April 1940 a number of Sunderlands were transferred from 15 Group to 18 Group, a move corresponding to operations from the south-west to the north-east of Britain.

One of the first to move on detachment was L5798 captained by A/F/Lt Van der Kiste who, on 1 April flew from Pembroke Dock to Stranraer and on the 2nd arrived at Invergordon. On the 8th he undertook searches for enemy warships off Norway under adverse weather conditions. On the 12th he was deployed from Sullom Voe to raid enemy troopships in the Hardanger fjord. On reaching the Norwegian coast heavy snowstorms were encountered but a search was made and, while over Haugesund, there was much AA fire. The starboard middle tank and the hull were pierced. Over Garvin there was further AA which pierced both the port middle tank and the tailplane. The troopships were not located and Sunderland L5798 returned to Sullom Voe with 400 gallons petrol in the bilges.

Another Sunderland from 210 Sqdn was detached to Invergordon – L2167 – captained by F/Lt Kite. On the afternoon of the 9th he was airborne to undertake a reconnaissance of Oslo. Sunderland L2167 failed to return. Postwar its fate was learned. While over Oslo it was attacked by two Me110s from Fornebu. During air-to-air combat over Sollihøgda and Holsfjorden the Sunderland caught fire and exploded over Maidalen. The explosion blew out Sgt Ogwyn George who fell about 3000 feet without a parachute but into very deep snow. A Norwegian who had witnessed the combat, went that night to the scene and found the wrecked aircraft and the sole survivor – Sgt George. With help he was taken to Drammen hospital, later to be a POW in Germany.

In April 1972 Ogwyn George returned to Norway and met his rescuer – Johan Bråthen.

A pilgrimage was made to the graves of his former crew members at Sylling church. Ogwyn George and his wife were later received by King Olav at the palace in Oslo. The crew of Sunderland L2167 represented for the Norwegians the first British casualties from the RAF following the German invasion and on 10 June 1990, a granite memorial stone was unveiled near Maridalshytta, north-east of Finnemarka, Lier.

Number 204 Sqdn was at Mount Batten on 1 April 1940 but made an initial move to Pembroke Dock leaving Mount Batten to be taken over by No. 10 Sqdn RAAF. Some of 204's aircraft were handed over to 201 Sqdn, but 204 moved to Sullom Voe on 2 April and the crews were accommodated on ss *Manela*. Number 204 Squadron's operational strength there was L5799, N9046, N9047 and N9044 but with S/Ldr Thomas to follow with N9021.

On the 3rd, N9046 captained by F/Lt Phillips was airborne from Sullom Voe at 1125 hrs on a convoy escort. Four hours later and 20 miles from the convoy, two enemy aircraft were sighted, low on the water and eight miles from the Norwegian coast. At 50–100 ft altitude the enemy circled the Sunderland for two minutes before attacking from 800 yds on the starboard beam, flying past successively on a parallel course. The intention was to draw the fire of the Sunderland while four more Ju88s appeared. These four made a line astern attack on the Sunderland's tail after three minutes combat with the first two who then drew away. Corporal Lillie, the

A South Wales newspaper report of W/O George who survived falling from Sunderland L2167 of 210 Sqdn lost over Norway 9.4.40.

rear gunner, held his fire until the leading attacker was at 100 yds range then shot him down, with the Ju88 banking steeply and diving into the sea. The second Ju88 was also hit and, (from a BBC broadcast), later force-landed. The first two Ju88s now attempted to bomb the Sunderland from 1500 ft altitude but their bombs fell 100 yds away. After the attacks by the four had broken up, the now remaining five Ju88s made off.

The Sunderland returned to base losing on the way 500 gallons of petrol from bullet holes made in the port inner, starboard middle and outer tanks. There were bullet holes in the hull, tail fin, instrument panel, trimming gear, fuel jettison systems and bomb rack. Two of the crew had cuts to their faces from splinters – P/O Armitstead and P/O Goodwin. On 5 April the AOC No. 18 Group – AV-M Breese – visited 204 Sqdn in the Shetlands and awards were made of the DFC to F/Lt Phillips and the DFM to his rear gunner – Corporal Lillie.

The Home Fleet had sailed from Scapa Flow at 2015 hrs on 7 April and the 2nd cruiser squadron from Rosyth the same evening. The 1st cruiser squadron sailed the following evening, but by that time the German battlecruisers *Scharnhorst* and *Gneisenau* were off Narvik with ten destroyers and the gallant HMS *Glowworm* had been sunk by the heavy cruiser *Admiral Hipper* off Trondheim.

At 0600 hrs F/O Johnson of 204 Sqdn was airborne in Sunderland N9047 detailed to escort the Home Fleet. Thirty-five minutes later he made contact at position 6100N 0109E between the Shetlands and Bergen with HMS *Warspite, Renown, Aurora, Southampton* and *Nelson* steaming on a course of 30° true at 18 knots and escorted by ten destroyers.

At 1030 hrs a second Sunderland – L5799 of 204 Sqdn captained by F/Lt Harrison was airborne from Sullom Voe to make a reconnaissance of the Norwegian coast. It was understood through a German broadcast that this aircraft was shot down 30 miles east of the Shetlands.

Meanwhile, the Admiral Home Fleet ordered F/O Johnson in N9047 to make a landfall on the Norwegian coast and head north to locate enemy sea forces. He did, and reported a battleship, three cruisers and destroyers. While shadowing the enemy warships, the Sunderland suffered damage from AA with pieces of HE shell in the hull and two fuel tanks. That evening, 204's CO – W/Cmdr Davis – was airborne, searching for the lost L5799 along its last known bearing, but to no avail.

The following day W/Cmdr Davis was airborne again taking N9844 on a reconnaissance of Trondheim fjord. At the entrance to the fjord were two enemy aircraft acting as guards.

W/Cmdr Davis made for the first – an Arado floatplane – which with great speed attempted to dive on the Sunderland's tail. The Sunderland's tail gunner opened fire with the enemy closing to 200 yards but the turret door opened putting it out of action temporarily. W/Cmdr Davis by a steep turn brought the front gunner in range who however did not fire. The Sunderland was undamaged and the Arado made off. The second enemy – a Blohm & Voss – attacked the Sunderland's tail putting the turret out of action for the second time and with machine-guns and cannon holed the two inner tanks of the Sunderland. However, the Blohm & Voss gave up the fight with black smoke emitting from its port engine. F/Lt Hyde climbed into the wings of the Sunderland and blocked the leaks to both port and starboard tanks with Plasticine. One crew member – P/O Wakeley – was cut by splinters. Before returning to base they had sighted correctly a 'Hipper' class cruiser near the entrance to Trondheim fjord.

On the 13th a floatplane with two Norwegian officers and a Naval W/T operator arrived at Sullom Voe. They were to be taken on 204's reconnaissance flights to Norway because of their local knowledge.

By that time German troops had been landed in Norway and the heavy units of the German fleet had returned to Wilhelmshaven – the battlecruisers *Scharnhorst* and *Gneisenau* and the cruiser *Admiral Hipper*. The first phase of *Weserübung* – the invasion of Norway was over.

Number 204 Sqdn personnel moved ashore from their temporary accommodation on ss *Manela* during the 16th and 17th April to be based at Sullom Voe; their baggage party arrived by ss *Rutland* two days later.

Number 228 Sqdn had Sunderlands detached from Pembroke Dock to Invergordon on the Cromarty Firth but

during the Norwegian campaign operated from both Invergordon and Sullom Voe in the Shetlands. One of their first missions was a reconnaissance of Trondheim fjord to report on enemy forces there. F/Lt Brooks captained L5806 which was airborne from Sullom Voe on 10 April at 1145 hrs. Brooks was aware that the day before a 204 Sqdn aircraft had been driven off by enemy aircraft and he elected to make his approach from the north, inland and then undertake the reconnaissance flying westwards. Using cloud cover he made landfall at Vikten island at 1600 hrs going inland above broken cloud at 7000–9000 feet and Trondheim was approached from the east through gaps in the cloud. In the harbour he reported sighting a Hipper class cruiser, two destroyers and three large merchant vessels, while in a fjord north of Trondheim, the *Nurnberg*, a cruiser was located north-east of the harbour. There were heavy snowstorms and the Sunderland experienced considerable icing. At 1700 hrs, Brooks set course west from Froene island, remaining in cloud for thirty minutes before setting course for base in the Shetlands, landing at 1955 hrs. A signal was sent to 18 Group from the AOC-in-C Coastal Command and the Navy at Rosyth: 'Captain and crew of Q/228 on a difficult task particularly well executed in spite of difficult circumstances. Excellent detailed reports made here. Well done indeed.'

F/Lt Brooks made a further reconnaissance in Sunderland L5806 two days later of fjords from Bjornsund to Bremanger and adopted similar tactics. On maps and charts, the positions of enemy vessels were plotted including a dozen merchant ships, a destroyer and the cruiser *Nurnberg* which fired on the Sunderland. Shortly after making landfall, the pocket battleship *Lutzow* was sighted with steam up at moorings.

On 15 April the officer who was to command the first Allied landings in Norway – Major-General A. Carton de Wiart, VC – was flown by a 228 Sqdn aircraft from Invergordon to Namsen fjord. This was in Sunderland N6133 captained

Namsen fjord 15.4.40. Major-General Carton de Wiart VC is ferried by N6133 captained by F/Lt L. Skey then with 228 Sqdn.

by the Canadian F/Lt Larry Skey with L.L. 'Slim' Jones as second pilot. It was intended to rendezvous with a Tribal class destroyer in Namsen fjord where the Sunderland touched down at 1645 hrs. Five minutes later bombing attacks began on the destroyer by four Ju88s and two He111s which were to last for one and a half hours. Some bombs burst within 10 yards of the destroyer's bows. A boat was launched and three of the Sunderland's passengers disembarked. The Sunderland had exchanged fire with the enemy aircraft and one on board – 2nd/Lt Eliot – was wounded in the knee. One aircraft had dropped a stick of incendiary bombs on the Sunderland, but with avoiding action they fell 250 yards away. During the return flight to Invergordon, the battleship HMS *Warspite* and four destroyers were sighted heading north.

F/Lt Brooks with Sunderland L5806 was detailed on 19 April to take one and a half tons of explosives from Invergordon to Molde in Romsdal fjord. A landfall was made at Ålesund to contact the sloop HMS *Bittern*. This was one of four sloops which after a diversion, had sailed on the sixteenth for Åndalsnes as a diversion from a major landing at Namsos.[6] F/Lt Brooks found cloud down to sea level in Romsdal fjord and landed 10 miles from Molde before taxying for four miles. After five tries, the cargo was unloaded into a rowing dinghy as enemy bombing attacks had put other marine craft out of action.

A pilot who served with 228 Sqdn during the Norwegian campaign, now Sir Robert Craven, recalls:

'My first trip to Norway was on 25 April 1940 in N9025 to Namsos where I met Major-General Carton de Wiart who commanded the northern section of the BEF. There was virtually no communication between the UK and Norway and I was taking messages which were "phoned from Downing Street to Invergordon".'

On 27 April he captained N9025 with a Canadian from Saskatoon – P/O 'Slim' Jones – as co-pilot. They were airborne from Invergordon to transport personnel to Åndalsnes. En route the weather was exceptionally bad but cleared near the Norwegian coast, where a landfall was made at Ålesund in under four hours. While flying along Sula fjord, Sir Robert adds: 'Our first sign of hostilities was of German aircraft bombing a radio station.' He changed course and while flying low towards Molde fjord, the Sunderland was attacked by three Ju88s with bombs which fell 50 yards astern. HMS *Witherington* was located and a touch-down made alongside the destroyer. At this point, twelve Ju88s were seen bombing Molde in flights of three. Three Ju88s then made for the Sunderland and the destroyer. Although avoiding action was taken, some bomb splinters damaged N9025's tailplane.

The passengers were disembarked and F/Lt Craven went with them to ascertain the situation. He was invited by the destroyer's captain onto the bridge to advise regarding the German bombers so that evasive action could be taken. The whaler used to take the passengers was sunk by a bomb in an action which persisted for half-an-hour.

P/O Jones in the Sunderland had been taking constant avoiding action on the water and the engines were overheating. He was forced to take-off and was promptly attacked by a Me110. His tail and midships gunners fired 700 rounds and the Me110 was shot down – this confirmed by the ground party. 'Slim' Jones then touched down at Åndalsnes to meet up again with HMS *Witherington*. Of this episode, Sir Robert concludes: 'We went into Åndalsnes

which by then was being laid flat and spent the night under some trees on the shoreline.'

Both F/Lt R. Craven and P/O L.L. 'Slim' Jones were awarded the DFC. F/Lt Craven undertook a further series of ferry trips to and from Norway. These included one on the 30th when some Army officers were flown from Invergordon to Namsos for an intended rendezvous with HMS *Bittern* but to find that the sloop had been sunk by enemy aircraft that day.

Sunderlands of 204 Sqdn were no less active during this period in the Norwegian campaign. They were closely involved in co-operation with the Royal Navy acting as escorts to the cruiser HMS *Arethusa*, Southampton-type cruisers, the destroyer F22, and the damaged sloop HMS *Pelican* – apparently with its stern blown off.

When F/O Johnson, captain of N9046 of 204 Sqdn returned from Namsos on the 29th, he reported the quay at Namsos as 'blazing' and that a destroyer and French transports had departed but leaving a British destroyer and a county-class cruiser.

That same evening King Haakon and the Crown Prince of Norway embarked on the cruiser HMS *Glasgow* which was escorted by two destroyers from Molde to Tromsö.[7] On 5 May the Norwegian Government was set up in London. On 7 June King Haakon embarked in HMS *Devonshire* at Tromsö.[8] It was to be almost five years before he could return to Norway in that same cruiser.

The success of Germany in taking Norway in *Weserübung* is emphasized by the official historian Denis Richards as being due to overwhelming air power, quoting three Army commanders: Maj-Gen Paget, Maj-Gen Carton de Wiart, and Lt-Gen Auchinleck plus the enemy – General Jodl.[9] John Terraine gives over 1000 aircraft being used by Germany in the initial invasion.[10]

Naval historian Captain Roskill sums up the Norwegian campaign by stating that Germany's supplies of iron ore were safeguarded, increased control of the Baltic had been achieved, and very valuable bases for both ships and aircraft able to threaten our trade routes had been captured.[11] Both John Terraine and Captain Roskill refer to Churchill's involvement in the Royal Navy's operations.

Churchill's final paragraph covers the Naval aspect with the loss of the carrier HMS *Glorious*, two cruisers, one sloop and nine destroyers. Disabled were six cruisers, two sloops and eight destroyers. For the end of June 1940, he gives the effective German fleet as one 8-inch cruiser, two light cruisers and four destroyers.[12]

Peter Cremer, a German naval officer who took part in *Weserübung* sums up with: 'The Allies had landed at three places in Norway but then withdrawn. The battle for Narvik had been decided in our favour. Norwegian forces had capitulated at Trondheim. But all in all the Navy paid a heavy price.'[13] (The loss of three cruisers, ten destroyers and *Admiral Hipper* out of action).

Many Norwegians made their way to the United Kingdom and two Norwegian squadrons came to be formed within Coastal Command – numbers 330 and 333. Number 330 Sqdn was initially equipped with Northrop floatplanes but later operated Catalinas and Sunderlands. Number 333 operated Catalinas but also had a flight of Mosquitoes.

Aftermath

On 10 May 1940 Germany invaded Belgium and Holland. On that same day Prime Minister Neville Chamberlain resigned for Winston Churchill to form a National Government. It was decided that Allied forces still in Norway should be evacuated. The Netherlands capitulated on 15 May, the Belgian port of Antwerp was captured by the Germans on the 18th and the Belgian army capitulated on 27 May.

By then the evacuation of British and other Allied troops through Dunkirk had begun, and by 3 June the evacuation was considered over with 338,226 troops having been rescued.14

German troops entered Paris on 15 June, and the French signed an armistice on the 22nd.

RAF Coastal Command aircraft now had the task of covering potentially hostile forces leaving ports from Narvik in the north, down to Bordeaux in the south.

In the Mediterranean, the former friendly French fleet was to prove hostile through some of its units, and via French colonies, a 'back door' could be opened to British controlled territory.

On 10 June 1940 Italy had declared war on Britain and France.

The deployment of the Sunderland squadrons reflects these events.

Number 201 Squadron remained at Sullom Voe having converted to Sunderlands, sharing that base with 204 which had a detachment at Reykjavik, and 210 moved from Pembroke Dock to Oban in July. A major change was for 230 to return from the Far East to the eastern Mediterranean in May, while 228 followed in June with both initially based at Alexandria.

References
[1] WSC I p. 480
[2] WSC I p. 483
[3] WSC I p. 484
[4] SWR I p. 163
[5] SWR I p. 164
[6] SWR I p. 183
[7] SWR I p. 188
[8] SWR I p. 197
[9] DR I pp. 104–5
[10] JT p. 115
[11] SWR I p. 201
[12] WSC I p. 592
[13] PC p. 14
[14] SWR I p. 603

Chapter 5
The Eastern Mediterranean

Number 230 Sqdn had by 11 May 1940, seven of its Sunderlands based at Alexandria with HMT *Dumana*, having returned from Ceylon. From Alexandria they came to have detachments in Malta, Greece, Crete and Bahrein.

At 1930 hrs on 10 June, the squadron received the news that Italy had declared war. On that same day, from Pembroke Dock, No. 228 Sqdn flew three Sunderlands L5806, L5806 and N9025 routed to Alexandria via Marignane and Malta with a total of 42 personnel including the CO – W/Cmdr Nicholetts, F/Lts Ware, T.M.W. Smith, DFC, D.C. McKinley, DFC, and F/Os Ellis, Bevan-John and P/O Jenks. They were requested to look out for Hudsons and Hurricanes also bound for the Middle East.

At 0400 hrs, L5807 and N9025 were airborne from Malta due to an impending air attack which followed half-an-hour later. All three aircraft flew to Aboukir but with L5806 direct from Bizerta. Number 228 Sqdn personnel were to be accommodated on HMT *Dumana* at Alexandria with office and stores at the Imperial Airways depot but on the 15th W/Cmdr Nicholetts made arrangements for the squadron to be transferred to Aboukir.

The Mediterranean was considered second only to the Home theatre due to trade routes to India, the Far East and oil supplies from the Persian Gulf.[1]

Allied strategy had been based on a French fleet able to control the western Mediterranean with the Royal Navy concentrated in the eastern basin. The collapse of France meant another potentially hostile fleet in addition to possibly hostile land and sea bases in North Africa. The entry of Italy into the war

introduced a large submarine and surface fleet in addition to another enemy air force. Capt Roskill gives the total of forty-six Italian submarines being immediately deployed but that the dominant factor in the control of the Mediterranean was to be air power.[2]

On the outbreak of war with Italy the strengths of the fleets in the Mediterranean are given as 262 Italian, 118 French, and 64 British.[3] The Italian total included four battleships and 115 submarines. Neglecting the French fleet, the Royal Navy was in all respects, apart from having five battleships as opposed to the Italian's four, greatly outnumbered.

The island of Malta in the central Mediterranean and lying only sixty miles south of Sicily, covered the Allied route from Gibraltar to Alexandria but, for the Axis powers, threatened convoys from Italy to Libya. Malta's proximity to Italian air bases precluded its use as a main base for the Royal Navy which opted for Alexandria. In 1939 the Imperial Defence Committee had decided that Malta should be defended and there was a flying boat base at Kalafrana in addition to three airfields.

One of the first to operate successfully from Malta was 228's CO – W/Cmdr Nicholetts. In co-operation with the Royal Navy, he began on 27 June with Sunderland L5806 on a reconnaissance between Alexandria, Malta and Crete for the Italian fleet. On the 28th while on a similar search in the approaches to the Adriatic, he attacked an enemy submarine. From the official Italian history[4] this must have been *Anfitrite*, one of four detailed to operate in that area. At about 1400 hrs in position 3718N 1954E, *Anfitrite* was subjected to a bombing attack which caused damage to its side forcing it to return to base. W/Cmdr Nicholett's record gives 3731N 1955E for his attack that day. During the same sortie, he reported sighting three Italian destroyers which he shadowed for 15 minutes.

S/Ldr Woodward in Sunderland L5803 en route to Malta from Alexandria also reported destroyers giving the position 3600N 2026E at 1630 hrs. Admiral Cunningham acknowledges[5] these sightings with his 7th cruiser squadron intercepting at 1830 hrs, 75 miles WSW of Cape Matapan and with the sinking of the Italian destroyer *Espero*.

The Sinking of *Argonauta* and *Rubino*

The first anti-submarine success for 230 Sqdn was during a routine patrol by F/Lt Campbell on 28 June 1940. Campbell was airborne from Aboukir at 1015 hrs in L5804 (NM-S) but as one of his crew – Roy Diss – recalls:

' .... the majority of alarms were due to birds or fish, but on this day, way off on the beam, was a sub travelling at periscope depth.'

'We turned away to wind out the bomb racks and prepare for the attack. In the early marks of boat the loading and winding out of the racks was manual and our earlier practice paid off. As armourer I had the responsibility for the bombs and all weapons on board and acted also as tail gunner.

'We turned to come out on to the sub from astern which was oblivious of our presence. The attack was made with four 250 lb A/S bombs which fell close enough to damage and disable; the second attack finished it off. The debris and oil were positive proof to us, but the claim of the sinking was not confirmed "as there is no knowledge of a submarine in that area" – this was later changed.

The Italian submarine *Argonauta* had been attacked by escort vessels on the 21st and returned to base on the 22nd, but on the 28th it must have been in transit between Tobruk and Taranto when sighted at

ITALIAN SUBMARINES DESTROYED

R.A.F. SAVE SURVIVORS

FROM OUR CORRESPONDENT

CAIRO, JULY 7

The successful cooperation of the R.A.F. in action against enemy submarines in the Mediterranean is strikingly shown by the exploits of a flying-boat attached to the Middle Eastern Command which accounted for two submarines recently.

While patrolling, the aircraft sighted the periscope of an enemy submarine, whereupon it immediately delivered a dive-bombing attack and released some special bombs, two of which burst abaft the conning-tower. The force of the explosion almost blew the submarine out of the water. Her nose rose sharply to the surface and then the boat appeared to slide vertically downwards. Huge air bubbles were seen at once, while smaller ones continued to rise for some time and oil also appeared on the surface of the sea. Returning two hours later, the pilot saw a huge patch of oil, 300 by 500 yards in extent.

The next day the same flying-boat, with the same crew, again sighted an Italian submarine on the surface. Again a dive-bombing attack with special bombs sank the submarine. Some of the crew of the submarine were blown into the sea by the force of the explosion. The pilot brought his aeroplane down to the water and picked up three lieutenants and one petty officer, all unwounded but suffering from shock. A search for more survivors had to be abandoned as a local storm was blowing up.

While returning to its base the aircraft spotted yet another Italian submarine. All its bombs having been used, the aeroplane swooped down and raked the conning-tower and bridge of the submarine with all its available machine-guns. The operation was repeated a second time before the submarine crash-dived.

One of the two submarines thus destroyed was included in the four which were claimed to have been sunk in the naval *communiqué* of July 2.

REFUGEE CHILDREN

A report in *The Times* of F/Lt Campbell sinking two Italian submarines in two days and picking up survivors from *Rubino* in L5804 (NM-S) on 29.6.40.

periscope depth by Sunderland L5804's crew. The disbelief in Campbell's success was countered the following day.

Sunderland L5804 was airborne at 0835 hrs and as again recalled by Roy Diss:

'The second submarine was spotted on the surface, our preparation time before attack was now much shorter and again from astern. The bow turret was instructed to pour concentrated fire into the conning tower, no-one could be seen on watch on the submarine. The first four bombs dropped two on either side of the sub which promptly broke in half forward of the conning tower; the second four almost lifted the stern section out of the water.

'We stood off and wound in the bomb racks and as we circled, survivors were seen in the water. Bill Campbell calmly advised us over the intercomm, that he was landing to pick up our proof from the sea. Against normal practice I was to remain in the tail turret in case we were attacked. How we managed to land and take-off in that swell I shall never know, I was looking up at wave crests above the tail fin. Our message to Malta to lay on a POW escort caused confusion; we arrived with only three survivors, to be met so it seemed, by most of the Brass of Malta.'

From the Italian official history,[6] *Rubino* was in position 3910N 1849E at 1400 hrs on the 29th, 45 miles off Cape St. Maria di Leuca when attacked by an English aircraft with the number L5804 releasing two bombs which struck the boat's stern and the conning tower, causing its rapid sinking and loss of most of the crew. *The Times* dated 8 July 1940 reported these two successes under a headline 'Italian Submarines Destroyed' and stating that three lieutenants and one petty officer were picked up. Roy Diss was apparently wrongly identified as that 'petty officer'. One of the three lieutenant's was Arturo Maroni whose son wrote to me from La Grazie in 1990 as a Lt-Cmdr in the Italian Navy.

There was further action on the 29th when W/Cmdr Nicholetts flew Sunderland L5806 from Malta on a patrol to Cape Colonne and Corfu. He reported attacking a submarine in position 3812N 1806E. The Italian record gives their *Sirena* responding to an attack 80 miles SE of Cape Colonne at 0630 hrs in position 3754N 1804E but apparently suffering no damage.[7] The following day when returning to Alexandria from Malta, but serving to protect a convoy en route, F/Lt Woodward in L5803 of 230 Sqdn attacked an Italian destroyer off Tobruk. He released four bombs from 5000 ft. One fell close to the stern and the ship stopped.

On 4 July, F/Lt Brooks of 228 Sqdn captained P9621 on a reconnaissance of Oran and Algiers. He was attacked by three French Curtiss 75As. One was shot down and a second probably.

Although badly damaged, the Sunderland returned to Gibraltar with one of the crew – P/O Pyne who had been on the starboard midships gun – wounded. This was to be just one of a series of attacks on RAF aircraft in the Mediterranean by our former allies.[8]

The Battle of Punta Stilo

The first major encounter between the Royal Navy and the Italian fleet occurred on 9 July and was referred to by the Italians as the Battle of Punta Stilo. On that day both 228 and 230 Sqdn Sunderlands were involved. F/Lt David McKinley of 228 was airborne from Malta at 0515 hrs in L5807 detailed for an endless chain patrol over the approaches to the Adriatic sea. After flying for 15 minutes he sighted the Italian fleet comprising two battleships, four cruisers and six destroyers which proceeded to shadow. Later, while east of the battle fleet, a further six cruisers and eleven destroyers were seen. Later still, to the west, seven cruisers. At one period, 39 Italian warships were visible, three battleships, 13 cruisers and 23 destroyers. It was suspected that there might be more in the vicinity. McKinley shadowed the Italian warships for nine hours and during that time witnessed the bombing of the Allied fleet by enemy aircraft which attempted also to bomb the Sunderland.

F/Lt Woodward was airborne from Malta at 0800 hrs. At 1245 hrs he bombed an Italian submarine claiming a direct hit abaft the conning tower. At 1442 hrs he sighted the Italian battle fleet in position 3750N 1750E. At 1515 hrs he saw the British fleet and gave HMS *Warspite* the enemy's position. Woodward returned to Malta at 1840 hrs with U/S engines and a gun turret. The submarine he attacked was possibly *Zoea* which had left Taranto on 29 June.[9] F/Lt Woodward's reported position agrees with Admiral Cunningham's account which gives the Italian fleet as 50 miles from Cape Spartivento. Within 40 minutes of Woodwood's signal to Cunningham's flag-ship, HMS *Warpsite* opened fire on the leading Italian battleship scoring a direct hit at the base of its funnel. The Italians turned away.[10]

S/Ldr Menzies with N9020 was also engaged in shadowing and was subjected to heavy AA from Italian warships. He was in air-to-air combat with a Heinkel 115 floatplane for 30 minutes before the enemy broke off the action. Menzies witnessed the engagement of the Allied and Italian fleets with one of the Italian ships being hit before they retired under a smoke screen. This, according to Capt Roskill,[11] was the first engagement between the Italian navy and Admiral Cunningham's main fleet and was off the Calabrian coast. Both fleets were concerned with covering convoys; for the Italians, theirs to North Africa, and for the British, two convoys to Alexandria from Malta. It was indicative of the Italian reluctance to enter battle and the superior speed of their ships.

Three days later, S/Ldr Menzies was again airborne from Malta at dawn to patrol between Sicily and the Ionian islands. He had been flying for almost six hours when from 2000 feet he sighted a submarine on the surface. The vessel zig-zagged and the first stick of three 250 lb A/S bombs released by Menzies fell just astern. A second attack was made with two bombs as the submarine was submerging but they struck abaft the conning tower. A final bomb was released ahead of the vessel's track. This must have been the Italian submarine *Settimo* of 954 tons which had sailed from Augusta and one of five submarines in the area about position 3730N 1730E at that time. It reported being struck astern by bombing from a Sunderland on the 12th but had suffered only slight damage (*lievi danni*).[12]

Shipping Attacks and Enemy Fighter Action

F/O Lywood was airborne from Malta on 23 July as captain of N9029. While on patrol off Cape Spartivento in Southern Italy, a small enemy convoy of five merchant vessels including three tankers and escorted by a destroyer, was sighted. Due to a fault in the release mechanism, only three A/S bombs were dropped. The second pilot, Dundas Bednall saw one bomb burst under the bow of a ship, but the squadron record gives two ships believed to have been damaged. The destroyer, however, had promptly made smoke and headed away from its charges. On return to base, the Sunderland captain was severely reproved by the operations officer as it was considered that reprisal bombing of Malta would result.

During such 'standard' Ionian Sea patrols, the Sunderlands were expected to recce the harbour of Augusta in Sicily and in daylight, despite the heavy defences. They were attacked a number of times by Italian fighters and on 25th N9029 was approached by two Fiat CR42s. In the combat, one CR42 was seen to break off and go into the sea, while hits were claimed on the second CR42. The Sunderland reached Malta despite receiving hits.

Three days later, F/Lt Garside while on patrol from Malta was attacked by three Macchi 200 fighters. These were faster than the CR42s and were armed with cannon. In a combat lasting fifteen minutes, one enemy aircraft broke off in the first attack with smoke pouring from its engine. During the third attack, another fighter broke off and crashed into the sea. The remaining Macchi 200s withdrew. Garside's crew suffered no casualties and returned safely to Malta.

S/Ldr Ryley on this same day, the 28th was en route from Alexandria to Malta in Sunderland L5804 and by 1048 hrs had made a recce of Syracuse. Fifteen minutes later he was attacked by four Macchi 200s. The engagement lasted almost an hour and in that time one Macchi was shot down in flames and the remaining three made off with one apparently badly damaged. Three of the Sunderland's gunners were wounded in their legs but continued to man the guns until the enemy broke off the engagement. The second fitter LAC D.A. Campbell went into the wings to plug holes made in the tanks until overcome by petrol fumes. He was 'revived by bullet splinters'. Damage to the aircraft had been serious due to large calibre shells and incendiaries but she was beached at Malta in a sinking condition at 1215 hrs. A passenger on board was the *Daily Mail* correspondent Alexander Clifford who gave 'valuable assistance'.

The Loss of Sunderland N9025
On 6 August 1940 S/Ldr Menzies in N9020 sighted an enemy tanker escorted by a destroyer when he was near to his PLE. His signal resulted in a call from Alexandria to Aboukir where David Bevan-John was in the operations room.

The Navy decided to send out a strike force of Swordfish but a Sunderland was needed to take over shadowing from S/Ldr Menzies. Number 228 Sqdn's CO – W/Cmdr Nicholetts – considered it a suicide mission to the Tobruk-Derna area in broad daylight and in range of enemy fighters. His wish to undertake the sortie himself was refused and it was left to Bevan-John to find a scratch crew with his captain – F/Lt Thurston Smith.

As G/Capt Bevan-John recalls:

'I did not rate my chances of survival very highly and asked a friend to see my kit got home safely and off we went. On our way out we had two warnings regarding fighters but found the tanker escorted by a destroyer and shadowed it. Our orders included the instructions to land and pick up survivors from any Swordfish which was shot down. They

didn't turn up and after a wait of about 40 minutes anxiously scanning the skies, we were attacked head on by three CR42 Italian fighters firing cannon. Their first burst severed our hydraulic lines putting both nose and tail turrets out of action leaving us with the two K-guns midships.'

This, (from the operational record), was in position 3219N 2342E with the rigger – LAC Jones, killed, and three of the crew wounded.

Bevan-John continues:

'We were forced to land with our inner petrol tank on fire and all guns silent. After a magnificent landing by Smithy we began to take in water as we leaked like a sieve. We managed to plug the worst of the holes with leak stoppers and finally stabilised with the tail well down and all watertight bulkheads shut. We then awaited rescue by the destroyer which was standing off. I had the fire axe to hand and posted a look-out while attending to the wounded. Shortly there was a shout, "lifeboat is coming" so we gashed holes in the hull to sink the aircraft. I'd just finished when there was another cry: "The lifeboat has stopped". "Get the Aldis lamp and send an SOS" I ordered. It was a near thing. The whaleboat came alongside as we were very low in the water and we managed to get the wounded aboard leaving the pilots behind – the Italians refused to take any more. So by the time the boat returned the Sunderland was under the sea and we were swimming but fortunately it was warm. N9025 sank in 25 fathoms taking the dead with her.'

W/Cmdr Nicholetts went out in Sunderland N9020 for a rescue attempt but was ordered back on hearing that the crew of N9025 had been taken prisoner.

Submarine *Gondar's* Last Voyage
On 21 September the Italian submarine *Gondar* sailed from La Specia in the Gulf of

Genoa under the command of Naval Lieutenant Francesco Brunetti. Its intended mission was a raid against the British naval base at Alexandria and with, perhaps, the prime target of an aircraft carrier.

At Messina, *Gondar* took on board a special group – six officers, one NCO and three divers before departing on the 25th for Alexandria. While on the surface off Tobruk on the 29th Brunetti sighted an Allied unit 1500 metres away. Brunetti submerged but was attacked with depth charges. The first stick of charges caused some damage with partial flooding and during the night *Gondar* suffered further attacks causing serious damage.

On the 30th, F/Lt Alington was airborne at 0530 hrs in Sunderland L2166 of 230 Sqdn to undertake a patrol which was to last five hours. He was signalled by the Australian destroyer HMAS *Stuart* which had used up its supply of DCs during the night attack on the submarine. *Stuart* marked the position with a lifebelt. Alington noticed some air bubbles appearing on the surface of the sea and released some of his anti-submarine bombs which caused flooding of the submarine.

This was apparently more than enough for *Gondar's* crew which had already experienced 14 hours of depth charge attacks. The submarine was scuttled in position 3202N 2754E.[13] Most of the crew appear to have been picked up by HMAS *Stuart*, although from photographs taken by the Sunderland, there were three surface vessels in the vicinity. The photographs showed also, the provision on the deck of *Gondar* for 'human torpedoes' which might well have been released against units of the Royal Navy in Alexandria. F/Lt Alington was sent for by Admiral Cunningham who wished to gain a direct appreciation of the action.

The Sinking of the Italian Destroyer *Artigliere*

In October 1940 230 Sqdn had detachments at Suda Bay, Scaramanga and Malta although based at Alexandria. Their CO – W/Cmdr Geoffrey Francis – was at Malta on the 12th and was asked by the Navy to make

sure that the Italian Navy could not leave from their bases in Sicily undetected as there were two Allied convoys at sea. From the Italian official naval history, 2000 British troops were being transported to Malta.[14]

The Italians had received a sighting report of 15 Allied warships with five other vessels at 0845 hrs on the 11th from a civil aircraft and that same night four of their destroyers including *Artigliere* had sailed with three torpedo boats.

Number 230 Squadron had daily routine patrols south of Sicily but W/Cmdr Francis decided to make an additional reconnaissance himself. He was airborne at 0350 hrs in L5803 with S/Ldr Woodward's crew whose aircraft (2160) was u/s.

As G/Capt Francis recalls:

'We passed the Mediterranean fleet at first light and set course on the search pattern. Soon after, we sighted two destroyers. They fired at us; we did not wish to scare them so made no W/T sighting report but flew towards our fleet and signalled by Aldis lamp. *Warspite* and *Illustrious* were in line and both acknowledged our signal. Shortly after the whole fleet altered course onto the bearing we had given. I told *Warspite* we were continuing our patrol but it flashed "Q" telling us to wait. We flew at about 4000 feet and about eight

The Italian submarine *Gondar* after attacks by HMAS *Stuart* and F/Lt Allington of 230 Sqdn 30.9.40. Tubes for 'human torpedoes' are on the deck which were intended for the British fleet in Alexandria.

Swordfish formed on us and with one third flap out we led them towards the destroyers. Fighters from one of the carriers[15] attacked the Swordfish once, thinking they were Italians attacking us but there was no damage.

'When close to the destroyers we waggled wings and the Swordfish attacked with torpedoes, perhaps bombs. A destroyer was by then steaming home at very high speed. The leading British ship, HMS *York* had meanwhile opened fire but all shells fell just short of the destroyer except when the vessel had to jinx violently to avoid a well-aimed torpedo; the shell dropped close alongside. *York* torpedoed the burning destroyer *Artigliere* as she passed, causing a spectacular explosion. There was a mass of survivors in the water. I asked Malta to send another aircraft to take over my search and they did. We then went after the fleeing destroyer with a view to trying the effect of some A/S bombs on it. However the target was entering harbour at Syracuse so discretion was the better part of valour.

'En route to Malta we sighted two large and several smaller warships. By the time we had decided they were 8-inch Italian cruisers, we were right on top of them and they were firing at us with their main armament causing . . . great splashes which made it difficult to stay low to counter attacks made by their escorting fighters. The latter fired from such long range that our ·303s were not used but we remained untouched.

'We reported our sightings by W/T and made a landfall on Malta to check the position we had given. We suggested returning to shadow but Malta replied that a striking force had left, which, however, did not find the target, the Italians had presumably turned for home on being sighted and reported.'

The action between surface forces began on the 12th at 0137 hrs and ended at 0233 hrs after the *Artigliere* had been seriously damaged by the light cruiser HMS *Ajax* which had engaged at 3000 metres.

Artigliere was located later by HMS *York* which, after sinking the vessel, signalled its position as 3550N 1622E for rescues to be undertaken. A hundred survivors were saved from *Artigliere* and 125 from two Italian torpedo boats.

The Battle of Cape Matapan

Italy had invaded Greece on 28 October 1940 but by 14 November had been forced back to Albania. The British and French had committed themselves to assist Greece if attacked and Allied forces landed in Greece on 7 March 1941 just before an Italian counter-offensive against the Greeks.

The British were prepared to jeopardize their successes in North Africa and in operation *Lustre* began moving land and air forces to Greece. The Italians, prompted by Hitler, deployed their naval forces with the intention of attacking Allied convoys sailing from African ports.

On 26 March the Italian battleship *Vittorio Veneto* with eight cruisers and some destroyers left port. Admiral Cunningham was aware of the Italian intention; convoys were cleared and the British fleet comprising the battleships HMS *Barham*, *Valiant* and *Warspite*, the carrier HMS *Formidable* and nine destroyers, sailed from Alexandria on the 27th.

Number 230 Squadron had maintained a detachment of Sunderlands at Scaramanga in support of naval forces and on the 27th NM-P with F/Lt McCall was airborne at 0410 hrs on a dawn-to-dusk patrol. When off Sicily, he reported sighting two 8-inch cruisers and one 6-inch cruiser with a destroyer steaming at 15 knots on course 120° when 84 miles from Cape Passero.

F/Lt Alan Lywood in NM-V N9029 was also airborne from Scaramanga at dawn. After flying for just over two hours, at 0620 hrs three unknown ships were located; when in position 3412N 2414E, two 8-inch cruisers, one 6-inch cruiser and three destroyers were identified and reported as steaming due east.

Over the next nine and a half hours Lywood and his crew transmitted a series of reports during which the presence of two enemy naval forces was identified with the

NM-V N9029 of 230 Sqdn which, captained by F/Lt A. Lywood, reported Italian fleet movements leading to the Battle of Cape Matapan.

final report at 1550 hrs giving one force at position 3609N 2019E steaming at 30 knots on course 300°T, and the other force at 3526N 2110E on course 325°T at 30 knots. For this Sunderland crew it was a 13-hour sortie.

Of these sightings, W/Cmdr Lywood writes in retrospect:

'We were proceeding to our patrol area when Dundas Bednall in the 2nd pilot's seat thought he saw ships on the starboard bow. It was early morning and still a lot of mist with some broken cloud, a calm sea and visibility 3–10 miles. We closed on what were 8-inch Italian cruisers steaming in line ahead at high speed towards Taranto. We were mystified by what appeared to be a signal light, until the tail gunner reported shells landing in the sea just astern of us, and we were flying at 70 feet. We checked our position by flying to Kithers on the western tip of Crete before J. Hughes our W/Op sent out sighting reports. On inadvertently heading back towards the 8-inch cruisers, we sighted a second Italian force of 6-inch cruisers, and we thought, two "Cavour"-class battleships on courses which would lead them to join the first force.'

(From the operational record, N9029 reported two 'battleships' at 0859 hrs at 3418N 2347E and at 0935 hrs, 'five cruisers and 3 destroyers at 3455N 2324E).

On this same day, the twenty-eighth, Admiral Cunningham had ordered light forces, four cruisers and four destroyers, to join him south-west of Gaudo Island. A series of engagements were to follow including aircraft from HMS *Formidable* and from bases on Crete. The battleship *Vittorio Veneto* was damaged but escaped and, in a brief night action, three Italian cruisers, *Zara*, *Fiume* and *Pola*, were sunk. The Allies lost only one or two aircraft.

It was the report from McCall which prompted Admiral Cunningham to set sail with his battle fleet and to instruct Admiral Pridham-Wippell with his cruisers and destroyers to meet him.[16] Sunderland N9029, however, of 230 Sqdn was the only aircraft involved in shadowing the Italian cruisers and had reported correctly positions, courses and speeds. Alan Lywood was awarded the DFC and his engineer – Sgt J. Waterland the DFM. The aftermath of the naval battle involved Sunderland NM-X being airborne from Scaramanga at 0350 hrs on the twenty-ninth to search the area around 35°N 21°E to locate any crippled ships.

The search was changed later to an area 40 miles further north-west. At position 3522N 2050E about 25 liferafts with about 600 survivors either on or clinging to them were seen. The survivors were believed to have been from the Italian cruisers *Zara*, *Pola* and *Fiume* which had been sunk in the action by *Warspite*. The Sunderland landed and its captain attempted to verify who the survivors were but they made a request only for water, and the aircraft was ordered to continue on patrol. It returned to base at 1615 hrs. The following day Sunderland NM-P reported Greek destroyers proceeding to pick up survivors. Sunderland NM-V airborne from Scaramanga on 2 April sighted an Italian hospital ship *Gradisca* at 3557N 2053E apparently still engaged in rescue operations following the battle off Cape Matapan.

For the Italians, the Battle of Cape Matapan was *Operazione Gaudo* and in their summing up of that operation, their conclusion begins with the role of the Sunderland.[17]

For Churchill and Admiral Cunningham it removed the threat of a naval challenge in the eastern Mediterranean for that year.[18]

Yugoslavia and Greece

Mussolini had invaded Greece on 28 October 1940 from Albania which had been annexed. The British had given a guarantee of the security of Greece and occupied Crete and Limnos on the 31st.

For Hitler, the Balkans represented bases for either attack or defence of the Ploesti oilfields in Romania and on 4 November he ordered plans for operation *Marita*, the invasion of Yugoslavia and Greece via Bulgaria.

For the Russians, interest lay in the ports of Bulgaria which covered the exit to the Black Sea.

The RAF established a headquarters in Greece which by 15 November was commanded by AV-M J.H. d'Albiac and three squadrons of Blenheims and one with Gladiators became operational.

By December, despite greatly superior forces, the Italians were forced back from Greece into Albania.

Yugoslavia signed a pact on 25 March 1941 with the Axis Tripartite states but a military *coup d'état* followed in Belgrade with the young King Peter being used to displace the Regent Prince Paul.

On 6 April the Germans began a merciless aerial bombardment of Belgrade in operation *Strafgericht*. The German invasion was through Germany, Romania, and Bulgaria with the Yugoslavs capitulating on the 17th. Macedonia was invaded in the same month and Greece surrendered on the 24th.

On 16 April S/Ldr Woodward and F/O Brand in Sunderlands L2160 and L2166 'X' and 'U' of 230 Sqdn, flew to Kotor on the Yugoslav coast to evacuate 'important passengers' returning on the 17th with '48 passengers conveyed to Greece' (Scaramanga). It appears likely that the

'important passengers' included King Peter of Yugoslavia, as N9029 captained by F/Lt Lywood flew from Scaramanga to Suda Bay with King Peter, and as W/Cmdr Lywood recalls:

> 'King Peter came up to sit in the second pilot's seat. His aide threw a scarlet cloak over the seat but air currents blew it over the King.'

From the squadron's operational records Sunderland N9029 must have taken King Peter together with General Simonovitch via Suda Bay to Alexandria arriving at 1255 hrs on 18 April.

By 22 April 1941 the British withdrawal from Greece had begun and the Sunderlands of 228 and 230 Sqdns with additionally two BOAC flying boats served to evacuate personnel. This was in addition to their reconnaissance role acting as 'the eyes of the fleet'.

At 0320 hrs on that day NM-X L2160 captained by S/Ldr P.R. Woodward was airborne from Scaramanga with passengers which included members of the Greek Royal Family. The Crown Princess, Princess Katherine, Princess Alexandra, Admiral Prince George and the children of the Crown Princess. They were flown to Suda Bay on the north coast of Crete.

The following morning S/Ldr Woodward flew a further eleven passengers from Scaramanga to Suda Bay including King George of Greece, Prince Paul, the British Minister in Athens – Mr Palairet – and his wife and daughter. L2160 made a further trip that day from Suda Bay, but this time to Nauplia, Morea where the Sunderland was anchored away from the town at 1730 hrs to take on board thirty-seven RAF personnel during the night. It left at 0134 hrs on the 24th for Suda Bay.

F/Lt Frame of 228 Sqdn made a series of trips to evacuate RAF personnel including one of the 25th in Sunderland T9046 to the Kalamata area of Greece. This was where the main party under G/Capt Lee were supposed to have collected. Some firing against the aircraft soon stopped, and RAF men not seen from the flying boat appeared

King Peter of Yugoslavia, wearing a trilby hat, being evacuated by a 230 Sqdn Sunderland N9029 on 18.4.41.

from their hiding places. After landing in the harbour enquiries were made. Down from the hills came G/Capt Lee with 50 others; they were embarked and flown to Suda Bay. On an earlier trip to Nauplia, F/Lt Frame had found the whole of the Bay in dense smoke from shipping which had been bombed. He made a blind take-off using a course given by F/O Austin his navigator and was able to land evacuees at Suda Bay.

For F/Lt Lamond and his crew of 228 Sqdn, the 25th was no less eventful. In a flight from Suda Bay in T9048 a search was made of the Githeon area for an RAF party before landing in the harbour. Greek officials arrived in a rowing boat and explained in French that the RAF had moved to a bay in the south-west. One Greek Flt/Lieutenant was taken aboard. On reaching the area flashes by a hand mirror from a ground party were seen. Lamond flew low over the area twice to check the people being sought. On landing the Sunderland was anchored 100 yards from shore. Contact was made with a party of 101 officers and men of 112 Sqdn from Janina. Fifty-two were evacuated but a message was left that the Sunderland would return to pick up others unless a contrary order was given, but that they

should make their own escape if the aircraft was not back by 2000 hrs.

F/Lt Lamond did return, but to Kalamata rather than Githeon. He took on board seventy-two personnel in addition to his own crew. His fuel load was then 350–400 gallons. Take-off was reported as not excessively long and stability of the aircraft was not affected. The final trip of Sunderland T9048 was that night from Suda Bay to Kalamata. It was first ordered to take 1800 gallons of petrol for next day; a message was then flashed from ashore to take only 700 gallons and fly to Kalamata to deliver a message from the AOC Greece to G/Capt Lee. A take-off was made without a flare path. At 2330 hrs over Kalamata harbour a landing was attempted using the Sunderland's landing lights. In a calm sea, the aircraft crashed and broke up immediately. Survivors were Lamond, P/O Goldfinch, P/O Briscoe and Sgt Davis. Lamond attracted a fishing boat from a section of the hull after a search party from the shore had given up. P/O Briscoe was taken to a local nursing home, the other three to a Kalamata military hospital. It was then believed by the Squadron that Lamond, Goldfinch and Davis were made POWs. P/O Briscoe was evacuated with the RAF party under G/Capt Lee.

Evacuation from Greece and the Shell Refueller

At Scaramanga in April was a Shell refueller which had been used by No. 230 Squadron's detachment. On the 25th S/Ldr Alington who had just been released from hospital, took command of the vessel as salvage as much of the RAF stores as possible. Two Pegasus engines which could not be taken were machine-gunned, but equipment such as a Vickers gun and a portable radio were embarked. The vessel was manned by P/O Kirkpatrick, two wireless operators and a Greek; passengers were two Territorial Army nurses – Sisters Stoner and M. Williams. W/Cmdr Francis, OC Number 230 Sqdn, was then in charge of evacuation with the Sunderlands of 228 and 230 Sqdns and two Empire flying boats – *Coorong* and *Cumbria*. He was then at Suda Bay but arranged by W/T to meet Alington at Nauplion, Argos to pick him up with his crew.

S/Ldr Alington, with the refueller, left Scaramanga at 1730 hrs arriving at Hydra Bay at 0500 hrs on the 26th but leaving shortly afterwards for Myli which was reached at 1700 hrs.

At Myli, G/Capt Pelly was embarked as a passenger and the refueller headed for Kyparissia arriving at 0400 hrs on the 27th.

G/Capt Francis writing in retrospect, recalls taking L2160 X/230 from Suda Bay and landing at Argos at last light, i.e. after German aircraft had returned to base. While making his approach, the Sunderland was narrowly missed by a Greek Bofors gun. As he relates:

'We anchored off Argos and Alington came alongside . . . and he ferried General Maitland Wilson and about seventy assorted soldiers, sailors and airmen; his two nurses came aboard.'

'The firing was getting closer (the Germans I think were across the Corinth Canal). So after consultation with the very exhausted General, we taxied five miles down the coast using two starboard engines in a very strong offshore wind and to save batteries until those engines had charged them. We

stopped engines and drifted until near dawn . . . we landed at Suda Bay at first light (0605 hrs 28th).'

S/Ldr Alington, after leaving Kyparissia, arrived with the refueller at Cape Malea at 0400 hrs on the 28th. He turned back for two miles to find an anchorage until night, due to the potential danger of crossing to Suda Bay by day, where, however, he arrived safely on the 29th. He was still seriously ill and returned to hospital near Alexandria.

One of the lightest loads for a Sunderland from Scaramanga was taken on 20 April by F/Lt Bednall who was shown written instructions to pick up the AOC's wife – Mrs d'Albiac. He embarked that lady complete with one parrot and one other passenger – an RAF corporal, flying them to Crete.

By the end of April, evacuation of Greece was practically over with both Navy and Air Force stretched to the full. Capt. Roskill gives 50,732 as the total brought out from Greece representing 80 per cent of the number taken there in operation *Lustre*.[20] Attention of the Sunderland squadrons was now directed to the Crete to Egypt routes.

Crete

The Greek island of Crete with its small southern port of Sphakia 440 miles from Alexandria became the scene of the first major airborne invasion in history.

In May 1940 with Allied troops in Greece, Suda Bay on the north coast of Crete served as an Allied naval base. There were airfields at Maleme and Heraklion plus a landing strip at Retimo but both air forces and troops were ill-equipped and aircraft were limited. The crucial factor for Army, Air Force and Navy was the overwhelming superiority of the Luftwaffe which was able to land or drop fresh and highly trained troops.

The German attack on Crete began on 20 May 1941 with, according to Churchill,[21] 5000 troops dropped on that day, subsequently increased to totals of 15,000 airborne and 7000 seaborne[22] troops, supported by 650 operational aircraft, including 180 fighters and 430 bombers. The bombers and fighters were able to 'soften up' defending forces before the use of 700 transport aircraft and 80 gliders. Maleme was taken on 20 May by the Germans who then concentrated their attention on Suda Bay. With the airfield captured, German forces were built up and on the 26th[23] they reached Suda Bay; the evacuation of Allied troops from Crete was decided.

Denis Richards gives 14,500 out of 28,000 safely evacuated with 361 out of 618 Air Force personnel; Churchill states 16,500 men were taken safely to Egypt with a further 1000 helped to escape later. He estimates 13,000 were killed, wounded or taken prisoner but adds 2,000 naval casualties.

The Navy evacuated personnel using Heraklion, Sphakia, Plaka Bay and Tymbaki, but port facilities were only at Heraklion. In the Crete action, three cruisers and six destroyers were sunk, one battleship and one aircraft carrier damaged, also six cruisers and seven destroyers. Despite such losses, Capt Roskill assesses that it was necessary, politically and strategically to fight in Greece and Crete.[24]

The Germans had lost their *Fliegercorps* with, according to Churchill, 5,000 graves in Crete but over 15,000 casualties, killed or wounded.[25]

Evacuation from Crete by Sunderlands
On 1 May, 230 Sqn's detachment on Crete at Suda Bay was instructed to reduce its commitment to the care and maintenance of W/T equipment and marine craft. That same morning, V/230 flew the main body of the detachment to Aboukir including two stretcher cases. Five days later, F/Lt Lywood captained V/230 and embarked 25 passengers from Suda Bay and flew them to Alexandria. They included six members of the Greek Royal Family; Prince George of Greece and Denmark, Queen Marie, the Princesses Frederica and Alexandra, the latter with her two young children – Sophie and Constantine. Alan Lywood recalls the

Royal *entourage* included two maids and two dogs 'which fought'. They landed safely at 0850 hrs in Alexandria on 6 May . Sunderland V/230 N9029, after undertaking a patrol, landed some freight and passengers at Suda Bay from Egypt and embarked others to be flown to Egypt.

On the night of the 22/23rd, the destroyers HMS *Decoy* and *Hero* took on board from the south coast of Crete, the King of the Hellenes, the British Ministers and other VIPs before sailing to Alexandria.[26]

F/Lt Frame of 228 Sqdn in T9046 and U/230 were sent to the south coast of Crete on 30 May touching down at Spaki Manch. Two of Frame's crew rowed ashore in a rubber dinghy but found no trace of RAF personnel. F/O Austin from the Sunderland, however, obtained a bearing on a flickering light on Gaudo Island which gave the aircraft's position 6 miles SW of Sphaki Manch. Frame taxied to that position where a boat with twenty-five service personnel was located. They were flown to Aboukir. U/230 embarked about seventy RAF and Army personnel from Sphakia and returned to Aboukir. The last combined effort of the two Sunderland squadrons appears in their records for 31 May for evacuating personnel from Crete. F/Lt Frame in T9046 arrived at Sphaki Manch and flashed a pre-arranged signal at places likely to conceal personnel; there was no reply. He landed ten minutes later and an SOS from the shore was received. T9046 took on board six Greeks and an RAF officer before taxying westwards to where the Navy was embarking passengers and where the other Sunderland-N9029 was similarly engaged taking aboard seventeen passengers. Both Sunderlands returned safely to Aboukir after 0100 hrs on 1 June. About this time, General Wavell and Maj-General Freyberg were flown back to Egypt by Sunderland.

After its role in the evacuation of Crete, 228 Sqdn in June began a move to Bathurst for some of its personnel; 230 Sqdn Sunderlands remained based at Aboukir.

For Admiral Cunningham, the loss of Crete meant difficulties in supplying Malta

An engine change for a 230 Sqdn Sunderland using floats from a Dornier seaplane.

from the east due to German aircraft from Crete flanking Allied convoy routes and his appreciation gave the need for a Coastal Command organization equipped with torpedo, bomber and reconnaissance aircraft and able to take over the function of aircraft-carriers.[27]

Yugoslav Aircraft and Personnel with 230 Squadron

Following the invasion of Yugoslavia by Germany in April 1941, a number of aircrews escaped with their aircraft. Number 230 Squadron gives, in its record for 4 June, two Dornier floatplanes flown by Yugoslav crews operating from Aboukir on routine patrols.

By 19 June, 230 Sqdn had completed its move to Aboukir under the CO – W/Cmdr Francis – who, with his HQ staff, took over the buildings previously occupied by 228 Sqdn. The move from Alexandria was due to the risks of collision in a crowded

harbour where night flying was impractical and that Alexandria was obviously an enemy target.

Number 2 Yugoslav Sqdn commanded by Cmdr L.V. Petrovitch came under 230's control but was considered almost self-supporting but with some RAF ground crew assisting with maintenance and equipped with two workshop lorries. They had eight Dornier 22 seaplanes and one twin-engined seaplane and by 1 July appeared to be fully operational with Dorniers Nos 303 and 307 patrolling off Alexandria in trips of about 2½ hours.

G/Capt Francis, writing in retrospect recalls that the Yugoslav crews were pleasant and courageous but that the Yugoslav unit was later to be removed for political reasons.

Mr M.J. Vracaric writing from London gives the following:

'The Royal Yugoslav Navy Air Arm had no connection, operational or administrative, with the land-based Yugoslav Air Force. There were in peace-time 50–60 floatplanes in the Fleet Air Arm and after capitulation of Yugoslavia on 17 April 1941, members of the various units who did not want to lay down their arms and surrender to the Italians or join the new independent state of Croatia Air Force under Italo-German protection, bunched together and flew down to Crete, then Alexandria and finally Aboukir. They

Dornier 22s flown by Yugoslav personnel attached to 230 Sqdn.

Yugoslav personnel with 230 Sqdn at Aboukir being inspected by HRH The Duke of Gloucester.

came to the Middle East as a unit, and as Naval personnel, possessing good knowledge of English, almost immediately started flying under 230 Sqdn RAF. On arrival in Egypt towards the end of April 1941, plans for the organization of the Yugoslav Air Force were made during the month of May which envisaged one fighter squadron to be called No. 1 RYAF Sqdn and one maritime squadron to be called No. 2 RYAF Sqdn; one heavy bomber squadron to be No. 3 RYAF Sqdn. Numbers 1 and 3 were to be manned by the personnel of the land-based Yugoslav Air Force evacuated from Greece by sea.

'Because of lack of material, training and knowledge of English, Nos 1 and 3 were disbanded in autumn 1941 while No. 2 Sqdn carried on flying until the end of 1942. Towards the end of 1942 all personnel of No. 2 RYAF were transferred to the land-based British RAF units in North Africa and with their Yugoslav comrades from the disbanded squadrons, resumed flying.

'In Yugoslavia before the war, all aircraft, sea and land-based, had the same markings on the upper and lower surfaces consisting of blue, white and red concentric rings with a white cross superimposed. There were no markings on the fuselage except the National tricolour of blue, white and red painted on the aircraft rudder. On arriving in the Middle East, to avoid confusion, as the aircraft were German, and German and Italian aircraft had crosses in their markings, the white cross was overpainted and only roundels remained and these were also painted on the fuselage.'

One of the Yugoslav officers who flew Dornier 22s with No. 230 Sqdn RAF was Dinar Stanic who recalls:

'We landed in Aboukir Bay on 22 April 1941 with seven Dornier 22s and one Sim XIV (twin-engined low-wing monoplane on floats, made in Yugoslavia). The crews consisted of 15 R.Y. Navy officers and 11 NCOs.

'With the help of 203 MU and assistance of 230 Sqdn RAF, the unit soon started operational sorties under the command of No. 201 Group RAF (the first sortie on 6 May, I believe).

'Of great help to us were the eight Free French fitters that the RAF managed to find and posted to our unit to service the Dornier 22 engines. We were also joined by a Greek Dornier 22 crew.

'Now the R.Y. Air Force HQ in Cairo decided to form our unit into a squadron and went in search of the required personnel amongst escaped R.Y. Air Force men gathered in various camps in the Middle East. Soon RYAF personnel started to arrive and we received also, mobile workshops. The unit was then designated No. 2 RYAF Sqdn. We continued the operational sorties up to and including 26 April 1942. On 27 April the squadron was disbanded and personnel sent to Allassia camp near Heliopolis for some obscure political reasons.'

New Equipment for Number 228 Squadron

In May 1941, 228 based at Aboukir, was by then receiving new equipment. W/Cmdr Nicholetts air-tested L5806 which had been fitted with a two-gun dorsal turret. His gunnery officer P/O Mason stated that the cone of fire was good but that the balance of the guns was bad, making their movement very difficult. Later in the month Mason gave a series of lectures on the Vickers Gas operated (VGO) gun and the Browning which were new to some airmen remustering as aircrew.

Additional navigational equipment included a Mark II drift recorder and an astro compass, both installed on T9046. Compass swinging in flight by F/Lt Frame was achieved with the use of the astro compass.

On 1 June, 228 Sqdn received an Air Ministry signal to embark on HMT *Dumana* as soon as possible for Bathurst; another signal the following day was for 228 to hand over three of their aircraft to 230 Sqdn.

Two of 228's Sunderlands were scheduled to fly on the 10th and 12th. Meanwhile, still at Aboukir, F/O Rees in T9046 made a search for two Wellingtons which had ditched. He located the crew of one and picked up in an open sea landing F/O McArthur, P/O Kemp, and Sgts Anderson, Lamb, Dovey and Crooks.

W/Cmdr E.J. Brooks had succeeded W/Cmdr Nicholetts as CO of 228 in May 1941 and on 23 June left Aboukir in L5803. He reached Kampala the following day but with one engine which needed replacement. During his time at Kampala he conducted the native King of Buganda on a tour of the Sunderland.

The squadron personnel which had embarked on HMT *Dumana*, met up with the crew of HMS *Exeter* while at Mombasa and a rugby match was arranged. With temporary goal posts erected on a ground which had been located, the *Exeter* team beat the 228 Sqdn side 36–0. Later while en route to Durban, HMS *Exeter* overtook *Dumana* and a signal was received about the match score.

On 20 July, 228 Sqdn then based at Bathurst, received a signal that it was to be replaced by 204 Sqdn and personnel not due to return to the UK were to be absorbed into No. 95 Sqdn and aircraft to be allotted to 95 Sqdn.

Sunderland T9046 however, captained by F/Lt Frame, returned to Calshot in August. While en route at Gibraltar, General Viscount Gort and Vice-Admiral Somerville were taken aboard as passengers. Later, at Calshot, an airman who was working in the wing, was attacked by a poisonous snake which must have hidden behind a starboard tank when the aircraft was at Bathurst. It was stunned with a spanner, removed and put behind glass.

No. 230 Squadron at Aboukir

While 228 moved to Bathurst, 230 Sqdn remained in the eastern Mediterranean and from June 1941 was based at Aboukir. The role reverted to largely reconnaissance and A/S patrols.

On 15 June a 230 Sqdn Sunderland sighted the Vichy French destroyer *Cavalier Paul* in position 3550N 3118E steaming a course of 084 degrees at 24 knots. The destroyer was shadowed until lost due to darkness although the Sunderland crew were aware of firing from the vessel. *Cavalier Paul* (from 230's record), was

No. 230 Sqdn at Aboukir July 1941.

attacked by Swordfish of 815 Sqdn FAA scoring a confirmed torpedo hit plus two possibles. This action was about 64 miles off Cape Greco where, in a later search, lifeboats, Carley floats and wreckage were sighted.

F/Lt Ted Brand as captain of Sunderland L2166 was airborne at 1642 hrs on 1 August from Aboukir. He had been detailed to undertake an A/S search in conjunction with four destroyers off the Gulf of Sollum.

Meanwhile, the Italian submarine *Delfino* commanded by Capt. Corv. Alberto Avogadro di Cerrione had left Taranto on 27 July and on 1 August had submerged at 0440 hrs but at 1955 hrs surfaced to take a star shot to check his position. At 2323 hrs *Delfino* was in position 3212N 1446E when his lookouts sighted a Sunderland astern which flew over the submarine. The Italian gunners reacted promptly with machine-gun fire and the flying boat was shot down in flames. Six bombs released from L2166 fell a short distance away from the hull of the submarine but caused some internal damage.

The Italians were no less prompt in attempting to rescue survivors of the Sunderland and the four picked up were F/Lt Brand, F/O Packington, Sgt Yates and Sgt White.

Capt. Corv. di Cerrione was apparently aware of four destroyers on an A/S search and changed course from 230 degrees to 050 degrees returning to Taranto on 6 August. Number 230 Sqadron heard via a German broadcast on 5 September of their Sunderland crew being shot down by an Italian submarine with some of the crew taken prisoner. The mission of *Delfino*, a lone one, had been to patrol the waters to the north of Raz Azzaz and to attack Allied shipping heading for Tobruk during the period 30 July to 4 August; it had been effectively aborted.[28]

Anti-submarine Operations

S/Ldr Garside of 230 Sqdn was to make a series of attacks on enemy submarines. On 21 October 1941 he sighted one just breaking surface in position 3152N 3034E. He made a quarter attack from 300 ft

releasing two bombs followed by two further attacks. These may have been on the Italian submarine *L'Atropo* which was apparently undamaged.

In 1942, S/Ldr Garside gained a confirmed success. On 9 January he was airborne from Aboukir in Sunderland W3987 X/230 at 0905 hrs on an A/S patrol of the area bounded by 2500E to 2700E from the coast to 3300N, effectively a 'coast crawl' from Bardia to Mersa Matruh. This must have stemmed from the need to cover supply lines for the Allied 8th Army but to counter supplies scheduled for the Germans under Rommel.

When in position 3222N 2654E, Garside's ASV operator reported a blip six miles to port beam when the Sunderland was on a northerly track. Garside turned to port and homed onto the contact. At two miles distance a submarine was sighted ahead with its conning tower just visible and about to submerge. Three depth charges were released from the Sunderland, and in a second attack, four 250 lb bombs were dropped.

A huge bubble appeared, and on a further run over the target area, a large oil patch was seen with further bubbles. Garside considered that the submarine must have had some means of detecting aircraft as he had flown up-wind in poor visibility.

Alexandria harbour c. 1940–41 with Sunderlands of 230 Sqdn and Londons of 202 Sqdn.

Sunderland M/230 T9071 which had been captained by F/Lt Hughes, wrecked at Ras Amr, Libya 21.12.41.

Post-war lists credit 230 Sqdn with sinking U-577 on 9 January in position 3222N 2654E. It appears as the only Axis submarine sunk by aircraft in that month.

S/Ldr Garside made three more attacks on submarines in January 1942 but possible successes are unconfirmed. In the final one on the 31st at position 3150N 2654E, he narrowly missed a head-on collision with a Swordfish which was homing on to the same submarine.

A further unconfirmed attack was made by Garside on 6 February using 250 lb A/S bombs; here lack of success may be attributed to the use of bombs rather than depth charges as the bombs were reported to have straddled the vessel.

The first half of 1942 for the African campaign is given by Capt Roskill[29] as the period when the Allies struggled to control the sea routes to maintain Malta and to oppose enemy build-up in North Africa.

In March 1942 the Italians deployed four submarines off Tobruk and another five to the east of Malta.[30]

At the end of the month Sunderlands of 230 Sqdn made a series of attacks on submarines; four of these were in positions off Tobruk; two by F/Lt Milligan on the 27th and 29th; two by S/Ldr Garside on the 27th although any success appears unconfirmed. F/Lt Milligan's action on the 27th from L5806 is notable as details of the armament used are given more fully, with 250 lb A/S bombs set at 60 ft and 250 lb DCs set at 100 ft, the latter dropped after the vessel had submerged.

An additional duty remained for the squadron – ferrying freight and passengers to Malta.

In the following month of April, the Italians had six submarines off Tobruk;[31] attacks were made on the 19th, 22nd and 28th on unidentified U-boats by the Sunderlands captained by F/Lt Squires, F/Lt Brown and F/Lt Frame. W3987 NM-X was damaged by splinters from the DCs released by F/Lt Squires, requiring the aircraft to be flown to Alexandria for repairs.

Malta, ever subject to enemy bombing, had been awarded the George Cross on 16 April. In May, HMS *Eagle* and USS *Wasp* with the fast minelayer HMS *Welshman*, brought 61 Spitfires flown off from the carriers and supplies and munitions from *Welshman*. Although by such means, 123 fighters were delivered in four weeks,[32] Malta was losing seventeen fighters per week.[33] In June, two Allied convoys were scheduled to take further supplies to Malta, one from the west, one from the east.[34]

The Axis powers attempted to oppose such convoys but to maintain their supply lines to North Africa. Four Italian submarines were deployed off Mersa Matruh, twelve around Malta, and three groups of submarines covered the western route south of the Balearics and Sardinia.[35] Similar areas were covered in May, and the Sunderlands of 230 Sqdn operating from Aboukir made a series of attacks.

P/O Howell captained L5806 on 1 May to patrol the near convoy *Master*. After being airborne for almost three hours, a submarine was sighted 30 miles astern of the convoy. Howell attacked with A/S bombs and a salvo of four DCs which fell to starboard of the vessel. He reported the submarine losing forward speed before submerging and with quantities of thick oil rising to the surface. Although not so reported, P/O Powell may have attacked one of the group which included *Galatea* and *Nereide* although seemingly without causing damage.

F/Lt Frame, while escorting two destroyers on the 11th gained an ASV contact which was illuminated by firing cartridges. The surfaced submarine then seen was attacked with A/S bombs but no damage was claimed.

Number 230 Squadron records two more attacks in May including that by W/Cmdr Garside on the 26th. He reported using A/S bombs with a one second delay and with flash bombs attached. His 250 lb DCs fitted with Mk X pistols were set to detonate at 50 ft depth. This was in position 3229N 2449E off Tobruk. After his attack on the submarine, three hostile aircraft dropped flares. The only reference to a Sunderland

given by the Italian historian in this month is against the submarine *l'Argo*. *Argo*, captained by Ten. Vasc. Pasquale Gigli was operating 40 miles NW of Cape Caxine on the 27th when first attacked from the air at 2350 hrs with four bombs which caused damage to the submarine's batteries, and with the entry of water through the hull.

The damage was such that Gigli decided to remain on the surface and abandon his mission. At 1350 hrs the following day, *Argo* was sighted by the crew of W3983 RB-R of No. 10 Sqdn RAAF captained by F/L G. Pockley.[36] During his attack Pockley was subjected to AA fire but was able in further runs to release depth charges. After subsidence, damage was seen on the forward section of the vessel. Following the Sunderland's sighting report, Lockheed Hudsons were sent from Gibraltar and *Argo* suffered a further attack. Nevertheless, on the 30th *Argo* reached base at Caglieri.[37]

The other attack by 230 Sqdn was made by F/O Howell in L5806 while on a similar patrol to Garside but on the 28/29th. Howell sighted a submarine in position 3224N 2425E and released three A/S bombs and four depth charges. Evidence of damage to the submarine was an oil patch 100 yds in diameter.

The second half of 1942 was for 230 Sqdn largely 'routine'; anti-submarine patrols, escorts to surface vessels and with a number of sightings of submarines which submerged before attacks could be made. These operations were not without losses. F/O R.J. Murphy captained T9050 Y/230 on a patrol along the Egyptian coast beginning on 29 September. On returning to base at Aboukir at about 0250 hrs on the 30th he crashed on landing. Three of the crew were killed and nine injured. On 7 September Sunderland W3987 crashed on take-off from Aboukir in the sea near Fort Burg. Eight of the crew of thirteen were killed including the captain F/Lt A.F. Howell.

There was a further attack on a submarine by 230 Sqdn on 1 November. F/O R.H. Holcombe while on patrol at 1325 hrs noticed in position 3152N 3245E, a

W4021 NM-W captained by F/O Statham of 230 Sqdn at Kastelorizo, c. October 1943.

lengthening streak of bubbles coming to the surface. Two attacks were made using four DCs ahead of the streak but no evidence of damage was seen.

For 230 Sqdn the last notable event in 1942 was a visit by the AOC No. 201 Group – AV-M Slatter with Air Marshal Edwards AOC-in-C, RCAF Overseas, to meet Canadian personnel on the squadron.

1943 had a mixed beginning for 230 Sqdn while still based at Aboukir. Their CO – W/Cmdr C.R. Taylor – gained a 'Mention in Despatches' but they suffered a loss.

Sunderland N9029 NM-V had earlier served with distinction notably in shadowing the Italian fleet before the Battle of Cape Matapan but also in undertaking many evacuation trips from Greece and Crete.

It was airborne at 2400 hrs on 1 January captained by F/O Holcombe on an A/S patrol for a convoy eastbound to Port Said. N9029 failed to return. A search was carried out the following day by S/Ldr P.R. Williams in W4021. Wreckage had been located by a Wellington in position 3145N 3228E. S/Ldr Williams found an oil patch in that area with wreckage. He touched down in the Sunderland but found no survivors.

On 9 January the movement of the squadron from the eastern Mediterranean to British East Africa began with F/Lt Squires flying EJ136 via Wadi Halfa, Khartoum, Kisumu and Mombasa to Dar-es-Salaam which was to become the unit's base for the following year.

Following General Alexander's victory in North Africa, six Sunderlands were ordered back from East Africa to Aboukir in June. The Aboukir detachment came under 216 Group to undertake transport operations between Bizerta and Malta, but additionally under 242 Group to lay on ASR searches.

In the ASR operations from Bizerta, an Australian, F/O McNichol in JM659 was ordered on 17 July to search in the Bay of Naples. This was following the ditching of an American aircraft with survivors possibly in dinghies positions 4010N 1410E and 4028N 1247E. While approaching Maritimo Island, two E-boats were sighted and when in position 4020N 1300E a dinghy was located due to a torch being flashed from it. McNichol had flame floats dropped to act as a flare path for landing but with the presence of an enemy aircraft and his mid-upper turret u/s, he set course for base.

Another Sunderland, EJ141, was airborne just over two hours after McNicol's return and captained by another Australian – F/O G.O. Watson. With the position of the dinghy 70 miles SW of Naples, an escort of fifteen P38 Lightning fighters was provided. When 15 miles downwind of the position given by McNichol, the dinghy was sighted just two miles away. F/O Watson touched down and took on board a complete crew of six from a Marauder. One had a broken arm and leg, two others had minor injuries, three were uninjured. A call to base was intercepted by the squadron's W/T section and an ambulance awaited them on return. A search for the second dinghy had to be cut due to the limited endurance of the fighter escort. However, F/Lt Middleton in JM659 later located an empty dinghy in position 4010N 1410E. A signal was later received from No. 320 Bombardment Group signed by Col. E. Baumeister, US Army Air Corps, congratulating 230 Sqdn on the part they had played in this rescue mission.

F/O F.J. Statham attempted a quite exceptional rescue on 19 July. He was airborne from Bizerta late at night in EJ143, and after completing a square search off Sardinia, noticed a red flare fired from a Very pistol. After releasing some flame floats to make a flare path, he touched down in a heavy swell of 7–8 ft.

Despite further signal cartridges being fired from the dinghy and responses made from the Sunderland with an Aldis lamp, contact was lost due to the heavy swell. Statham was waterborne for over three hours and the Sunderland crew suffered some sickness. German voices were heard over the intercom and a brief glimpse of the dinghy showed it to be oval in shape. Unable to make contact, the Sunderland took off at dawn in a 10 ft swell with the sea

breaking right over it. Base was reached after a mission time of 8½ hrs.

On 29 July instructions were received for the aircraft in the Bizerta detachment to return to East Africa. W/Cmdr Dundas Bednall assumed command of 230 Sqdn on 25 August succeeding W/Cmdr C.R. Taylor.

References

[1] SWR I pp. 41–2
[2] SWR I p. 293
[3] GF p. 71
[4] MB I p. 54
[5] ABC p. 239
[6] MB I p. 59
[7] MB I p. 56
[8] WSC I p. 773
[9] MB I p. 70
[10] ABC p. 259 and GF pp. 99–110
[11] SWR I p. 298
[12] MB I p. 66
[13] MB I p. 91
[14] GF p. 204
[15] HMS *Eagle* or *Illustrious*
[16] SWR I p. 428
[17] GF IV p. 511
[18] WSC III p. 194
[19] Records give 65 including Gen. Rankin, the Greek PM and a 'Greek Prince'
[20] SWR I p. 436
[21] WSC III p. 253
[22] DR I p. 326
[23] WSC III p. 263
[24] SWR I p. 449
[25] WSC III p. 268
[26] ABC p. 374
[27] ABC pp. 387, 291
[28] MB p. 187 and *Delfino's* operational record
[29] SWR II p. 43
[30] MB chart 3
[31] MB chart 4
[32] SWR II p. 61
[33] SWR II p. 302
[34] SWR II p. 63
[35] MB chart 6
[36] MB II pp. 29–30
[37] Ibid.

Chapter 6
Iceland

ALTHOUGH A neutral country, Iceland would have constituted a serious threat if in World War 2, it had been occupied by German forces. This was due to its geographical position on the great circle route from North America to the United Kingdom – the vital Allied 'lifeline'.

One of the first indications of Iceland being considered as a base was a 'special mission' flown by the CO of 228 Sqdn – W/Cmdr Barnes – with Larry Skey and P/O Bevan-John during September 1939. This was in the RAF's PBY-4 P9630.[1]

At the time of the Norwegian campaign, Churchill, in a memo to the First Sea Lord, referred to the need for bases in Iceland for flying boats and for patrol ships to be refuelled.[2] An advanced party of Royal Marines arrived at Reykjavik on 10 May 1940 in the cruisers HMS *Berwick* and *Glasgow*; these were followed in June by Canadian troops from Halifax.[3]

For the British, Icelandic bases eased the task of covering the northern exits from occupied Norway and the North Sea through the 300 miles wide Denmark Strait and the 240 miles wide passage between the Faeroes and Iceland. Few escort vessels were available with the range to take convoys all the way across the Atlantic; bases in Iceland alleviated that deficiency. Initially however, a 'mid-Atlantic gap' remained devoid of cover by aircraft.

KG-G N9021 at Plymouth in 1940 while serving with 204 Sqdn. It crashed in the Cromarty Firth 15.12.40 when with 201 Sqdn.

Later, for the Americans, Iceland provided the shortest route to Russia from the Atlantic ports of New York and Philadelphia. A preliminary reconnaissance was made by the destroyer USS *Niblack* on 10 April 1941. While approaching the Icelandic coast survivors from a torpedoed Dutch vessel were picked up.[4] A U-boat approached and was attacked by *Niblack* with depth charges. It was the first action between American and German forces in WW2.

By June 1941, air escorts could be provided for 700 miles from the British Isles, 600 miles from Canada, and 400 miles from Iceland, leaving a 300-mile Atlantic gap.[5]

Hitler had intended taking islands from Iceland to the Cape Verdes as advance bases for U-boats, and Admiral Raeder had correctly feared that Iceland would be occupied by the Allies. For the Icelanders it was 'Hobsons's Choice', and on 7 July 1941 their Prime Minister Herman Jonasson invited the Americans when in fact they were approaching Reykjavik.[6]

On 4 September while USS *Greer* was off Iceland in position 6245N 2737W, U-652 made two torpedo attacks against her. This was *de facto* war according to Professor Morison.[7]

Initially, the RAF in 1940 had deployed Fairey Battles of No. 98 Sqdn in Iceland, but a number of other squadrons were to follow including Hudsons of 269, Liberators of 120, Venturas of VP-128 USN, and Catalinas or Cansos of VP-84 USN, 162 Sqdn RCAF, and 209 Sqdn RAF. Sunderlands were flown to Iceland by 201 and 210, while 204 Sqdn Sunderlands became based there. The Norwegian No. 330 Squadron operated Northrop floatplanes followed by Catalinas and Sunderlands. Whether British, American, Canadian or Norwegian, they came under Coastal Command control.

Number 204 Squadron was one of the first units to operate Sunderlands from Iceland but in June 1940 was based at Sullom Voe. On the 20th the battlecruiser *Scharnhorst* which had earlier been attacked by Skuas from HMS *Ark Royal*, was heading south for Germany from Norway. On the 21st a number of Coastal Command aircraft including Hudsons from 224 and 233 Sqdns flew to shadow or attack.[8]

Number 204 Squadron detailed F/Lt Phillips in Sunderland N9028 'A' to shadow *Scharnhorst* and he was airborne from Sullom Voe at 1237 hrs setting course for position 5919N 0342E. The Sunderland was initially escorted by three Blenheims from Sumburgh but en route a Dornier 18 was encountered and in air-to-air combat the gunner in one of the Blenheims was

A complete engine change for L5800 'J' while serving with 204 Sqdn.

killed and all three Blenheims returned to base. The Sunderland however, at 1445 hrs sighted *Scharnhorst* escorted by seven destroyers in position 6005N 0339E steaming due south at 20 knots.

Phillips shadowed them and 25 minutes later *Scharnhorst* altered course to 260 degrees. An attack on the battlecruiser by five Swordfish was witnessed with one of them crashing into the sea. The Sunderland itself was now shadowed by an He60 which attempted to bomb the flying boat. For an hour Sunderland N9028 was subjected to AA from the warships which used possibly 5·9-inch and 4·1-inch calibre when F/Lt Phillips was flying at 600 ft 4–7 miles from *Scharnhorst*.

The Sunderland was now approached by three Me109 fighters, and then a fourth. One was shot down in flames but the Sunderland's rear turret was put out of action and fuel tanks were holed, albeit without casualties in the crew.

N9028 returned to base and was succeeded by S/Ldr Thomas in N9046 who sighted *Scharnhorst* with the destroyers in position 5925N 0415E at 1856 hrs. Cloud was at 11,000 ft and shadowing was made at 10,000 ft. At 1915 hrs two cruisers and five destroyers were sighted steaming north at 20 knots. They were challenged and the response was about 50 rounds which fell low and astern of the Sunderland. The vessels were escorted by six Me110s and four of these shadowed the

s.s. *Manela* in Iceland serving as a depot ship for 204 Sqdn c. 1941.

Sunderland but did not close. S/Ldr Thomas was recalled to base.

In August 1940, W/Cmdr K.F.T. Pickles assumed command of 204 Sqdn. On 9 November he undertook a cross-over patrol between Iceland and the Faeroes intending to intercept an enemy raider. He had been airborne from Sullom Voe at 0645 hrs and at 1310 hrs was signalled to return to Stranraer. Due to lack of fuel he decided to land in Iceland. Severe weather precluded Reykjavik and he turned east. Failing light and more bad weather made it necessary to touch down on Hornefjord where the Sunderland ran onto a sandbank but with no damage caused. At that time 204 had six operational Sunderlands spaced from Iceland to Pembroke Dock with three unserviceable.

Number 204 Squadron began its move from Sullom Voe to Iceland on 3 April 1941 with F/Lt Armitstead in T9072 and F/Lt Lovelock as captain of N9024. They were followed by F/Lt Hughes in N9023 the following day. Two more Sunderlands were flown in on the 6th and 7th – N9047 and T9070.

Ground staff were embarked on the transport ss. *Manela* on 1 April to arrive at Reykjavik on the 5th. The ground staff included such as John Loader of the Marine Craft Section and Roy Barton a Halton-trained fitter IIE. One of the latter's first tasks was to work on T9072 which had run aground. So that two barges could be run under the Sunderland's wings for her to be refloated, two inner propellers were removed.

After an air-test of Sunderland N9023 on the 23rd, F/Lt Hughes undertook a convoy escort taking off at 2015 hrs. While returning the following morning at about 0500 hrs, he crashed into a mountain near Fragjadalsfjall, ENE of Grindavik in SW Iceland. The aircraft caught fire and blew up. The rear gunner (Sgt Taylor) was trapped in the turret and killed; another of the crew – Sgt Cook – died later. The second pilot and a fitter – Bill Doddington – walked for help probably to Grindavik or Keflavik rather than Reykjavik as stated in the squadron record. Doddington returned to the site of the crash with a rescue team and did much to save others – he was awarded the DFM. It was believed that a total of three were killed and ten injured, the third fatality being Copping who died on the 28th.

Another of 204's early sorties while based in Iceland was by F/Lt Stead in T9070 on 3 May. He had been detailed to escort a convoy bound for the UK from Halifax – SC29 – and then to search for a Norwegian merchant vessel *Taranger* and locate an outward bound convoy from Liverpool – OB316. He found a destroyer also searching for *Taranger* which however, had been sunk by U-95 by torpedo and gunfire in position 6107N 2520W, at probably first light that day. Two days later survivors from *Taranger* were picked up by a corvette.

Battleship *Bismarck*
Under Exercise *Rhine*, the German battleship *Bismarck* with the heavy cruiser *Prinz Eugen* sailed from Gdynia on 13 May with the intention of attacking Allied Atlantic convoys. *Bismarck* would have engaged escorts while *Prinz Eugen* would have sunk as many merchant vessels as possible, perhaps leaving one to pick up survivors.

En route they were sighted by a Swedish vessel on the 20th and by a reconnaissance Spitfire on 21 May. There was a further report from a FAA Maryland indicating the departure of *Bismarck* and *Prinz Eugen* from Bergen, and by the 23rd they had entered the Denmark Strait.[9]

The Denmark Strait was patrolled by the cruisers HMS *Norfolk* and *Suffolk* which the German raiders attempted to evade by increasing speed to 30 knots. Coastal Command deployed a number of aircraft including Catalinas of 240 and 209 Sqdns and Sunderlands of 201 Sqdn.

On the 22nd, Sunderland L5800 of 201 captained by F/Lt Rae flew a cross-over patrol at 05°W between 62°N and 65°N to locate the German warships which had been reported at Bergen on the 21st. This was followed by Sunderland P9606 with F/Lt Alexander patrolling between Iceland and the Faeroes on the 23rd. That same day,

F/Lt Fletcher in T9076 escorted the Home Fleet which had sailed from Scapa Flow the previous night. Number 201 Squadron's record correctly records HMS *King George V, Victorious, Galatea, Kenya, Hermione* but with six destroyers.[10] This force was due south of Iceland at first light on the 24th. Fletcher had contacted the fleet at 1445 hrs in position 6030N 0930W steaming at 16 knots. A message was flashed by the fleet to the Sunderland: 'At 1605 my posn is 6026N 0956W 270° 16 knots.' At 1845 hrs the Sunderland received another message from the force: 'Failing development 0800 posn 6030N 1815W'. F/Lt Fletcher left the Home Fleet at 1930 hrs position 6030N 1200W and was recalled to Oban.

F/Lt Vaughan of 201 Sqdn had been detached to Iceland from Sullom Voe with Sunderland L5798 ZM-Z on 12 May, but late on the 23rd was briefed to search for and shadow an enemy force. He was airborne in L5798 at 2025 hrs. Sighting reports had been received from the cruisers HMS *Suffolk* and *Norfolk* of an enemy battleship and battlecruiser heading south through the Denmark Strait with the last position given by *Norfolk* as 6617N 2543W at 1945GMT. F/Lt Vaughan flew a calculated intercept course. At the time of Vaughan's take-off, HMS *Hood* and *Prince of Wales* must have been at about 27° roughly due west of Reykjavik.

Weather conditions were bad with 10/10ths cloud at 300–500 ft with frequent showers and poor visibility. The need for frequent W/T watches resulted in the Sunderland's ASV being used only occasionally. At 0205 hrs on the 24th Vaughan returned to Onverdarnes, Iceland to make a landfall and then set course 240°T to intercept the enemy whose course and speed had been estimated at 200° 30 knots, but following another signal, Vaughan's interception was amended. At 0355 hrs gun flashes were seen in position 6330N 3200W and four ships were reported to be engaged in battle. At that time, the Sunderland's first wireless operator – Bam Martyn – was taking his turn in the rear turret and with the second operator – Les Archer – at the radio. Bam Martyn recalls:

'As we approached the ships we saw and heard, or perhaps felt, the gunfire before we had sorted out which group was British and which was German. I have an abiding memory of the unbelievable flash of the explosion that killed *Hood* and the shock of the realisation that a ship had sunk.'[11]

Number 201 Squadron records that a ship was seen to explode, catch fire and sink within a few minutes. Only later was it realised to have been HMS *Hood*. F/Lt Vaughan identified two ships as German which at 0420 hrs were signalled as being on course 220° at 30 knots. HMS *Prince of Wales* and *Norfolk* were reported on the beam of the enemy at 12 miles range with

Sunderland T9072 KG-F of 204 Sqdn after running aground in Iceland, April 1941.

HMS *Suffolk* on the starboard quarter and following the enemy course.

The naval engagement was over within ten minutes of the Sunderland's arrival which reported the larger enemy ship emitting smoke and losing a large quantity of oil, (later to be proved significant).

At 0500 hrs Vaughan approached within five miles of the enemy ships on their starboard beam and identified them as *Bismarck* but the *Prinz Eugen* incorrectly as *Admiral Scheer*. Twenty minutes later, Martyn in the Sunderland was called to the flight deck to signal by Aldis lamp to HMS *Suffolk* 'Can direct you to survivors'. The reply came: 'No, what is bearing of enemy?' '216°T'. *Suffolk*: 'Thank you, destroyer will pick up *Hood*'s survivors.' At 0605 hrs the Sunderland received a signal from the cruiser HMS *Norfolk*: '*Suffolk* reports enemy battleship on fire, investigate and report course and speed.' F/Lt Vaughan complied and ¾ hour later confirmed the enemy's course and speed as 220° 30 knots with *Bismarck* losing oil but no fire visible. The two cruisers were still maintaining contact with the enemy, *Norfolk* on the port beam and *Suffolk* astern.

By now, weather conditions were improving with good visibility; Vaughan signalled to *Suffolk* that he was returning to base and set course for Reykjavik. En route, six destroyers were sighted in the position of HMS *Hood*'s demise.

In the engagement the *Prince of Wales* had scored hits on *Bismarck* with 14-inch shells causing damage below the bow waves and to oil tanks. Admiral Lütjens decided to abandon his mission and head for St. Nazaire. The escape of *Prinz Eugen* was covered by *Bismarck* turning towards the shadowing cruisers; they, however, lost contact just after 0300 hrs on the 25th. The Royal Navy withdrew many ships from other duties to counter *Bismarck* and RAF Coastal Command laid on many patrols by Catalinas, Hudsons and Sunderlands.

From 201 Sqdn on 26 May, F/Lt Vaughan in L5798 was deployed from Reykjavik to position 6030N 1430W and then to follow a 300 mile track of 240° with F/Lt Alexander in P9606 on a parallel track and with two more Sunderlands from 204 Sqdn. North-west of the Faeroes, F/Lt Rea in L5800 flew a cross-over patrol from Sullom Voe following F/Lt Fletcher in T9076. Air Chief Marshal Sir Frederick Bowhill, AOC-in-C, Coastal Command, on his own initiative, deployed Catalinas of 209 and 240 Squadrons well south and it was to be P/O Dennis Briggs, captain of Catalina AH545 of 209 Sqdn who sighted *Bismarck* west of southern Ireland.[12]

Subsequent attacks by the Fleet Air Arm damaged *Bismarck*'s steering gear and in an engagement with units including HMS *King George V*, *Rodney* and *Dorsetshire*, the *Bismarck* was sunk.

Number 204 Squadron remained based at Reykjavik and on 29 May F/Lt Stead took the CO – W/Cmdr Coote – with W/Cmdr Collins on a survey of Iceland. They first flew to the east coast touching down at Budareyri for 1½ hours before heading north to Akureyri. They remained there before a return flight on the 30th to Reykjavik. About 200 photographs were taken of possible landing areas and conspicuous landmarks. On 4 June S/Ldr Laws undertook a DF calibration survey lasting ten hours in which a further 100 photographs were taken. While leaving Reyharfjordur (Budareyri) on the east coast, the wreckage of a Heinkel 111K was sighted halfway up the cliff on the north side of the fjord.

F/O Wood in Sunderland N9047 flew from Reykjavik to Thingvalla Lake on 9 June. He landed there and a check was made on facilities available for flying boats and personnel before returning to Reykjavik the following day. After this same aircraft had been refuelled at moorings on Skerjafjordur, smoke and flames were seen rising above the mainplane, this by a signaller who happened to be watching from ss. *Manela*. Within 2½ minutes the aircraft's mainplane broke off and tipped over. Those on board were taken off by launch. Within seven minutes of the fire breaking out, two-thirds of the Sunderland was under water and sinking fast. Some attempts were made at salvage, and coxswain John Loader recalls

that the engines of N9027 were recovered within 24 hours.

Five PBYs of the United States Navy arrived on 3 July followed by two more on the 4th. They became based in Iceland with the tender USS *Goldborough* and later, two squadrons of the American Navy's PBYs – VP73 and VP84 – operated with success under the control of RAF Coastal Command.[13] On 10 July the AOC-in-C of Coastal Command – Air Chief Marshal Sir Philip Joubert de la Ferte – visited Iceland to inspect aircraft and crews. By then there was an awareness that 204 Sqdn was due to move.

One of the last sorties for 204 from Iceland before the move was by F/Lt Armitstead on 7 July when he escorted convoy OB341A. On return he witnessed the American forces arriving with battleships, cruisers and destroyers and merchant ships heading for Reykjavik. Photographs of the event were taken by W/Cmdr Coote in N9044.

The operational strength of 204 Sqdn at this time was seven Sunderlands – five at Reykjavik, one at Pembroke Dock, and one under repair at Shorts, Rochester.

In July 1941, 204 Sqdn moved from Iceland to Gibraltar with the CO – W/Cmdr Coote – leaving in W3981 initially to Pembroke Dock on the 13th with three other aircraft T9074, N9044 and L2158 following. Some landed at Stranraer due to bad weather. A further stage was for four aircraft flying to Gibraltar from Pembroke Dock on the 15th. The ground party sailed from Reyjavik in ss. *Manela* on the 17th in charge of the adjutant A/F/Lt Dance and P/O J. Dewar.

References
1   AH 'FC' p. 34
2   WSC I p. 687
3   SWR I p. 345
4   SEM I p. 76
5   SWR I p. 459
6   SEM I p. 74
7   SEM I p. 79 and SWR I p. 472
8   AH 'S&S' p. 49
9   AH 'FC' pp. 21–24
10   SWR I p. 397 map 30
11   In letter to author
12   AH 'FC' pp. 22–24
13   AH 'FC' pp. 34–41

Chapter 7
Gibraltar

T HE ROCK of Gibraltar, 1,400 ft high, three miles long and ¾ mile wide is connected to southern Spain by a flat sandy stretch. It was taken by the British in 1704 and in WW2 was of great strategic importance controlling the western entrance or exit to the Mediterranean Sea.

For the Royal Navy it provided a base for Force H; for the Army it was a fortress, and for the RAF, a base for flying boats and land aircraft, serving also as an important staging post for aircraft in transit.

British strategy in WW2 was based on France as an ally which would be responsible for the western Mediterranean, while the Royal Navy would control the eastern basin.[1] The collapse of France and the entry of Italy into the war required the British to contend not only with a powerful Italian fleet supported by an Air Force, but a potentially hostile French fleet supported by aircraft. Much British effort was devoted to countering some French naval units, suffering also, losses due to Vichy French aircraft.[2]

A number of RAF squadrons came to be based at Gibraltar or to provide detachments including notably, 233 and 48 Squadrons with Hudsons, 179 Sqdn Wellingtons and 202 Sqdn operating Londons, Swordfish, Catalinas and Sunderlands.

For the Hudsons, Wellingtons and Swordfish, the former racecourse was transformed into a west to east runway and which, in 1943 was being extended into the harbour lying to west of the rock.

Swordfish of the FAA were used to patrol the Straits of Gibraltar and this task was later taken up by PBYs of VP-63 USN equipped with MAD gear.[3]

N6138 coded TQ for 202 Sqdn which was detailed to recce the North African coast for French fleet units, and shown here at Aboukir, July 1940.

Some of the potentially hostile French fleet at Oran 5.7.40 after the Royal Navy's action.

A feature at Gibraltar was the sight of 'Spitfire boxes'; wooden packing cases from which Spitfires were removed for assembly and then flown off from the North Front runway. Petrol for aircraft came in 4-gallon tins and both wood from the Spitfire boxes and the empty tins were put to various uses. Food for both Army and RAF personnel came as 'Fortress rations' and included corned beef, 'M&V' (meat & vegetables), tinned potatoes, tinned herring and soya sausages. Hard biscuits but white bread. There was a free issue of 50 cigarettes per week and, for RAF aircrew, a ready supply of sweet tea seemingly at the direction of the Medical Officer. The additional rations for those who flew operationally were shared in at

A group of No. 10 Sqdn RAAF aircrew including the two pilots – F/Lt Cohen and F/O Stewart who took Lord Gort to Rabat.

W9024 H/204 at Gibraltar 28.7.41 while float repairs were undertaken on HMS *Ark Royal.*

least one squadron with the ground staff who maintained the aircraft.

Possible diversions for personnel included bathing near the east end of the runway, the shops of Main Street, and for the virile who were so minded, official arrangements were made for some feminine contact in either Algeciras or La Linea. In addition to cinema shows, celebrities such as Solomon, John Gielgud and Elizabeth Welch gave performances from time to time.

An Area Combined H.Q. was formed at Gibraltar and with aircraft within Coastal Command control. Coastal's published record for Gibraltar gives 24 enemy submarines sunk and 10 damaged. Of those sunk, two were credited to Sunderlands operated by 202 Sqdn, all the others sunk or damaged were by Hudsons, Catalinas and Wellingtons. Some of the sinkings were shared with the FAA or HM ships.[4]

One of the first Sunderland flying boat detachments to Gibraltar was made by No. 10 Sqdn RAAF in July 1940. This was by F/Lt I.S. Podger as captain of RB-K P9605 and intended to reinforce 202 Sqdn against possible Italian fleet and French hostility from Oran. After a series of sweeps east from Gibraltar, Podger made a

reconnaissance of Casablanca on the 19th followed by one on the 21st from Oran to Cape de Gata.

Following a request for another Sunderland to operate from Gibraltar, F/Lt Birch was sent in P9602 on the 29th. En route west of Brest he attacked a Dornier 18 and in an exchange of fire, the enemy appeared damaged but the front turret of the Sunderland was put out of action and the gunner was wounded; the hull was holed also by a cannon shell. F/Lt Birch returned to Mount Batten, and a third Sunderland, P9600, was despatched.

Following Italy's entry into the war, Admiral Cunningham had expressed the need for reinforcements to Malta and the aircraft carrier HMS *Argus* was used to take twelve Hurricanes to south-west of Sardinia from where they were flown off to Malta. The two Sunderlands served as cover for this operation and ferried also, airmen to Malta to service the fighters.[5]

When the French surrendered to the Germans, units of the French fleet were located at various ports. At Mers-el-Kebir, near Oran were the modern battlecruisers *Dunkerque* and *Strasbourg*, battleships *Bretagne* and *Provence*, a seaplane carrier and six destroyers. At Oran, seven destroyers and four submarines.[6] Winston Churchill contemplated the effect of such units against our trade routes.[7]

On 2 July a communication was sent to Admiral Somerville who was to command Force H based at Gibraltar. The text of that signal gave a series of options to the commander of the French fleet but concluded with an ultimatum of force being applied to prevent the French fleet falling to the Germans or Italians.[8]

On 30 June two Sunderlands from 228 Sqdn at Pembroke Dock were detached to 202 Sqdn at Gibraltar. They were P9621 with F/Lt Brooks and F/Lt Craven as captain of P9622 including in his crew, P/O L.L. Jones and P/O Goyen. The two Sunderlands flew in formation to Gibraltar.

F/Lt Brooks made a reconnaissance of Oran the following morning and reported sighting *Dunkerque, Strasbourg, Bretagne, Provence* and the six destroyers at Mers-el-Kebir. F/Lt Craven followed that afternoon in P9622 and confirmed no change in the disposition of the French fleet.

On 3 July F/Lt Craven patrolled east from Gibraltar to look for enemy surface vessels and while off Algiers, sighted the Italian fleet. He touched down that evening

off Sfax before returning the next day to base. F/Lt Brooks made a reconnaissance of both Algiers and Oran on the 4th and while entering Oran, his Sunderland was attacked by three French Curtiss 75As. P/O Pyne at a starboard midship's gun was wounded and the Sunderland was badly damaged but one French fighter was shot down and a second probably. P9621 returned a few days later to Pembroke Dock for repairs.

Of Force H action against the French; a destroyer was sent on 3 July with Capt. C.S. Holland to attempt a peaceful negotiation – it failed. At 1725 hrs the French were preparing for action; at 1754 hrs Admiral Somerville opened fire. *Bretagne* was blown up, *Dunkerque* and *Provence* were damaged together with other ships. *Strasbourg* escaped to Toulon with five destroyers.[9] F/Lt Craven made a reconnaissance of Oran and Mers-el-Kebir on the afternoon of the 5th to find French warships beached and destroyed. Although the Free French were later to form a Sunderland squadron, there were Vichy French who remained prepared to shoot down such as Hudsons, and Catalinas, if not Sunderlands.[10]

The flying-boat squadron at Gibraltar in

Anthony Eden's telegram commending the No. 10 Sqdn RAAF crew captained by F/Lt Havyatt 17.2.41 on a flight to Gibraltar in very severe weather.

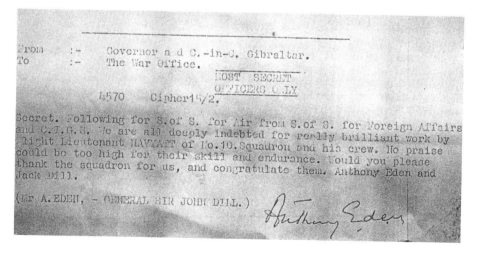

WW2 – No. 202 – was initially equipped with Saro Londons but by May 1941 was receiving Catalinas and the following year, some crews were flying Sunderlands. Number 204 Squadron moved down to Gibraltar from Iceland in July and by the 20th, six of their Sunderlands were there including one u/s. A seventh was still at Rochester. Roy Barton, a fitter with 204, had drawn tropical kit on the 16th and had flown down to Gibraltar in KG-M L2158. This Sunderland smashed off the starboard float on the 20th damaging the securing lug on the mainplane. There were no spares but

Ferrying and Detachments to Gibraltar

Number 10 Squadron RAAF although based at Mount Batten to undertake A/S patrols and convoy escorts, was required from time to time to ferry VIPs to Gibraltar. F/Lt H.G. Havyatt was detailed for such a trip on the night of 14 February 1941. His crew had been working on their aircraft P9605 RB-K that day and as one of them, Bill Vout recalls:

'That night the weather began to blow up and we realised that take-off was very unlikely (but). . . . Geoff Havyatt

N9027 DA-J of 210 Sqdn which sank at Gibraltar in a gale 11.4.41.

naval personnel on the carrier HMS *Ark Royal* made a mild steel replacement.

While based at Gibraltar, 204 undertook a number of convoy escorts. At that time, as throughout the war, convoys were being run at great cost to keep Malta supplied. Despite the dangers in the Gibraltar to Malta run, Churchill considered that convoy route less hazardous than from Alexandria.[11]

During August, 204 returned to Pembroke Dock and prepared for a move to Bathurst, West Africa where W/Cmdr Coote arrived on the 26th in Sunderland T9074.

came out to us and remarked, "Our passengers are VIPs who have to attend an urgent conference in the Middle East. They are game to risk the storm if we are."

F/Lt Havyatt later returned with the VIPs and gave a list of their names: R/Hon Anthony Eden, Foreign Secretary; General Sir John Dill, Chief of Imperial General Staff; his ADC Brigadier Mallaby; Mr Pierson Dixon, Foreign Office; and Mr Ralph Stephenson, Eden's principal secretary. This trip had been prompted by a meeting of the Defence Committee on the

11th following General Wavell's victory in Cyrenaica.[12] It would be for Eden and General Dill to discuss Middle East problems related to Greece and Turkey.

Sunderland P9065 was airborne at 2335 hrs, and there were two other flying-boats also attempting the trip at intervals. Eden gives details of this flight in his memoirs referring to the storm being so violent that headway could hardly be made. As Bill Vout recalls: 'We tried at least twice to climb above the storm but being without oxygen, were limited to 12,000 feet.' They had needed to use rich mixture and began to run short of fuel. They cut across Portugal and reverted to weak mixture, now no longer climbing, and with the wind to beam instead of head-on. They adopted a procedure normally avoided, i.e. draining a tank dry before switching to another. This meant a cut in engines before the switch was complete. Exceptionally, most of the crew suffered air-sickness. The passengers suffered similarly.

As Gibraltar was approached, turbulence abated a little but there was a heavy swell. Havyatt touched down outside the harbour and taxied in through the entrance. A check on the remaining fuel indicated 20–30 gallons. From Mount Batten to Gibraltar had taken 13 hrs 10 mins. The rigger of P9605 was worried that the rough conditions would tear the normal mooring gear from the aircraft and a heavy manilla hawser was passed round the buoy and taken up through the Sunderland to the main spar. Of the two other Sunderlands, one from 95 Sqdn was forced down in Portugal, the second arrived shortly before Havyatt having made a shorter cut across Portugal.

Sir John Dill and Anthony Eden sent a signal to the Air Minister stating:

'We are deeply indebted for really brilliant work by F/Lt Havyatt of No. 10 Sqdn and his crew. No praise could be too high for their skill and endurance. Would you please thank the squadron for us and congratulate them.'

As Lord Avon, Eden later endorsed that tribute in his memoirs. He must have checked the service of F/Lt Havyatt and refers to him being killed in action.[13]

In the following months of 1941, No. 10 had a series of detachments to Gibraltar. Some flights extended to Malta and Alexandria and some links were made with 230's operations in the eastern Mediterranean area.

Detachments of Sunderlands from No. 10 Sqdn RAAF were made from Mount Batten to Gibraltar in April and May 1942. F/Lt Stokes left on 28 April for Gibraltar before flying on to Malta with the Australian Minister Mr R.G. Casey on the 30th. On 7 May, F/Lt Stokes, with the same aircraft W3993, flew General Lord Gort from Gibraltar to Malta. Stokes returned the following day with the retiring Governor of Malta – Lt-Gen Sir William Dobie – and Sir William's wife and daughter. In May, No 10 detached another Sunderland to Gibraltar – W3983. Captained by F/Lt Pockley it achieved No. 10's first positive success for 15 months. Convoys were still sailing eastwards to supply Malta, and the Italians had a group of submarines, *Veniero*, *Brin*, and *Argo* deployed off Cape Caxine.

Veniero, as for *Argo*,[14] was one of a group of Italian submarines deployed south of the Balearics to counter Allied convoys routed from Gibraltar to Malta during May and June 1942. *Veniero* was on station by 19 May and, (from the Italian account), nothing was heard from it after 29 May.[15] British and American lists differ[16] in respect of date, type of aircraft and squadron for the loss of *Veniero*, but it appears likely that a Sunderland of 202 Sqdn may claim its sinking.

Gibraltar from Sunderland PP118 J/201.

Another encounter was perhaps with the Italian submarine *Brin*. Sunderland W3983 of No. 10 Sqdn RAAF was airborne from Gibraltar on 6 June captained by F/Lt Marks. At 0351 hrs an ASV blip gave a contact three miles on the port beam. A fully surfaced U-boat was sighted and Marks dived from 1000 ft to 100 ft releasing eight DCs spaced at 36 ft and set for 25 ft depth. The centre of the stick fell 30 yards from the submarine's beam. AA fire damaged the Sunderland's starboard outer engine and the starboard float. F/Lt Marks reported to base and requested beaching gear for the Sunderland's return. *Brin* had reported an attack on the 7th but was apparently undamaged.

Another Australian but serving with 202 Sqdn was F/O R.M. Corrie. He was airborne in M/202 at 0702 hrs on the 7th in a hunt for a U-boat. After flying for over four hours, an ASV contact was obtained 16 miles to port. Three minutes later, a surfaced U-boat was sighted and Corrie lost height to attack. Four DCs were released from the port racks. They exploded dead centre straddling the vessel. There was an exchange of gunfire and light flak and Sgt Lee, one of the Sunderland crew, was hit above the heart. In another gun duel, an aerial was shot away and the wing was hit. During another circuit, the submarine turned until heading north-west and began submerging. Corrie again attacked releasing four DCs which exploded 50–60 yards ahead of the swirl but five yards to port. The whole of the action took place in less than twelve minutes. An oil patch appeared and covered an area 300 yards by 150 yards. About 40 minutes later foam and bubbles appeared 20 yards diameter. Corrie made a landing at Anciola Point before returning to the area and making a square search. The loss of *Veniero* in position 3821N 0321E was attributed to these attacks.

After being airborne from Gibraltar at 0313 hrs on 13 June, S/Ldr Burrage of No. 10 Sqdn RAAF, flew on an A/S sweep. Just over five hours later he sighted a submarine on the surface and attacked with seven DCs. They straddled the vessel

between the conning tower and bows. The submarine listed heavily before righting itself and remained on the surface for over an hour. The Italian submarines *Bronzo* and *Otario* were operating south of the Balearic Islands in June and an attack was reported by them from a Sunderland on the 13th.[17]

In WW2 there were a number of occasions when men were prepared to risk much to help those on opposing sides who were in difficulties. Such an incident appears in 202's records. On 15 July Sunderland 0/202 captained by P/O Lawrence was detailed for an A/S cross-over patrol to the east of Gibraltar. After flying for eight hours Lawrence was near to the coast of Majorca where an Italian Cant 501 was seen to touch down on the sea and burst into flames. The crew of six jumped into the sea but with two of the Italians apparently in difficulties. The Sunderland landed and picked up all six Italians. P/O Lawrence returned to Gibraltar where the 'enemy' were fit enough to be entertained in the Mess before being taken to the frontier.

There was a less happy ending for Sunderland TQ-M W4029 captained by P/O Rimmington in August. On the 21st he flew as escort to convoy OG88 outward bound from the UK. At 0235 hrs on return to Gibraltar, the aircraft was seen to circle the bay before crashing 1000 yards short of the first flare. The Sunderland burst into flames and two depth charges exploded. Only one of the crew survived – P/O K.G. Grey – and he was dangerously ill. The bodies of Sgts Orr and Hay were recovered on the 3rd and 9th September.

TQ-R W6002 with F/O Walshe was airborne at 0725 hrs on 21 August for an A/S patrol west of Gibraltar. Two hours later engines cut due to an air lock and a forced landing was made off Cape St Vincent. An SOS was transmitted and after a further two hours, it was sighted by a Hudson which directed the tug *Jaunty* to the Sunderland. The flying boat was taken in tow and arrived back at base on the 24th undamaged and none of the crew injured.

With that same aircraft R/202, F/O Walshe was detailed for a U-boat hunt on 14 September. He headed east from

Gibraltar at 1005 hrs. In September the Italians had deployed a group of five submarines covering the area between the Balearics and the North African coast, and with a sixth – *Alabastro* – which had only recently come into service, heading west to the area.[18] F/O Walshe had been flying for almost 4½ hours when a submarine was sighted on a course 250° at 18 knots. Walshe made a circuit before approaching for a bombing run at 20° to the vessel's starboard quarter. At two miles range the vessel opened fire with heavy flak and Walshe took evasive action. Within four minutes of the first sighting he attacked, releasing five DCs. Four of these exploded, two against the port bow and two within 5 ft of the conning tower to starboard. The submarine's gunners were still firing as the Sunderland circled out of range. The vessel lifted out of the water and then circled to port but with its forward gun still trained on the aircraft. Circling for both continued over half-an-hour by which time about 20 of the submarine's crew were on deck. At 1507 hrs the submarine began to submerge, with some of the crew jumping into the water. Twenty men were counted in a dinghy but with another sixteen in the sea being hauled aboard. Sunderland R/202 was waterborne at base by 1910 hrs. The official Italian history gives the same position for the loss of *Alabastro* as appears in 202's record, i.e. 3728N 0434E and credits a Sunderland with that sinking.[19]

Gibraltar and Operation 'Torch'
When a second front was being considered in 1942, the American – General Marshall – proposed Cherbourg. Churchill favoured landings against the French in Morocco, Algeria and Tunisia.[20] Churchill gained President Roosevelt's support who briefed his delegation to London in a memorandum dated 16 July 1942.[21]

At a meeting of Chiefs of Staff on 22 September, with both Churchill and General Eisenhower present, 8 November was fixed for Operation *Torch* – the invasion of French bases in North Africa.[22]

Admiral Andrew Cunningham arrived at Gibraltar in HMS *Scylla* on 1 November and General Eisenhower flew in on the 5th as Allied Commander-in-Chief.[23] Admiral Cunningham was responsible for all Naval operations. The RAF at Gibraltar became officially under the command of Eisenhower before reverting to Coastal Command control in October 1943.[24]

The Eighth Army battle against Germans and Italians at El Alamein was reported to Churchill by General Alexander on 4 November as being won. This, for Churchill, was the turning of 'The Hinge of Fate'.

Operation *Torch* represented for the Army, about 70,000 troops which were to be deployed in attacks on 8 November against the areas of Casablanca, Oran and Algiers. For the Navy, about 340 ships were to pass Gibraltar between 1930 hrs on the 5th and 0400 hrs on the 7th in a definite sequence.[25]

Of Air Forces; at Gibraltar were fourteen squadrons of fighters to be deployed in Operation *Torch*, these in addition to Coastal squadrons such as 233 and others which had moved down from the UK to Gibraltar in 1942.[26] Capt Roskill refers to Gibraltar as the 'hub' for the whole of Operation *Torch*; Churchill states that Gibraltar's greatest contribution in WW2 was its airfield, and General Eisenhower refers to Gibraltar making possible the invasion of North Africa.[27]

About the time of *Torch* there were 25 U-boats in the Mediterranean[28] and the Italians deployed 34 submarines off the North African coast between 02°E and 11°E in November.[29]

By November 1942, 202 Sqdn must have been mainly equipped with Catalinas rather than Sunderlands. Sorties from Gibraltar were being given largely to Hudsons and Wellingtons. All the successes against U-boats by Coastal Command, Gibraltar are listed in that month to Hudson-equipped squadrons Nos 233, 500 and 608. For Sunderlands, Gibraltar was to remain a staging post and a base for detachments.

References

1   SWR I p. 42 and WSC II p. 388
2   AH 'FC' p. 62 and WSC IV p. 773
3   AH 'FC' pp. 65–9
4   CCWR pp. 14, 18
5   SWR I p. 298
6   SWR I pp. 240–1
7   WSC II p. 206
8   WSC II p. 209
9   SWR I p. 244
10 AH 'S&S' and 'FC'
11 WSC II p. 393
12 WSC III p. 56
13 W/Cmdr H.G. Havyatt, KIA 21.5.44 (JH p. 64)
14 Ibid.
15 MB II p. 30
16 USSL p. 178 and SWR II p. 472
17 MB II p. 41
18 MB II chart 9
19 MB II pp. 76–7
20 WSC II pp. 288–9
21 WSC II p. 398
22 WSC II p. 488
23 SWR II pp. 312–13
24 SWR II p. 359
25 SWR II p. 320
26 AH 'S&S' pp. 111–38
27 SWR II p. 315
28 SWR II p. 333
29 MB chart 11

Chapter 8
East and West Africa

IN THE early stages of WW2 shipping losses due to U-boats were confined to the areas north of Gibraltar.[1] Towards the end of 1940 however, U-boats were operating with success off the coast of West Africa. To counter the U-boats and give additional cover to convoys, a number of squadrons became based in West Africa.

On 15 January 1941, No. 210 Sqdn then at Oban was instructed to detach three Sunderlands with captains and crews, together with maintenance staff for service at Freetown, Sierra Leone. The three Sunderlands with personnel were to form No. 95 Sqdn. The three captains were F/Lt Evison, F/O S. Baggott and P/O Bailey with Sunderlands P9623, L2163 and T9041. Two other officers from 210 to be CO and F/Cmdr of 95 Sqdn were W/Cmdr Fressanges and S/Ldr Lombard. The Sunderlands were modified with an additional fuel tank in the bomb compartment to take 355 gallons giving a total fuel capacity of 2400 gallons. Spares necessary for one month's operations in

A group of 210/95 Sqdn officers at Oban in 1940. The one with the pipe, Fergus Pearce, was as senior RAF officer in W. Africa, able to organise a Hurricane fighter Flt with 95 Sqdn to counter hostile French aircraft.

Freetown were to be taken. L2163 was replaced by N9027.

The ground party in the charge of F/Lt Gibson, left Gourock in ss. *Highland Brigade* on 8 February. The aircraft flew down via Pembroke Dock, Mount Batten and Gibraltar. En route to Gibraltar on 14 February, P9623 with S/Ldr Lombard, force-landed in Portugal and both aircraft and crew were interned. The crew was later released following help from British officials and the Royal Navy. ss. *Highland Brigade* arrived in Freetown harbour on 2 March where F/Lt Gibson and three other officers disembarked to arrange accommodation. For some, this was at Fourah Bay College, and for others, at Lumley Camp with a battalion of the Essex Regt.

S/Ldr Leggate left Gibraltar in N9050 and was fired upon by the Spaniards and a bullet entered above the wireless operator's head.

Number 95 Squadron's first operational flight was made by F/O Baggott in N9050 from Freetown on 24 March. It was to cover convoy SL69 comprising 40 merchant vessels escorted by six warships, homeward bound from Sierra Leone.

On the 25th a survey with soundings was made at Bathurst with the help of two BOAC captains – Lock and Brooke-Williams – and with the conclusion that the area was suitable for emergency landings in rough weather. W/Cmdr Fergus A. Pearce assumed command of 95 Sqdn and in April a detachment was formed at Bathurst where W/Cmdr Pearce arrived on the 4th in T9078. This was the first Sunderland 95 Sqdn had which was equipped with Mark II ASV and de-icers.

The squadron's record during 1941 gives sightings of a number of ships sailing independently or which had become detached from convoys, and also signs of ships which had been sunk. On 19 May P/O Bailey was airborne from Freetown on an A/S search and after sighting the Dutch vessel *Monterland* located a British sloop which had just picked up 64 survivors from *Piako* which had been sunk by U-107 in position 0752N 1457W. It was the fourth vessel lost during four days in that area; two claimed by U-107, and two by U-105.[2] The four merchant vessels formed part of 30 ships of 176,168 tons mentioned by Capt Roskill which were lost in May within 600 miles of Freetown and Bathurst.[3] With potentially hostile French shipping in addition to German U-boats, checks were

A fully-stalled landing of a Mk III Sunderland demonstrated by W/Cmdr G. Francis of 230 Sqdn.

No. 228 Sqdn personnel crossing-the-line on HMT *Dumana* 7.7.41 en route to Bathurst from Egypt.

made on all traffic sighted and on the 20th F/O Robertson in Sunderland L5805 located a Spanish vessel ss. *Manu* with a boarding party from HMS *Boreas* H77.

On 12 June President Roosevelt's envoy – Averell Harriman – together with American embassy officials, was shown over RAF bases at Hastings and Jui where building work was in progress. Hastings was used by a Hurricane fighter flight organised by W/Cmdr Pearce to counter Vichy French Martin Marylands which were quite prepared to shoot down RAF aircraft. This Hurricane flight then on the strength of 95 Sqdn, formed the nucleus of No. 128 Sqdn in October 1941. At 1630 hrs on 7 August when French recce aircraft were sighted, the first Hurricane was airborne within 3 minutes, the second within 7 minutes.

No. 228 Sqdn based at Aboukir in June, received signals from HQ Middle East that the unit was to move to Bathurst with sufficient personnel and equipment to operate on arrival. Two aircraft were to fly via the Nile valley and the Belgian Congo with the first scheduled to leave Aboukir on 10 June.

The ground party embarked on HMT *Dumana* at Port Tewfik on the 17th with A/S/Ldr Ellis in charge. They arrived at Bathurst on 28 August and by then 228

Sqdn had been posted back to the United Kingdom. Some of 228's personnel were however transferred to 95 Sqdn which was still in West Africa. Two Sunderlands of 228 Sqdn captained by W/Cmdr Brooks and F/Lt Frame left Aboukir in L5803 on the 23rd and T9046 on the 24th respectively for Khartoum. At the next stage – Kampala – the landing area was cleared of hippos and crocodiles for Frame to land. W/Cmdr Brooks had engine trouble but with an all-up weight of 56,000 lb at an altitude of 3,700 ft on Lake Victoria, made three attempts at take-off. W/Cmdr Brooks reached Bathurst on 30 July having covered 5,908 miles at an average speed of 117·4 knots in total flying time of 50 hrs 20 mins. F/Lt Frame in T9046 took 72 hrs 35 mins. W/Cmdr Brooks assumed the duties of Senior Air Officer, Gambia having under his control 200 Sqdn, Jeswang, the flying-boat control unit Bathurst, 228 Sqdn at Half Die, and the RAF transit camp, Bathurst. After consultation with diplomatic, naval and army staff, a combined operations room ·was set up at Cape St Mary and a co-ordinating HQ at the transit camp. The operations room was at Marina Base, Half Die.

The CO of 204 Sqdn – W/Cmdr Coote – arrived at Bathurst on 28 August 1941 in Sunderland T9074 to be followed the next

No. 204 Sqdn ground crew at Bathurst in February 1942.

day by F/Lt Stead, S/Ldr Laws, F/Lt Dagg and F/O Douglas as captains of T9070, N9044, N9024 and L5800. Meanwhile in the United Kingdom, some 204 Sqdn personnel sailed from Liverpool in HMT *Northumberland* routed to Freetown. On arriving there on 15 September, they transhipped to another vessel *Abosso* for Bathurst. The ss. *Dumana* became a depot ship for such as engine fitter Roy Barton, serving for him and others as 'home and workplace for many months'.

Two of the Sunderlands were attacked by French fighters. On 29 September N9044 was detailed for a convoy escort but, while near Dakar, encountered four or five French aircraft. According to Roy Barton, three of the Sunderland crew were wounded with one – Jock Simpson – shot in the leg.

KG-V T9041 of 204 Sqdn on air test at Jewsang in 1942.

The Sunderland returned fire and possibly one of the French fighters was shot down. N9044 returned with 70–100 bullet holes. F/O Douglas in L5800 was on an A/S patrol and also attacked by the Vichy French aircraft but returned at 1730 hrs. This same Sunderland captain – F/O Douglas – flew a sortie of exceptional length in October. He was airborne at 2325 hrs from Bathurst on the 10th, and after completing a convoy patrol, returned to base at 1530 hrs on the 11th – a flight of over 16 hours. That same night F/Lt Ennis was on a convoy escort in T9074 and at 2149 hrs set course for base. At 0031 hrs on the 12th he encountered a storm and turned to the north. At 0250 hrs shortage of fuel made it necessary to force-land five miles south of Dakar. W/Cmdr Coote made a search and on locating the overdue Sunderland, landed alongside in T9070 to be joined by a launch – ML274. Another launch ML242 was also directed to the scene and F/Lt Ennis had his Sunderland refuelled.

HMT *Manela* arrived at Bathurst on 13 October en route to Freetown. On board were A/Cmdre E.A.B. Rice and personnel for the new AHQ to be set up in West Africa. The American ship ss. *Lehigh* or (*Lea High*) of 4983 tons was torpedoed by U-126 in position 0826N 1437W on the 19th. Two days later thirty-five of the survivors were entertained by 204 Sqdn personnel. U-126 had earlier that year been refuelled by the German merchant raider *Atlantis*. On the 10th U-126 had torpedoed *Nailsea Manor* and on the 20th, her third victim in eleven days – the *British Mariner*. All three of these ships were apparently sailing independently. *Atlantis* was sunk the following month by HMS *Devonshire* when again refuelling U-126.[4]

Sunderland KG-L T9074 was airborne from Bathurst for an A/S patrol on the 23rd captained by F/Lt Ennis. After flying for just eight hours he force-landed and was towed in by HMS *Challenger*. This aircraft had presented many problems and when checked, water and grit were found in the fuel system, there were only four good cylinders on the aircraft, and thirty-two valve guides needed changing.[5]

Despite the losses of such as ss. *Lehigh* and others which were to follow, W/Cmdr Coote was able to inform 204 Sqdn on 20 January 1942 that no ships were lost within range of the Sunderlands' patrols while they were on convoy duties. A rare sighting and attack was made by F/Lt Dart on 18 April. He was airborne at 0458 hrs in KG-C N9044 to locate and escort a convoy. After two hours flying, a submarine was seen in position 1015N 1848W but it submerged before it could be reached. Fifty minutes later there was a further sighting when the submarine was heading north at eight knots. At 0922 Dart was in a position to attack; six DCs were released but the only evidence of damage was a patch of oil. The convoy was located at 1200 hrs in position 1000N 1910W. There were twenty-nine merchant vessels then with only two escorts, but two destroyers were searching for the U-boat.

The following month, 204's workshop and hangar were located at Half Die and personnel left *Dumana* on the 21st to be accommodated ashore.

Sunderland KG-V T9041 was lost on 28 June. It had been airborne from Half Die at 0500 hrs to escort a convoy OS31 and was last seen by the convoy at 1830 hrs. From two reports it appeared that shortage of fuel resulted in all four engines cutting. At 1045 hrs on the 30th Hudson E/200 sighted a dinghy with ten crew on board about 100 miles out. The survivors were sighted again the following day by the same Hudson. They were picked up by the destroyer HMS *Velox* and landed at Freetown where the captain – F/Lt Ennis – was admitted to hospital. One of the crew had failed to exit from the Sunderland, another died while in the dinghy. These were Sgts Humphrey and Thompson. The other survivors returned to base on 6 July.

Air-Sea Rescue Operations by No. 204 Squadron

In the second half of 1942 204 Sqdn undertook a series of searches for survivors from both ships and aircraft. These sorties were in addition to the usual A/S patrols and convoy escorts. On 23 July S/Ldr

Wood in KG-E T9070 located survivors from the American vessel ss. *Honolulan* which had been torpedoed by U-582 on the 22nd. Three days later, L2168 captained by F/O Inglis was searching for survivors from a Norwegian merchant vessel *Tank Express* which U-130 had sunk by torpedo and gunfire on the 25th.

Number 204 Squadron suffered another loss on 17 August. L2158 captained by P/O J. Quinn was escorting convoy SL119 and flying at about 400 ft when there was an engine failure due to loss of oil pressure. Quinn was too low to jettison the depth charges and the Sunderland struck the water nose first. Those on the fight deck were saved by escaping through the Flt/engineer's hatch and taking the dinghy from under the navigator's table. When about 300 yards away the aircraft blew up with the DCs. This was witnessed by the convoy at 0800 hrs. The survivors paddled north and after four nights and five days reached land. They lived on berries for two days before being found by a native who took them to a village where they were well-treated and fed. This was in the Portuguese area and Quinn was able to send a signal to base. Five members of this crew arrived back at base on 5 September. On the 14th a memorial service was held for those who had been lost.

F/O P. Wall also had engine trouble on a flight to escort convoy SL123. He crash-landed Sunderland DV965 KG-A in the sea between Bathurst and Freetown on 24 September and lost the port float. The crew attempted to 'sail' the Sunderland using an awning as a sail with dinghy oars as a mast but with the constant need for some of the crew to lie on the starboard wing to compensate for the lost port float. They were met by a corvette which towed the Sunderland into Freetown arriving at 0850 hrs on the 26th.

On 15 October two Sunderlands searched for a missing Wellington HX636 which had been in transit. From the squadron record, F/Lt D.G. Hewlings in DV959 searched for 2¾ hrs before touching down at 0900 hrs. From Roy Barton's recollections, Hewlings found the Wellington crew 80 miles south in French territory and landed alongside the survivors' dinghy. Four of the Wellington crew were badly burnt, a fifth was satisfactory, and one died in hospital. Hewlings was waterborne for almost two hours during the rescue pick-up before returning with the survivors to Bathurst.

The Dutch vessel ss. *Polydorus* was torpedoed on 27 November by U-176 in position 0901N 2538W. Number 204 Squadron detailed Sunderlands to search for survivors and on 1 December the crew of DV959 located a lifeboat with about 20 men in position 1009N 2324W. A signal was made to the escort vessel *Bridgewater* which was also searching; food and flares were dropped from the Sunderland before it flew to *Bridgewater* and gave the bearing of the lifeboat. Two days later F/O Wall in DV965 was also searching for survivors from ss. *Polydorus*; he found only wreckage and two lifeboats, half-filled with water – not men.

Following the operation *Torch* landings in North Africa, the threat from some of the hostile Vichy French forces was removed but the Battle of the Atlantic was forever being fought. Off Freetown in April 1943, six U-boats were deployed supported by a 'milch cow' for refuelling.[6]

On 5 April H/204 N9024 was airborne from Half Die captained by F/O Cooper to escort convoy SL127. After flying for over six hours a U-boat was sighted in position 1718N 2133W. An attack was made releasing five DCs within 10 secs of the vessel submerging. No wreckage was sighted and no oil or bubbles, only a 'vivid green patch' was reported.

Another Sunderland from 204 took off shortly after H/204 but on a search for survivors from an American aircraft. Dakar had then been taken by the Allies as a base and the American aircraft, a B-17E commanded by Major Edgar B. Cole, was en route to Dakar from Natal, Brazil when oil pressure was lost in an engine. It could not be feathered and the reduction gear sheared and height was lost to 100 ft where flying speed could not be held. Not one of the crew was injured and all ten gained their dinghies.[7] Their sea marker and radio functioned and (from both British and American records), the Sunderland captained by F/Lt C.B. Hugall was airborne at the time the Americans ditched – 1255 hrs. They were located in position 1255N 1651W 30 miles west of Bathurst. this was at 1850 hrs and all returned to Bathurst 65 minutes later.

Sunderland JM669 A/204 flew from Gibraltar on 13 April in transit at the time of violent storms being reported. An SOS was heard at 1515 hrs and at 0336 hrs the aircraft sent 'Landing sea'. By DF bearings its position was estimated as 2008N 1733W which is off Port Etienne, and it was from there that an air-sea-rescue was commenced with P/95 and X/200 aircraft in co-operation with a Free French sloop. P/95 reported wreckage at 0834 hrs in position 2026N 1730W. There were no survivors.

In July 1943, 204 Squadron made one attack on a U-boat. F/O Mayberry was airborne from Port Etienne on the 9th and at 1930 hrs sighted a surfaced U-boat in position 2610N 1835W. It began to submerge when the Sunderland was ¾ mile distant. Mayberry attacked down sun from astern at 60° and released six DCs from 40 ft altitude but three of them hung up. Thirty feet of the stern of the submarine was visible when the DCs exploded centre of the swirl but slightly to starboard. No wreckage was seen, only bubbles.

A week later, 204 lost another aircraft and this was due to engine failure. EJ145 P/204 captained by F/O D.W. Pallett was on an escort to convoy OS51 outward bound from the United Kingdom to West Africa. At 0645 hrs distress signals were received giving the Sunderland's position as 2303N 1746W. At 0847 hrs it force-landed 100 miles north-west of Port Etienne. The crew of ten were picked up by a Spanish fishing boat and taken to Villa Cisneros and from there to Las Palmas. One of the crew had suffered a broken leg. An event occurred in August which was possibly unique. On the 11th a Liberator D/200 captained by F/O Trigg attacked and sank U-468 in position 1220N 2007W. The Liberator crew was lost with the aircraft but a dinghy came free and it was used by the U-boat's survivors. Sunderland H/204 on an ASR mission, sighted the dinghy in position 1228N 1918W and dropped Lindholme gear to the U-boat survivors. At 1835 hrs emergency packs and flame floats were dropped before the Sunderland returned to base at 2000 hrs. Sunderland F/204 flew on a night search to locate the dinghy and at 0110 hrs met the corvette *Clarkia* which was co-operating in the ASR mission.

At 0445 hrs the Sunderland located the dinghy with the aid of Very lights. A flare, sea-marker and flame floats were dropped; F/204 then homed the corvette to the dinghy, reaching it at 0631 hrs when it was in position 1225N 1913W. *Clarkia* signalled that the dinghy occupants were German survivors from the U-boat. The Liberator captain – F/O L.A. Trigg – who had gone down with his aircraft was awarded a posthumous VC following the testimony of the U-468 survivors.

During the latter half of 1943, 204's duties continued to be 'routine' – A/S sweeps, convoy escorts and with some ASR missions. They were not without loss. On 22 September L/204 JM710 captained by F/O J.G. Finney had returned to Half Die following an A/S sweep. At 2100 hrs the Sunderland was seen to crash straight into the sea and burst into flames. It was believed to have been from 800 ft in a left-hand turn when the aircraft must have stalled. The bodies of F/O Finney, F/Sgt Evans and Sgt Weston were recovered and buried at Fajara Military cemetery, Cape St Mary. Others in the crew went down with the aircraft. DV974 G/204 also crashed in a night landing. This was on 1 October when the aircraft was recalled to Bathurst while en route to Port Etienne. It sank almost immediately. Seven were rescued and taken to 55th General hospital. The captain – F/Lt Mayberry – with two of his crew – Sgts L. Hare and W.T. Barnes – went down with the aircraft.

Sunderlands with the Free French

Following the Allied landings in North Africa some French units still remained. It was decided in February 1943 that Sunderlands would be allocated to the Free French and in March some crews moved to Britain for familiarisation before returning to Dakar. Initially, two Sunderlands – DP182 and JM674 – were allocated to the 4th GR Squadron to be based at Bel Air, Dakar. They were coded 4E-5 and 4E6. Two more Sunderlands arrived at Dakar in July, followed by four more in August. They came under the command of Capitaine de corvette Fournier of the 1st Flotilla which comprised two squadrons – 4E and 3E – but by August, 3E was omitted in respect of Sunderlands.

On 10 October the 1st Flotilla (1F) became 7FE (7th GR Flotilla) and the aircraft were designated 7F-1, 7F-2, etc. In addition to Sunderlands, two large flying-boats of French construction, l'Antares, Potez 141 and l'Achernar Late 611, were attached to 7FE. The unit became incorporated into the RAF's West African Command and allocated a RAF squadron number 343 under No. 295 Wing, Bathurst. Operations by the Free French Sunderlands included convoy escorts, A/S patrols and recces until the end of the war. As the Service Historique de la Marine report: 'There were no effective engagements against the enemy, but there were a number of accidents.' Thus on 5 October Sunderland JM705 (the CO's aircraft), force-landed and waited 24 hours before being taken in tow and brought back to an Allied port. In 1953 the French continued to operate Sunderlands but under Flotilla 27F. They gradually returned to Toulon and Lanveoc-Poulmic with the last two flying to Lanveoc-Poulmic in November 1961. They were written off on 30 January 1962.

A Royal New Zealand Air Force Squadron

Number 490 (RNZAF) Squadron was formed at Jui, Sierra Leone in March 1943 and was initially equipped with Catalinas. In May 1944 it was taking delivery of Sunderlands, replacing Catalinas. Number 490 Squadron undertook A/S patrols, searches for U-boats and transport missions. In addition to the base at Jui, a detachment was made on Fisherman's Lake, Liberia. Transit flights included trips to Port Etienne, Bathurst and Abidjan. Sunderland ML852 was lost on 14 July when it was ditched off Cape St Mary due to engine failure. Two of the crew were killed and five injured.

Of merchant ships sunk in the Gulf of Guinea area, Churchill[8] gives nine losses between 19 September 1943 and 15 May 1944, and from Jürgen Rohwer's lists, none was lost in that area thereafter from U-boat attacks.[9]

Number 490 Squadron however, flew sorties in a U-boat hunt in October 1944 which included F/Lt Harvey as captain of Sunderland Y/490 EJ169 on the 7th, 8th and 10th.

No. 270 Squadron in West Africa

Number 270 Squadron was reformed in November 1942 at Jui and equipped with Catalinas. In July 1943 it became based at Apapa near Lagos and in January 1944 was taking delivery of Sunderlands. By the 25th three of the Sunderlands were exercising with HM ships, and at the end of February nine Sunderlands had been received with only one Catalina on strength.

Number 270 Squadron's duties were anti-submarine patrols, sweeps and convoy escorts. On 7 April, Professor Blackloch from the Liverpool School of Tropical Medicine came to report on anti-malarial measures at RAF Apapa. Five crews which had been on detachment at Abidjan reported lack of mosquito nets and bedding and 12 per cent were admitted to station sick quarters within a week of returning to Apapa. Aircraftman second class R.H. Anning was treated with penicillin (perhaps one of the earliest occasions of its use). This was for septicaemia of which he died three months later. In May there were 42 admissions to sick quarters, 21 of these from 270 Sqdn. Malaria and septicaemia were apparently the most common health problems.

On 3 June W/O Wall in Sunderland K/270 searched for ML811, a Sunderland in transit from the United Kingdom to SE Asia which had left Apapa for Libreville. ML811 crashed near Lakka where the aircraft burned out. There was one survivor, Sgt W. Best, who died later in hospital. On the 7th Sunderland EK585 at moorings with a maintenance crew on board caught fire. The crew had to abandon the aircraft which blew up and sank, when there was a second explosion due to depth charges. A happier event was the wedding of P/O W.S. Smith of 270 Sqdn to a nursing officer, Miss Barbara Page from the 58th West African General Hospital.

In July an intensive search was made by a 270 Sqdn detachment at Jui. This was for a U-boat following the sinking of a ship during the night of the 2–3rd. This may have been the Dutch vessel *Bodegraven* torpedoed by U-547 in position 0414N 1100W.[10]

At Apapa there was friendly liaison with the Royal Navy and on 30 July a hundred RAF personnel embarked on HMS *Fal* and *Kildwick* for a bombing, gunnery and depth charge exercise. Number 270 Squadron reciprocated by flying thirty naval personnel in Sunderland aircraft. In addition to football, cricket, hockey and baseball, swimming and tennis; yachting was organised with personnel building their own craft. Canadians organised a league of three teams and an unofficial 'Maple Leaf Stadium'. With four Australians and seven Canadians a 'dominion' team was formed. The US Army Air Force and Ensa provided an average of five films per week, some in advance of United Kingdom release.

An exceptional incident occurred on 3 October which was perhaps unique for a Sunderland. F/O Harper was airborne from Apapa in EJ164 detailed to escort convoy ST86. For reasons not stated in the record, he was forced to ditch in position 0457N 0335W. Emergency procedure was followed and all the crew of eleven escaped in three dinghies at 1404 hrs. Nine hours later the hospital ship *Chantilly* sighted distress signals fired from the dinghies and took all survivors on board and unharmed. The Sunderland had lost a float on touching down, capsized but floated on its back for about two hours before sinking. The survivors were put ashore at Freetown on 7 October. In that month the squadron's duties came to include many met. flights in addition to

PP153 at Congella, Durban after being delivered to No. 35 Sqdn SAAF. It is recorded as having crashed on 26.4.45 and was given the letter 'M' but received no SAAF serial number.

the routine ones of escorts, recces and searches.

F/O Collie was captain of N/270 on 17 February 1945 for an air test with only five in the crew. At 1456 hrs his lone wireless operator – W/O Johnson – picked up an SOS from Sunderland Q/490. N/270 had been fuelled with only 1,000 gallons and the crew was without navigational instruments, rations and water. Collie however, proceeded immediately to the position given by Q/490 – 0840N 1415W – arriving over the ditched aircraft at 1530 hrs. W/O Johnson transmitted a message to Freetown giving the position; this apparently was the first report received by any ground station. F/O Collie remained over the ditched aircraft until 2045 hrs, past his PLE but his wireless operator had homed a launch onto the scene; he was on W/T watch for seven hours.

A second Sunderland from 270 Sqdn captained by F/Lt Russell also on air test contacted the 490 Sqdn crew on a different wavelength and passed on a message to their base at Jui. The following month on the 10th, F/Lt M.E. Russell was again on air test with ML844. While over Lagos, without warning, the port inner propeller and the reduction gear sheared off. The

leading edge inspection platform was damaged and opened up and the propeller struck the side of the aircraft causing a six foot gash. Control was lost and the aircraft fell rapidly. Russell however, regained control and was able to land safely.

In May, 270's operational flights under West African Command ceased, and on the 23rd instructions were received that their Sunderlands were to be flown back to the United Kingdom some time after 1 June. In that month the squadron was disbanded.

Number 230 Squadron in East Africa
Number 230 Squadron based at Aboukir, commenced moving to Dar-es-Salaam in East Africa on 9 January 1943. This was by F/Lt P.D. Squires in Sunderland Y/230 EJ136 which was airborne at 0245 hrs for the first stage to Wadi Halfa. The CO – W/Cmdr C.R. Taylor – followed ten days later in EJ132 'X' arriving at Dar-es-Salaam on the 23rd.[11]

During the period 17–27 February, F/Lt Squires flew on a tour of the Indian Ocean islands. He took on board EJ136, the GOC-in-C, Lt-Gen Sir William Platt, Maj-Gen Smallwood and AV-M Wigglesworth, AOC East Africa. This tour commenced at

Mombasa with stops at Pamanzi, Diego Suarez, Mauritius, Rodriquez and the Seychelles before returning to Mombasa. At Dar-es-Salaam on 10 March the mosquito authorities inspected the squadron's camp and found evidence of yellow fever and malaria. Effective aircrew personnel were depleted due to malaria and assistance was obtained from No. 16 Sqdn SAAF which sent four officers and five NCOs on attachment. On the 25th the main ground party arrived aboard ss. *Takliwa*. They had embarked in Egypt and en route had picked up about 400 Italian civilian internees from British Somaliland before proceeding unescorted to Dar-es-Salaam.

During this period, 230 Sqdn had detachments at Aboukir, Bizerta, Kisumu, Mombasa and Pamanzi. The Allied battle for Tunisia was over on 23 May, and as General Alexander reported to Churchill: 'We are masters of the North African shores.'[12] This Allied victory is reflected in 230's record which anticipated the invasion of Sicily and the Italian mainland. Six of their Sunderlands were ordered back to Aboukir on detachment including DP180 'O' with W/Cmdr Taylor and W4021 'W' with S/Ldr D. Bednall. F/O G.O. Watson in EJ141 'R' left on 23 June and arrived in Aboukir on the 25th.

The malaria epidemic in Dar-es-Salaam had peaked in May with 94 cases, declining in June with 73 cases. On 29 July instructions were received for a detachment at Bizerta to return to East Africa. The following month W/Cmdr D.K. Bednall succeeded W/Cmdr Taylor as CO of 230 Sqdn. As W/Cmdr Bednall recalls in his book,[13] Japanese submarines had been active off the eastern coast of Africa and thus the deployment of 230 Sqdn. Ships had been sunk in the Indian Ocean by such Japanese submarines as I-27, I-129 and I-37 in addition to sinkings by the German U-177, U-178, U-181, U-198 and U-511.[14]

Sunderland EJ131 captained by F/Lt A.D. Todd was lost on 20 August. It had taken-off from Pamanzi at 0720 hrs to locate a naval force and at 2003 hrs sent a signal that a forced landing was being made. It crashed in Mozambique with the loss of nine. The strength of the squadron was brought up to thirteen Mark IIIs when DP189 'L' arrived from the United Kingdom on 16 November 1943 at Dar-es-Salaam.

There were sinkings of Allied ships in the Indian Ocean during November and December by the Japanese submarines in addition to U-178 and in December, 230 Sqdn undertook a series of A/S sweeps. Another Sunderland was lost on the 29th; this was EJ140 with F/O D.E. Lumsden who was on a calibration flight from Mombasa. While in thick cloud, he crashed at 3,500 ft into Sangala hill with all the crew killed.

By February 1944 the Allies controlled the Mediterranean and the Japanese were hard-pressed in the Far East; no sinkings of Allied ships were listed off the East African coast. While based at Dar-es-Salaam, 230 Sqdn had suffered 300 cases of malaria but were now scheduled to move to Koggala. The move was via Kisumu, Khartoum, Aden, Masirah, Korangi Creek, Bombay and Cochin. Nine Sunderlands were to move, eight in February, and one in March. F/O W.S. Fumerton with EJ136, left on 7 February and arrived in Koggala on the 16th after total flying time of 45 hrs 25 mins.

References
[1]   WSC III p. 135 (chart)
[2]   JR p. 52
[3]   SWR I p. 470
[4]   SWR I p. 245
[5]   Letter from Roy Barton
[6]   SWR II p. 371
[7]   B17E No. 42–3121, 95th Bomb Group, 336 Bomb Squadron
[8]   WSC V p. 14
[9]   JR pp. 181–95
[10] JR p. 182
[11] Ibid.
[12] WSC IV p. 698
[13] DB p. 100
[14] JR pp. 268–9

Chapter 9
The Battle of the Atlantic and the
Bay of Biscay

IN JUNE 1942, Torpex-filled depth charges were coming into service with Coastal Command. They were 30 per cent more efficient than the earlier Amatol-filled charges and a pistol which could cause detonation at 34 ft depth was available.[1] The depth for detonation was later reduced to 25 ft. These developments are reflected in No. 10 Squadron's attacks on submarines made in the summer of 1942. The first of these was at the end of May.[2]

On 5 June, F/Lt Wood as captain of W3986 'U' was airborne from Mount Batten at 1125 hrs. The crew was detailed for an A/S patrol which commenced at 1545 hrs when a radar contact was made at eight miles on the starboard bow. Wood was flying at 5000 ft but immediately made a steep dive to 50 ft reaching the U-boat only 25 seconds after it had dived.

Eight Torpex DCs were released set at 30 ft and spaced at 25 ft which straddled the U-boat's track 130 yards ahead of the swirl. A minute later the U-boat re-surfaced bow first at a 40° angle before settling at the bow with the stern raised and with a 15° list to port. A large air bubble appeared together with oil alongside the vessel which remained stationary for 10 minutes before moving in figures-of-eight and with smoke and steam rising.

Men appeared at the conning tower but disappeared when the Sunderland opened fire with machine-guns. The U-boat responded with AA before increasing speed to eight knots and then submerging. It was U-71 which had to return to base due to the damage it had suffered.

The Sunderland, after leaving the area, was attacked by a FW200 which opened fire at 1000 yards with cannon. In one of the attacks the hydraulic line from the rear turret was cut needing it to be operated

manually. Hits were scored by the midships gunners on the FW200 which broke off the action and headed east at a low altitude. The Sunderland suffered five large and eighty small holes, the R/T aerial was shot away and both flaps were damaged. There were slight scratches to two of the crew.

The Italian submarine *Luigi Torelli* commanded by Naval Lt. Augusto Migliorini sailed from La Pallice, Bordeaux with another submarine *Morosini* on 2 June 1942. They had been detailed to operate within a 200 miles radius, 330 miles NE of San Salvador and 600 miles NE of Puerto Rico.[3] At 0227 hrs on the 4th when *Luigi Torelli* was in the Bay of Biscay about 90 miles NNW of Gijon it was surprised by a searchlight directed at its conning tower. This was from a Leigh-light Wellington of 172 Sqdn captained by S/Ldr J.H. Greswell. The DCs released resulted in a heavy explosion under the hull causing damage. The compass was put out of action and a fire near the batteries threatened the munition store. Migliorini put in at the Spanish port of Aviles.

On the 7th, two Sunderlands of No. 10 Sqdn were airborne from Mount Batten both detailed for A/S and anti-shipping patrols in the Bay of Biscay. These were 'X' W3994 with P/O T.A. Egerton and 'A' W4019 captained by F/Lt E. Yeoman. After flying for almost six hours, Egerton sighted a submarine five miles away near the northern coast of Spain. Then flying at 1500 ft, he approached the U-boat which opened fire at 3000 yards range with a 'heavy gun' but Egerton attacked out of sun at 30° on the port bow releasing eight 250 lb DCs set at 25 ft depth and 35 ft spacing. One large explosion was seen to starboard of the vessel's stern. Both front and rear gunners had fired about 600 rounds in total but two of the Sunderland's crew had been wounded by shrapnel.

While Egerton circled at 1½ miles radius, Yeoman's Sunderland appeared on the scene. Yeoman had been flying on a westerly course at 1800 ft when he correctly identified an Italian submarine at six miles range. As he approached, AA from *Luigi Torelli* scored hits in the Sunderland's tail. Yeoman now attacked from 80 ft releasing seven Torpex DCs set for 25 ft depth and 35 ft spacing. Light flak was silenced by his front gunner, but a shell caused a large hole in the aircraft's hull and one of the crew was wounded.

Two of the depth charges were thought to have exploded below the submarine amidships with the others at 30 yards on the starboard beam. A wake of 300 yards was seen from a torpedo, released due to the Sunderland's attack. One of those sailing in *Luigi Torelli* was Eugenio Franzitta, who in a letter to me, confirms damage to the motors, the batteries with the evolution of chlorine gas, a fire endangering the munitions, and a torpedo tube being affected. There were nine wounded on board and Migliorini sought refuge at Santander. On 14 July, evading surveillance of the Spaniards, the *Luigi Torelli* sailed for Bordeaux which was

T9115 K/461 which ditched 8 miles off Plymouth on 22.2.43. It was towed in by a minesweeper and escorted by DV869 E/10 captained by F/Lt Mainprize.

reached on the 15th. Both Sunderlands returned safely to base although Yeoman had a brief encounter with an Arado which turned tail after the Sunderland's gunners responded in two attacks.

There were further attacks to follow by the Australian Squadrons Nos 10 and 461. On 11 June F/Lt E. Martin of 10 Sqdn while flying at 200 ft altitude on an A/S patrol sighted a fully surfaced U-boat at five miles on the port bow. He attacked from astern after diving to 40 ft and released six Torpex DCs set at 25 ft and spaced at 30 ft. All burst near the vessel which almost stopped and listed to starboard. It pitched and tossed before moving out of the area and submerging. A minute later, the U-boat resurfaced and Martin made two runs, releasing a 250 lb bomb during each run. The second bomb fell a yard from the U-boat's bow and five men were seen on the conning tower. For 10 minutes there was a steady stream of smoke from the U-boat. During an exchange of fire, a wing-tip on the Sunderland was hit by a shell. The U-boat had been so damaged that it returned to port. It proved to be U-105 which during its service was credited with successful attacks on 25 ships.[4]

On 1 September, the Italian submarine *Reginaldo Guiliani* was returning from operating off Brazil and the West Indies and that morning was about 170 miles from the Gironde when it suffered its first attack from a Sunderland.[5] F/Lt S. Wood was airborne from Mount Batten in W3986 at 0600 hrs followed 5 minutes later by F/Lt H. Pockley in W3983.

Both were detailed for anti-shipping patrols. At 1014 hrs Pockley's crew obtained a radar contact at eight miles and then sighted a fully-surfaced submarine. Pockley used cloud cover until four miles from the vessel before attempting a diving attack. Orders were received not to attack but at two miles he was subjected to AA fire. He circled at 1–2 miles radius and as the submarine was still surfaced, decided to attack.

Meanwhile F/Lt Wood's crew at 1023 hrs also obtained a radar contact and after closing to five miles, dived through cloud to attack despite AA from the submarine. Four 250 lb bombs were released from 400 ft with 12 seconds delay and spaced at 25 ft. There was an explosion 30 yards to port and forward of the conning tower. A second intended attack was abortive.

Pockley witnessed this and then attacked from stern to bow diving from 1,500 ft releasing two bombs which failed to explode. He made another run diving from 1,500 ft to 400 ft releasing another bomb which exploded 70 yards astern. There had been intense AA to which his gunners responded. A third Sunderland – A/461 – entered the scene and a concerted attack was considered but all three were ordered to resume their patrols. In these attacks, *Guiliani*'s commander – Lt-Cmdr Giovanni Bruno, was killed and his second in command – Naval Lt. Aredio Calzigna took over, and a lookout on the bridge was wounded. The following day, the submarine was attacked by a Wellington – A/304, when there were six more casualties and the vessel was seriously damaged but was able to enter Santander on the 3rd.

1942 ended with 212 U-boats operational out of a total of 393[6] but a turning point in the Battle of the Atlantic in favour of the Allies was to come in 1943 and with the initiative passing to the Allies.

Anti-Submarine Operations – The Turning Point

By March 1943 there were over one hundred U-boats constantly at sea[7] and still able to use the French ports of Brest, Bordeaux, Lorient, La Pallice and St Nazaire.

By the first half of 1943 however, Coastal Command's aircraft were being flown by experienced crews, some on their second tour of operations. Both equipment and armament were being improved such as a change from 1·5 to 10 centimetre wavelength ASV, and Torpex-filled depth charges were increasingly available. More attention was being given to both offensive and defensive guns, with the need to have more forward-firing to counter AA when attacking. Troubles which appear to have prevailed in Sunderlands were failure of DCs to run out in time, 'hang ups', and the cutting of hydraulic lines to the turrets during air-to-air combat. Engine problems prevailed until the advent of Mark V Sunderlands. None-the-less, the records for Sunderlands operating under 15 Group and 19 Group control from March 1943 onwards show considerable success.

Those U-boats which were sunk and those which returned to port as a result of Coastal Command attacks are recorded: but there remain those unassessed factors – harassment of U-boat crews, the numbers of ships which must have been saved from torpedoes, and the boost to morale of Merchant Navy crews who saw friendly rather than hostile aircraft circling convoys.

An opening Sunderland attack was by F/Lt G.A. Church in DD837 V/228 on 19 March. He was on an A/S sweep covering

F/Lt Les Baveystock DSO,DFC,DFM of 201 Sqdn who sank U-955 and U-107.

convoys SC122 and HX229 en route from Halifax to the United Kingdom when a U-boat just surfacing was sighted. Church released DCs from 60 ft which straddled the vessel's track 150 ft ahead of the conning tower. Credit was given of causing damage to an unknown U-boat.[8] The following day F/O W.C. Robertson of 201 Sqdn captained W6051 on a parallel track sweep to cover the same convoys. After flying for almost six hours, a conning tower was sighted seven miles away. Robertson dived to attack at 170 knots but the periscope had disappeared 80 seconds before the position could be reached and only a marker was dropped before resuming patrol. Half-an-hour later, a surfaced U-boat was seen six miles to starboard. As the Sunderland turned for attack, the U-boat altered course through 180 degrees to operate its forward gun which opened fire at 800 yards. At 400 yards a small cannon was brought into action and the Sunderland responded with machine-gun fire. Explosions from DCs released obscured the vessel but its bows reared into the air for three minutes before sliding down stern first. It is given in American and British lists as the sinking of U-384, but by Martin Middlebrook as only damage to U-631.[9]

F/Lt Dudley Hewitt in DD829 ZM-Z was also on a parallel track sweep to cover the two convoys on the 20th. At 0850 hrs he attacked a U-boat with six DCs and only a minute later made another attack on a U-boat which had surfaced bows first. The two remaining DCs were released. For the 20th however, the Coastal Command War Record credits only T/201 with a kill. Middlebrook's account gives Hewitt as having attacked U-527 and U-598 with some damage to U-527.[10] The U-boat battle against convoys HX229 and SC122 are given as extending from 6 to 22 March 1943 during which twenty-one ships were lost, against the loss of one U-boat out of 41 deployed.[11]

From 201 Squadron's 'line book', Coastal Command at that time had limited Sunderlands to 12-hour sorties, although later in May, they were to fly on trips of 15 hours carrying 2,400 gallons fuel but armed with six instead of eight DCs.

It had been decided in March that Canada would take responsibility for protecting convoys as far as 47° West but that the range of their aircraft would be limited only by their endurance. In April, Admiral Dönitz instructed his U-boats to charge their batteries during the day; this order followed a series of attacks at night by Coastal Command aircraft.[12]

May 1943 marked a turning point in anti-submarine warfare; for that one month alone, the Americans list 41 U-boats sunk, and Capt Roskill gives 47 Axis submarines sunk by all means.[13] Capt Roskill's chapter covering the Battle of the Atlantic for the period 1 January – 31 May 1943 is sub-headed 'The Triumph of the Escorts'; the 'escorts' must surely include Coastal Command aircraft which are credited wih 40 enemy submarines sunk and 26 damaged in that period. Two of the 40 were shared with HM ships.[14]

One of Coastal's first anti-submarine successes in May was achieved by No. 461 RAAF Sqdn. F/Lt E.C. Smith was airborne from Pembroke Dock in 'M' DV968 on the 1st and at 1136 hrs sighted a U-boat 10 miles away moving at 6 knots on the surface. This U-boat (U-415) had earlier been attacked by a Leigh-light Wellington of 172 Sqdn. Smith released depth charges 18 seconds after the vessel had submerged. U-415 escaped to suffer another attack, this by Whitley E/612, before returning to port damaged.

The following day at 1354 hrs, F/Lt Smith was airborne again in the same aircraft. Over five hours later a U-boat was seen at ten miles on the port bow. Smith flew into cloud at 2,500 ft breaking out from it when the U-boat was five miles ahead. At one mile there was AA from the U-boat, but at 60 ft altitude, Smith released DCs which straddled the vessel. In a circuit for a second attack, the tail-gunner raked the U-boat with machine-gun fire. The vessel was by then listing to port and losing oil when a further four DCs were released. The U-boat began to settle and many of its crew came out of the conning tower and jumped into the sea. They were from U-332 which sank in position 4448N 0858W. During its service, U-332 had sunk nine Allied vessels.[15]

The other Australian squadron – No. 10 – followed on 7 May when F/Lt G. Rossiter captained W3993 'W' from Mount Batten. He had been flying for almost six hours when a conning tower and the wake of a U-boat were sighted 10 miles away on the starboard beam. The vessel disappeared before an attack could be made and Rossiter adopted baiting tactics. At 1220 hrs he was at 2000 ft just below 6/10ths cloud when the wake of a fully-surfaced U-boat was seen by using binoculars in position 4706N 1058W, 17 miles away. Rossiter climbed into cloud and broke out again when four miles from the submarine which was still fully surfaced. As the Sunderland dived to attack, the U-boat altered course but Rossiter followed across track at 60° to the starboard quarter armed with eight 270 lb Torpex DCs set at 25 ft depth and 100 ft spacing. Four were released from 50 ft straddling the vessel with two exploding within 50 ft. Both nose and tail gunners had opened fire scoring hits on the conning tower. A second attack was made after completing a very tight turn, releasing the remaining four DCs, the first of which fell within 20 ft to port and aft of the conning tower.

The U-boat made a series of tight circles at 4–5 knots but was gradually losing speed and trailing oil, finally becoming still with the stern and conning tower awash. At 1300 hrs the U-boat slowly submerged still trailing oil and 30 minutes later a large crescent-shaped patch of oil appeared. The Sunderland remained until 1415 hrs during which time there were more patches of oil surfacing. Post-war records give U-465 being sunk in the position of Rossiter's attacks.

In May 1943, No. 228 Sqdn lost both Sunderlands EJ139 and DD837. F/O W.M. French while on patrol on the 15th sighted 'V' DD837 turn to port and disappear from view. 'V' had been captained by F/Lt G.A. Church with a crew of nine and had taken off from Pembroke Dock at 1100 hrs; it failed to return. On the 24th F/O H.J.

Debnam was detailed for an A/S patrol in the Bay of Biscay. Some time after being airborne from Pembroke Dock at 1400 hrs, he, (from the Coastal Command records), must have attacked U-441 causing such damage that the submarine returned to port. F/O Debnam and crew in EJ139 however, failed to return.

The month ended with Sunderlands involved in the sinking of two U-boats. F/Lt D.M. Gall was airborne from Lough Erne in R/201 DD835 at 1034 hrs on a creeping-line-ahead (CLA) search. He had been flying for over six hours when a fully surfaced U-boat was sighted eight miles away. Gall approached along the U-boat's track but as four DCs were released, the vessel turned sharply to starboard and the charges straddled at 45° to the stern, but all four exploded. The U-boat continued on course for a minute before sinking stern first with the bows rising above the water. F/Lt Gall circled and was aware of two heavy explosions with flashes. These were followed four minutes later with large eruptions which lasted for about five minutes. This represented the demise of U-440 which, with another commander (Geitzler) had sunk two ships from convoy HX228 in March.[16]

Sunderland DV969 of No. 10 Sqdn RAAF was airborne from Mount Batten at 1345 hrs on an A/S patrol but at 1645 hrs was signalled to search for a damaged U-boat in position 4638N 1042W. At 1730 hrs while flying at 2000 ft the Australian crew captained by F/Lt Mainprize sighted the U-boat five miles ahead. Two Halifax aircraft were circling the vessel which was low in the water. Mainprize made his first attack with four 270 lb Torpex DCs set at 25 ft and spaced at 100 ft. One burst 20 ft from the port side, another close to starboard. The U-boat was trailing oil but able to steer. It stopped and men were seen on the conning tower. Mainprize made a second attack with his last four DCs; the U-boat went down at the bows with its stern clear of the water and apparently sinking. Its crew appeared on deck with life-jackets. One of the two Halifax aircraft from 58 Sqdn now attacked with machine-gun fire.

This was at 1750 hrs when a second Sunderland came on the scene. This was DD838 captained by F/O W.M. French of 228 Sqdn who made two attacks releasing four DCs on each occasion. Number 228 Squadron reported the U-boat as having 'shuddered and disappeared'; No. 10 Sqn's account as 'seen to disintegrate'. The AOC of 19 Group congratulated the three squadrons, 58, 10 RAAF, and 228. The U-boat, U-563 had in its service, sunk seven Allied ships and damaged four. It was lost off Brest in position 4635N 1040W.

Earlier in March, some Leigh-light Wellingtons had been equipped with Mark III ASV and were able to undertake successful night attacks on U-boats without being detected themselves through their own ASV transmissions. Such attacks had prompted Admiral Dönitz to order his U-boats to surface during the day to charge their batteries. This order by Dönitz, naval historian Capt Roskill suggests was perhaps, 'his biggest mistake of the war'.[17]

Churchill gives the period 1 April – 1 July as the decisive phase in the U-boat war, and of 235 U-boats in action in April 1943. Fifteen U-boats were sunk in April, and 41 in May.[18] In May, Dönitz withdrew U-boats from the North Atlantic for rest or to be deployed in less hazardous areas. The lone Sunderlands with crews prepared to accept all the risks, could well claim to have made an appreciable contribution to the Allied success.

One of those risks was Germany's deployment of flights of Ju88 fighters intended to counter Coastal Command's operations of the Bay of Biscay such as is exemplified in the following account.

Sunderland N/461 Versus Eight Junkers 88s

N/461 with a crew of ten including the captain – F/Lt C.B. Walker was airborne from Pembroke Dock at 1331 hrs on 2 June for an A/S patrol over the Bay of Biscay. At 1900 hrs W/O R.M. Goode in the tail turret reported aircraft at six miles on the port quarter and above the Sunderland. They proved to be eight Ju88s and Walker attempted to reach cloud cover but there

was no time. The navigator F/O K.M. Simpson positioned himself in the astrodome to act as controller, DCs were jettisoned, and two of the crew manned the guns in the galley, Lane to port, and Miles to starboard. In the nose turret was L.S. Watson and in the dorsal turret – A.E. Fuller.

Three of the fighters appeared to starboard, three to port, one on the port quarter and one on the starboard quarter. In the initial attacks, the Sunderland's port outer was set on fire, and an incendiary bullet struck the compass with the burning alcohol released setting fire to Walker's clothing. The second pilot – Amiss – used an extinguisher on the burning clothing. Although the engine fire was also put out, the propeller windmilled and sheared off with the reduction gear.

All the gunners held their fire until they were sure of scoring hits, and in another attack, the midships gunner – Fuller – shot down an enemy in flames at 50 yards range.

On the Sunderland, wires to the rudder and elevator trims were shot away, the hydraulic lead to the rear turret was cut and the rear gunner collapsed, due possibly to concussion. Fuller and Watson concentrated their fire on another Ju88 which plunged into the sea. A shell which exploded against the radio bulkhead wounded three on the flight deck including Simpson who had shrapnel in his leg. The intercomm was lost and Simpson maintained control by shouting and passing messages. Below in the galley, Miles at the starboard gun was mortally wounded in the stomach. Constant violent corkscrewing twisted the Sunderland's airframe and all doors were jammed. Instruments were damaged including the airspeed indicator and fuel gauges. Miles was replaced by flight engineer Turner, and Amiss reached the rear turret to find Goode had recovered and was operating the turret manually.

Six Junkers 88s now reformed on the beams and quarters; Goode shot down one in flames, and from the nose turret, Watson scored hits on another with flames coming from its port engine.

After a battle lasting three quarters of an hour, two Ju88s remained and they elected to break off the engagement in which twenty attacks had been made. F/O Simpson, the navigator, obtained an astro shot, gave a course for return to base, and collapsed – due to loss of blood.

The pilots then flew back about 300–350 miles on three engines without an airspeed indicator or fuel gauges and with need to compensate on the rudder. Walker reached the village of Marazion in Penzance Bay with hundreds of holes in the hull, intending following ditching procedure. On touch-down it was found that water was not entering the hull as rapidly as expected and the Sunderland was run up onto the beach using two engines, by then having lost another.

This crew had earlier that year in February, experienced attacks by Ju88s and FW190s; many of the crew were later lost on 13 August.

In what the Chief of Air Staff described as '. . . this epic battle', Walker and his crew could claim three 'kills' and one probable kill. With just two Ju88s remaining after the battle, it appears likely that two other Ju88s were damaged.

Successes and Losses in the U-boat War
The limited number of recorded successes against U-boats by Sunderlands in June 1943 may have resulted from Dönitz having withdrawn them from the operational areas of the flying-boats. However, on the 13th both F/Lt G.D. Lancaster and F/O L.B. Lee of 228 Sqdn made encounters. Lancaster was airborne at 1058 hrs in DD834 and while on patrol at 1848 hrs made an attack with six DCs. Of three explosions seen, the nearest to the submarine's swirl was 50 ft.

F/O L.B. Lee airborne from Pembroke Dock in DV967 failed to return. He had attacked and 'heavily damaged' U-564[19] and its commander – Hans Fiedler – attempted to return to port but was sunk by a Whitley of No. 10 OTU. Both the Sunderland and the Whitley were shot down by U-564.

Early the following morning F/O Stan White was airborne from Pembroke Dock in JM678. His wireless operator intercepted a sighting report transmitted by Sunderland W3985 T/10 Sqdn. According to 228's record, White sighted three U-boats in position 4514N 1025W on a north-easterly course at 12–14 knots.[20] Two of the U-boats submerged, and when the third started to dive, White attacked from astern with four DCs, two of which exploded ahead of the swirl. White then intended using baiting tactics but was attacked by a Ju88 flying at 500 ft and sighted four more Ju88s. After an exchange of gunfire with one of the enemy aircraft, White escaped into cloud.

In June 1943, No. 201 Sqdn was based at Castle Archdale on Lough Erne. It was from there on the 27th that the New Zealander F/O B.E.H. Layne flew W6005 on an A/S patrol. He had been flying for seven hours when a U-boat was sighted five miles away. Layne dived to attack releasing two DCs from 75 ft when the vessel's conning tower was still visible. Three to four minutes later, the submarine surfaced and the Sunderland was subjected to AA fire as Layne turned for a second run. Further attempts were thwarted by intense AA fire. F/O Layne's attack had damaged the submarine U-518 and she returned to port. U-518 had begun sinking ships on 2 November 1942 when three were claimed. Her final torpedo attack is recorded for 12 September 1944 with a total of fourteen ships listed.

Coastal Command and the Royal Navy on the Offensive
July 1943 was 'disastrous' for the German U-boat Command.[21] Thirty-seven U-boats are listed as sunk[22] plus five damaged by Coastal Command controlled aircraft.[23]

At this stage in the war, not only were Coastal squadrons better equipped with aircraft, but some units had improved offensive armament including rocket projectiles and the 'Mark 24 mine' which was really an acoustic homing torpedo. Sunderlands however, were using depth charges.

The Royal Navy had at sea, groups of surface vessels devoted to anti-submarine operations such as the 2nd Escort Group commanded by Capt. F.J Walker, RN. An effective blockade of the French ports from which the U-boats crossed the Bay of Biscay to the Atlantic was being achieved. The German response was to arm the U-boats more heavily against aircraft attacks; have some sailing in small groups; to provide air cover, and to deploy destroyers from the Biscay ports.

The Sunderland crews became well aware of all these measures, and the crew of JM708 from 228 Sqdn were able to give confirmation on the 13th. JM708 captained by F/O R.D. Hanbury was airborne at 0304 hrs from Pembroke Dock on a trip which was to be of 13½ hours duration. On reaching position near 4502N 0914W, three U-boats were sighted on the surface. Hanbury circled for forty minutes during which there was an exchange of gunfire before one of the U-boats became detached from the others. Hanbury then attacked the separated U-boat releasing seven DCs. The bows and the conning tower were blown off and it sank immediately leaving twenty-five men in the water.

The Sunderland crew dropped a dinghy and saw six of the submarine's crew enter it. From Capt Roskill's account, these survivors were later picked up by HMS *Wren*, a sloop from Capt Walker's group.[24] The six were from U-607 captained by ObLtn. Wolf Jeschonnek which was lost in position 4502N 0914W.

Three U-boats Lost to Combined Air/Sea Forces

On 30 July 1943 three U-boats were lost while sailing in a group but accounts vary of what happened. According to Capt Roskill,[25] in the last four days of July, eleven U-boats sailed from French ports to cross the Bay of Biscay. Three of that eleven were U-504, U-461, and U-462; U-461 and U-462 were the tankers of particular value to Dönitz.

The captain of U-461 – Wolf Stiebler – recalls:[26]

'I received the order as the senior commander, to escort U-462 and U-504 (Vowe and Luis) in convoy through the Bay of Biscay . . . we travelled in formation at various depths and surfaced only for charging the batteries. The signal to surface was given by me. On the third day, U-462 did not surface and with batteries drained, it was necessary for the three of us to remain on the surface while U-462's batteries were charged.

'Half-an-hour later the first plane was spotted, and it wasn't long before several were above us. On the horizon, three more destroyers (sic)[27] appeared. Our defence with the quadruple guns worked very well. The manoeuvre of the boats excellent; each had room to move but they stayed together – we made a good defence force. My radio messages were never answered . . . U-504 moved away separately, and later Vowe also went; he scuttled his boat and I saw people from U-462 jumping into the water.'

Stiebler was shocked; U-461 was alone.

'Now it was more difficult as planes were flying from various directions. Two machines approached from different angles. I had only the quadruple guns and shot at a machine; the volley struck well as I saw the strikes using glasses.'

This aircraft, (from Roskill's account) would have been one of the two Liberators in the affray. The first sighting of the U-boats was credited to a 53 Sqdn Liberator followed by Sunderland JM679 of 228 Sqdn captained by F/O Stan White who recalls circling out of range of the light AA fire from the U-boats. He sent an accurate sighting report giving the position and commenced homing procedure but was attacked by a Ju88 and made for cloud cover jettisoning his depth charges.

Halifax aircraft of 502 Sqdn appeared and one of them made a successful high level bombing attack on U-462 apparently causing such damage that it was unable to submerge. A second Sunderland arrived captained by Dudley Marrows of 461 Sqdn, 'U' W6077. Marrows recalls:

'We were well south on patrol when we received a signal to divert to a position where a U-boat had been sighted. From wireless traffic it was obvious that aircraft were already there and reporting three subs. P/O Jimmy Leight, first pilot, sighted them through binoculars – three in tight formation . . . we were at the end of our outward endurance . . . when we got within 'attack' range aircraft were circling, the U-boats manoeuvring in formation, keeping bows-on to the aircraft, and putting up a formidable barrage of cannon and machine-gun fire. From our height of 1000 ft the RN sloops were not visible.'

F/Lt Marrows found the submarines could out-turn him, he could not effectively contact the other aircraft and with one Liberator having been hit, he followed one in its second attack but taking the Sunderland as low as possible believing that the guns on the U-boats would be so depressed that the first U-boat would act as a shelter. He released seven DCs at such low altitude that it was necessary to pull up to clear the U-boat's conning tower. He heard the voice of Jock Holland his second pilot say 'You got him'. Of this, the victim of that attack – Capt Stiebler – in U-461 states:

'. . . an almighty explosion, after which I thought the boat had been blown apart. I was dragged into the depths, then there was a jerk and I shot to the surface.'
    'We were drifting; on my command we tried to stay together. The depth charges of the destroyer against the surfaced U-504 were hellish torture. After a short time a dinghy was thrown to us by Dudley. There were still eleven of us; the injured got into the dinghy, the others held on tightly outside. Later the *Woodpecker* took us on. I was put in an officer's cabin and treated very well; a

Capt. Wolf Stiebler who commanded U-461 when it was sunk by U/461 Sqdn. Capt Stiebler was saved with some of his crew by the Sunderland's dinghy dropped by F/Lt Dudley Marrows. Post-war they became great friends.

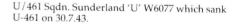

U/461 Sqdn. Sunderland 'U' W6077 which sank U-461 on 30.7.43.

guard in front of the door watched over me. Before leaving I was able to thank the English commander for taking us on board.'

Post-war, the two former enemies, Wolf Stiebler and Dudley Marrows of U-461 and U/461 respectively, became friends and it was thanks to Dudley that I was able to contact Capt Stiebler. HMS *Woodpecker* which picked up Capt Stiebler, was one of Capt F.J. Walker's group of sloops which concentrated on A/S warfare with much success and on this day had the support of a Catalina. In the final assessments, U-461 was credited to 461 Sqdn, U-462 to a Halifax of 502 Sqdn, and U-504 to HMS *Kite*, *Woodpecker*, *Wren* and *Wild Goose*. Survivors were picked up from the two 'milch cows'; U-504 went down with all hands. The approximate position for all three being 4530N 1100W. On that same date, 30 July 1943, three other U-boats were to be lost, U-591, U-43, and U-375, thus making a total of six.

In his summing up of this period, the official naval historian Capt Roskill gives credit to aircrews, 'mainly from Coastal Command– a welcome tribute indeed![28]'

On 1 August there were eight U-boats in the Bay of Biscay and with six more sailing from St Nazaire and Lorient.[29] Coastal Command Sunderlands claimed the first A/S successes in this month; these were in attacks by V/228 JM678 and B/10 W4020.

U-461, U-462 and U-504 in position 4540N 1055W on 30.7.43 before all three were sunk by air/sea forces. This photograph was taken from JM679 of 228 Sqdn.

F/Lt Stan White of 228 Sqdn was airborne from Pembroke Dock at 1450 hrs on a 'Musketry 2' patrol. After flying for six hours a surfaced U-boat was sighted to port. White now recalls:

'We attacked with the front gunner firing accurately at the conning tower and we released depth charges. I made a second run dropping the remaining DCs. During the attack we were hit by four shells, one knocked off the port float, another hit the wing damaging ailerons.'

One of White's crew, Fred Jackson recalls: 'The sub was straddled with DCs each time and was left listing badly to port.' The effect of two other shells from the U-boat Jackson gives as: 'Our aircraft was also holed below the front gun turret and in the rear end of the hull.' Of the Sunderland's return to base, F/Lt White adds:

'We were diverted to Poole due to bad weather, but requested to return to Pembroke Dock. On arriving at dusk we were instructed to fly round while the flare path was set up in Angle Bay. There was a five-foot swell and it was raining heavily. Just before finishing alighting, a number of the crew clambered out of the astro hatch onto the starboard wing to prevent the port wing striking the water. We were led into shore by one of the boats and beached it on the sand. How the crew managed to stay on the wing in such foul conditions I do not know.'

This Sunderland's victim – U-383 – sank the following night from lethal damage inflicted in F/Lt White's attacks.[30]

W4020 of No. 10 Sqdn RAAF was airborne from Mount Batten captained by F/Lt K.G. Fry with a crew of eleven and detailed for a Musketry 10-3 patrol. At 1440 hrs flying at 1700 ft they were in position 4536N 1023W and sighted five sloops six miles away escorted by a Catalina on a U-boat hunt. Fry altered course towards the sloops and then sighted a U-boat on a northerly course two miles away. The

Sunderland passed over the submarine before making a tight turn and attacking with six depth charges which were released from 50 ft. They straddled the U-boat – three on each side. The tail gunner saw it enveloped in explosions before sinking bows first. During the run-in, the front gunner had opened fire but the U-boat responded with three 20 mm cannon. One shell must have struck the starboard main fuel tank and the aircraft's bridge was flooded with petrol.

The Sunderland continued on that course for another six miles before turning 180° to port and ditching across wind into a 15–20 ft swell, bouncing twice before quickly settling due to a damaged hull. There were six survivors from the aircraft and five of these clung to part of the starboard wing which had a float attached. The sixth survivor – Don Conacher, who was swimming nearby, was picked up with the others by HMS *Wren* one of the sloops within 10–30 minutes. Four days later No. 10's CO – Wg Cmdr Geoffrey Hartnell – met the survivors at Devonport. F/Lt Fry had gained a 'mention' for the award of the DSO but such cannot be made posthumously. The captain of the U-boat, U-454, KL Hackländer who also survived the action, was picked up by

HMS *Kite*. His comments confirm Don Conacher's impression of how the vessel sank; its bows must have been blown off or split open.[31]

Sunderlands N/228 and M/461 Versus U-106

On 2 August, Sunderlands from 228 and 461 Sqdns were detailed for 'Musketry' sorties which were A/S patrols north-west of Finisterre in the Bay of Biscay. F/O R.D. Hanbury captained N/228 JM708 airborne from Pembroke Dock at 1100 hrs; F/Lt Clarke was airborne in M/461. On that day there were a number of U-boats and surface

U-106 settling in position 4635N 1155W on 2.8.43 after co-ordinated attacks by JM708 of 228 Sqdn and Sunderland M/461.

craft both Allied and German in the Bay. Clarke sighted three German destroyers heading westwards and while shadowing them, F/O Hanbury came on the scene. They exchanged signals before Hanbury flew off to warn the Navy's escort group.

At just after 2000 hrs while still shadowing the destroyers, Clarke sighted a U-boat, and at 2010 hrs it was reported also by the 228 Sqdn crew. From what one of Hanbury's crew – Alan Lacy – recalls it is apparent that there was close and efficient co-operation between the two Sunderland crews. At 2015 hrs Clarke attacked, covered by fire from Hanbury's Sunderland. The U-boat was straddled by seven DCs. Hanbury now followed with another seven depth charges. Further attacks were made by both aircraft but by then the U-boat had stopped and was settling by the stern.

Some of the U-boat crew jumped overboard but others who attempted to man the U-boat's guns were shot down by both aircraft. At 2040 hrs the U-boat blew up leaving many survivors in the sea. These were picked up by German destroyers and returned safely to port. This submarine, U-106 lost in position 4635N 1155W was the fourth in two days, and following losses in the previous month, resulted in Dönitz recalling the last six U-boats to leave port and to cancel group sailings.[30]

Sunderland DD852 Versus Seven Junkers 88s

Sunderland 'J' DD852 was the first of No. 10 Sqdn's aircraft to operate with armament modifications with four fixed ·303-inch Brownings in the nose to be operated by the captain and intended to counter U-boat AA fire during an attack. An additional modification for 10 Sqdn was the installation of guns to port and starboard in the galley. On 3 August DD852 was on an A/S patrol over the Bay of Biscay captained by F/O Alan Williams. He had been flying for one and a half hours when the first pilot sighted three aircraft at eight miles on the starboard bow. Williams headed for cloud but later, three aircraft caught up with the Sunderland – they were Ju88s. Shortly after, a further three,

followed by a seventh appeared on the starboard bow and attacked with cannon and machine-guns. F/Sgt H.A. Bird in the front turret was fatally wounded by a shell which struck below him. Williams took evasive action while his navigator – F/O Gross – acted as fire controller. The first three Ju88s were now astern and in an attack from the starboard quarter, a shell exploded at the wing root wounding Gross, cutting the control wires to fuel cocks, breaking hydraulic lines to front and dorsal turrets, and making the radar and intercom. u/s. Fire control orders were now passed to the 2nd pilot and a passenger. Attacks followed from the port quarter and then with all seven Ju88s attacking from various angles. Sergeant Owen at the starboard galley gun was seriously wounded in the legs by a cannon shell and was replaced by a Flt/engineer. F/O Williams was able to use his four fixed guns but they detracted from his prime need – to take violent evasive action and to obtain best position for his gunners. After a battle lasting an hour some cloud cover was gained, but when broken, the enemy again appeared. There were further attacks with cannon before the enemy broke off. Five of the seven fighters were seen heading away in formation. The squadron record gives one Ju88 probably destroyed and all others damaged by the Sunderland's machine-gun fire. There was a service for Sgt Bird at Mount Batten before he was taken to Haycombe cemetery, Bath. Sunderland DD852, apparently severely damaged, was handed over to Shorts.

The two Australian squadrons Nos 10 and 461, undertook a number of Sunderland modifications; another made by 10 Sqdn on 3 August was for a ·5-inch calibre gun in the nose of the aircraft. This was on a ball mounting, hand held and with limited movement both vertically and horizontally. Number 10 stated that it was of no practical use and prevented the installation of a low level Mk III bombsight. This opinion is however disproved by successful use in other squadrons, notably when the hydraulics to turrets were cut.

Further Encounters With Enemy Aircraft

There were more battles over the Bay of Biscay with enemy fighters such as occurred on 8 August. A No. 10 Sqdn Sunderland DP177 'F' was on an A/S patrol from Mount Batten. When far south over the Bay, F/10 captained by F/Lt N.C. Gerrard, was attacked by six out of eight Ju88s. They caused damage to the port wing and float but no members of the crew were wounded. When the enemy broke off the combat, F/Lt Gerrard continued with the patrol. From the phrasing of No. 10's record, it was considered almost routine! Three days later, that same aircraft, captained again by F/Lt Gerrard, failed to return from a patrol. A total of twelve crew were listed as missing, believed killed.

The following week, instructions came from No. 19 Group that in view of the presence of enemy single-engined fighters, aircraft proceeding to or from the 'Musketry' patrol area were to pass through position 5000N 0830W thence to datum and return to the same point. The varying 'Musketry' areas extended as far south as 4230N off the Spanish coast up to about 48°N and from approximately 0730W to 12°W thus covering the Biscay ports from south of Brest to just south of Cape Finisterre in a series of five 'boxes'.

During a trip on 14/15 August a Sunderland from 461 Sqdn captained by F/Lt P.R. Davenport was attacked by six Ju88s. Before the Sunderland could reach cloud cover it was damaged by cannon fire, a gunner, R.V. Woolhouse, was killed and the wireless operator – I.A.N. Jones – was wounded. Despite the loss of instruments, Davenport was able to use cloud cover to escape before eventually force-landing in the Scillies.

Six Junkers 88s Versus Sunderland EK578

On 16 September 1943 EK578 of 461 Sqdn was flown by a crew comprising men who for the most part were on their last trip in a tour of operations. At 1535 hrs they were returning to base from a patrol over the Bay

F/Lt de le Paulle's crew of 422 (RCAF) Sqdn at Bowmore, Isle of Islay. They spent 3 to 4 days in a dinghy before being rescued by a 228 Sqdn Sunderland captained by F/Lt Armstrong.

of Biscay and were near the position (4542N 1100W) where their captain – Dudley Marrows – had attacked U-461 earlier that year.

Two minutes later, Peter Jensen in the tail turret reported 'specks' at 20 miles on the port quarter. At 17 miles they were identified as aircraft, and when the distance closed, came the message: 'Tail to captain, five aircraft dead astern'. Marrows ordered his wireless operator to send an aircraft attack signal and 'immediately turned west to take the enemy further from base and reduce attack time'. Depth charges were jettisoned, additional guns were deployed in the galley, plus another from the 2nd pilot's seat. Already manned were the four in the tail turret, two in the mid-upper, while below the nose turret was a ·3-inch manually operated American

Browning. Cloud cover could not be gained and it was apparent that the enemy had pre-arranged tactics with one of the six Ju88s acting as a controller with a modified cockpit giving better visibility.

In the first two attacks the hydraulic line to the rear turret was cut, a gun in the mid-upper jammed, and there were hits on the fuselage. The Sunderland's violent evasive actions caused ammunition in the rear turret to twist out of the pans and the turret could not be operated even manually and Jensen left it just before a shell exploded in the turret. Another shell burst in the bomb compartment, the radio was put out of action and its operator wounded in the face. A 37 mm shell exploded in the nose of the Sunderland blowing a front gunner towards the wardroom and his gun out of its mounting. Bamber, the gunner,

L/Cmdr Peter Cremer of U-333 who, in addition to sinking a number of ships, shot down Sunderland ML880 of 228 Sqdn when attacked by F/Lt Slaughter 11.6.44.

The official 'Form Orange' from No. 461 (RAAF) Sqdn which reports the sighting of three U-boats sailing in formation.

although severely wounded, used his shoulder as support to fire his gun before being taken back for his wounds to be treated.

It was thought that three of the Ju88s had been hit in return fire with one of the three unlikely to reach base. The Sunderland was still being attacked, the two port engines were windmilling, the starboard outer caught fire and the port float support had been shot away.

It was impossible to maintain height and ditching was ordered. Dudley Marrows had well in advance considered the state of the sea and in Jensen's words, 'Put it down as a moth on a petal' despite a 12 ft swell. The port float was lost and the Sunderland heeled over before the crew could reach the starboard wing. The wounded gunner was passed through the hatch first and all the crew were able to reach dinghies, but two of the three burst due to damage by shrapnel, thus eleven men were crowded into one. Much equipment was lost with one of the dinghies but a flame float and some signal rockets were retained.

Jensen recalls:

'I looked at the man opposite me to see a strange face. He held out his hand "John Eshelby", he said. I took his hand, "Peter Jensen". Lance Woodland our engineer had gone to hospital and John replaced him . . . this was his first trip! I then introduced him to the rest of the crew.'

The night was spent in the dinghy and early next day a Catalina flew over. This was FP237 of 210 Sqdn captained by F/O John Cruickshank. At 0305 hrs the Catalina crew had sighted a faint glow at one mile from 800 ft and located the dinghy by switching on the Leigh-light. After dropping a marker and signalling base, homing procedure was ordered. During the five hours Cruickshank remained in the area, a Liberator and three sloops were sighted. The dinghy's position was given to the sloops which were from the five

comprising the 2nd Escort Group commanded by Capt. F.J. Walker. It was with these vessels that Dudley Marrows had co-operated at the time of sinking U-461. The sloops had seen the ditched Sunderland which had not sunk despite the loss of a float. HMS *Starling* (U66) lowered a boat and all the crew of the Sunderland were taken aboard; the wounded Pierre Gamber to sick bay, Marrows with some of the others, to be hosted by Capt Walker. They were presented with souvenirs of U-461. Although not his base, Capt Walker detached a sloop taking the Sunderland crew to Pembroke Dock. After debriefing, the 'Form Orange' was endorsed by the station CO: 'An example of what can be done by a well-trained and disciplined crew' – 461's Squadron Commander added: 'concur'. Two of the gunners – Sgts Bamber and Pearce – were awarded the DFM; F/Lt Marrows – the DSO

References
1 DR II p. 100
2 Ibid. p. 82
3 UMU XII p. 275
4 JR p. 296
5 UMU XII pp. 282–4
6 SWR II p. 218
7 WSC V p. 7
8 CCWR p. 16
9 MM p. 278
10 MM p. 277
11 SWR II p. 365 and map 38
12 SWR II p. 371
13 USSL p. 163 and SWR II p. 378
14 CCWR pp. 10–18
15 JR p. 298
16 JR p. 156
17 SWR II p. 371
18 WSC V pp. 8,9
19 PC p. 187
20 See also KB p. 292
21 SWR III pt 1 p. 24
22 USSL p. 164
23 CCWR pp. 16–18
24 SWR III pt 1 p. 25
25 SWR III pt 1 p. 27
26 Letter to author
27 Capt. Walker's sloops
28 SWR III/1 p. 29
29 SWR III/1 p. 27
30 SWR III/1 p. 28
31 KB p. 298

Chapter 10
Canadian Squadrons in Coastal Command

NUMBER 422 Squadron was formed at Lough Erne in April 1942 and was intially commanded by an ex 201 Sqdn officer – S/Ldr J.S. Kendrick. He was succeeded by the Canadian – W/Cmdr Larry Skey, DFC – who had served previously with 210 and 228 Sqdns. W/Cmdr Skey arrived at Lough Erne on 9 July and F/Lt R.E. Hunter, DFC, reported for duty as Flight Commander. The playwright F/O Terence Rattigan was posted to 422 Sqdn as W/AG and was later to be involved in the preparation of the squadron's badge and motto. Number 422 Squadron trained initially on Lerwicks before a brief operational period with Catalinas but in November became based at Oban and by 1 December had received four Sunderlands with more expected.

Number 423 Squadron similarly had an RAF officer as CO – W/Cmdr F.J. Rump – shortly after being formed at Oban in May 1942. W/Cmdr Rump had been ferrying PB2Ys across the Atlantic in flights typically of 28 hours duration. As A/Cmdre Rump recalls:

'It was quite a unique experience as up until then the Flying Boat Union had been very much a closed shop!' On arrival at Oban, I was joined by Johnnie Hughes, an operationally experienced flying boat captain. Together we had the task of forming and training with RCAF pilots and aircrew (who were mostly very inexperienced) in what was a very unusual change, and indeed, a challenge to us all. The nucleus of RAF ground crew was eventually built up to squadron strength as they were gradually replaced by RCAF tradesmen. Meanwhile the aircrews flew with another RAF flying boat squadron based at Oban to gain operational training and experience.

'After approximately six months, 423 was operational and in what was a well-planned and executed move the whole squadron of approximately 250 personnel flew to Lough Erne. At Lough Erne we settled into strange accommodation including a castle, stables and Nissen huts, and commenced our full operational role.'

The first A/S patrols undertaken by 423 Sqdn were flown by S/Ldr J.D.E. Hughes in Sunderland W6001 and F/Lt Lindsay in W6052 on 3 August 1942. Number 423 Squadron moved to Lough Erne in November and on the 21st W6052 had a fifteen minute combat with a Junkers 88. Sgt Clegg in the galley carried on cooking steak during the affray. The enemy broke off the engagement, probably damaged. In the Sunderland were only four bullet holes. Number 422 Sqdn became operational on Sunderlands on 1 March 1943 when six aircraft were available. Three more were allotted from 246 Sqdn in April and the

A 422 Sqdn Sunderland piloted by Larry Giles on Lough Erne 27.2.44 when the unit was based at St. Angelo.

No. 422 (RCAF) Sqdn aircrew having converted from Catalinas to Sunderlands.

following month, 422 moved to Bowmore, Isle of Islay but returned to Lough Erne in November.

The Canadians' First U-boat Kill

Aircrew from 423 Sqdn gained their first success against enemy submarines in May 1943 while operating from Castle Archdale on Lough Erne. F/Lt John Musgrave was airborne just before midnight on the 12th in Sunderland W6006 'G' to escort convoy HX237 which had sailed from Halifax, Nova Scotia. After flying for 8½ hours and then at 3000 ft, the Sunderland crew sighted a fully-surfaced U-boat heading north at 15 knots. Musgrave gained cloud cover before making a diving attack, but at one mile range the U-boat opened fire and it was obvious that it intended remaining on the surface.

Following Coastal Command's orders, Musgrave aborted his attack and signalled the convoy which was only ten miles away. The Canadian corvette HMCS *Drumheller* one of the escort vessels, had just rescued 15 survivors from a torpedoed merchant vessel when she sighted the Sunderland circling and signalling by Aldis lamp that the aircraft was over a U-boat. While *Drumheller* headed for the U-boat, the Sunderland carried on a running battle against the submarine's AA and in an

exchange of fire scored hits on and around the conning tower but itself was hit by a shell in the fight which lasted twenty minutes. When the corvette came in range, the U-boat began to submerge and Musgrave attacked while it was changing course. Only two DCs were released as by then the U-boat had submerged. Markers were dropped from both the Sunderland and a Swordfish which must have taken off from the escort carrier HMS *Biter*. *Drumheller* arrived on the scene six minutes after Musgrave's attack and released depth charges. On regaining Asdic contact, it led the frigate HMS *Lagan* which then began a 'Hedgehog' attack.[1]

Sunderland G/423, HMS *Lagan* and HMCS *Drumheller* shared the sinking of U-456 in position 4837N 2239W. U-456 had herself claimed seven Allied ships the last of these being *Fort Concord* a merchant vessel in the convoy, and possibly shared with U-403, another of four U-boats claiming sinkings from convoy HX237.[2]

The fifteen survivors picked up by HMCS *Drumheller* may have been from either of two Norwegian ships in the convoy *Sandanger* and *Brand* which had been torpedoed on the 12th. For convoy HX237, the score was even, three ships against three U-boats sunk.[3]

'Hedgehog' as used by HMS *Lagan*, could fire a pattern of 65 lb bombs ahead of the attacking vessel which did not interfere with Asdic detection, the bombs having contact fuses, unlike DCs which were released from astern and were detonated by water pressure.

Sunderland DD859, U-489 and HMS *Castleton*

On 21 June F/O Al Bishop together with his crew in 423 Sqdn collected Sunderland DD859 from Wig Bay and flew it to Castle Archdale where they were based. After a few hours training they started operations two days later. On 4 August Al Bishop was airborne with the same crew and aircraft at 0455 hrs. Two hours later they were on a 'Moorings' patrol. At 0910 hrs Bishop was at 4000 ft when a U-boat was sighted 4–5 miles away. The submarine was sailing westwards at 7 knots and almost immediately commenced zig-zagging and with no sign of diving. As Al Bishop recalls:

'During that period some of the U-boats were staying on the surface to fight it out with attacking aircraft so we did not find this unusual. As we circled the U-boat we soon saw that the advantage we might have was to attack down sun.

'We proceeded with such an attack and descended to sea level. As we approached the sub. they started shooting at us with what appeared to be cannons with exploding shells and machine-guns. I took evasive action by undulating the aircraft. As I levelled out at 50 ft for the final bombing, the shells began to hit the aircraft. Two of my crew returned fire with a ·5-inch on a swivel and a ·3-inch in the front turret. I was successful in tracking over the submarine and dropping a stick of six DCs which straddled the sub.'

This attack had been made with Torpex-filled DCs of 250 lb each when flying at 140 knots from directly astern of the U-boat. Bishop continues:

'. . . there was a fire in the galley and bomb bay areas with flames coming upstairs . . . the starboard engines were running at full power and there was very little aileron control. This was caused by a shell which had burst under my seat severing the exactor controls to the starboard engines. I had slight flak in the back of my knee which I did not know of at the time. I had to stop the starboard engines and attempt to maintain control with the rudder. I decided to attempt an emergency landing and advised the crew. All this happened in a very few seconds.

'In trying to land we bounced and I had trouble controlling the aircraft. As we hit the water again the port wing dropped a little, the float caught in the water and we cartwheeled into the sea. I recall putting my right arm in front of my face and the next thing was being under water and rising to the surface. I came up slightly behind the port wing. What was left of the aircraft was on fire and there was fire on the water around it. I swam through an open space. As I was swimming I heard Sgt Finn call, "Skipper, can you give me a hand?" I turned and swam to him to discover he had no Mae West and was badly hurt. I grabbed hold of him with my right arm.

'I saw one of the aircraft floats and was able to reach it, but it began to fill with water as soon as I grabbed it and sank.

'I could not see any of the other crew members but a short while later I saw the submarine stern down, not too far away. The crew were getting onto Carley floats or rafts. As the sub sank there was a big explosion. The crew made no attempt to come over and help us. For the fifty minutes I was in the water, I recall nothing. My right arm had been bruised in the crash and was sore and stiff. I attempted to change Finn to my left arm but every little move caused him to scream with pain.

'Next I recall looking round and seeing the Royal Navy's destroyer. Apparently they were patrolling in the same area and an alert look-out had seen the Sunderland dive down. Then after the crash they could see black smoke from the fire. They launched lifeboats and picked us up. I was able to climb up the scramble net at the side of the destroyer. While in the water I recall seeing a Sunderland overhead. It was from a Norwegian squadron and I later met the captain. Once aboard the destroyer we were taken into the wardroom. Then we started shivering violently. Before I could bed down I was called to the deck to identify the body of one of my crew and witness his burial at sea. After that I saw a doctor briefly and climbed into a bunk.

'I was awakened at about 0230 hrs 5 August as we were entering Reykjavik. We survivors were taken to the hospital. Two of us were able to walk, the other four were badly injured and were in hospital in England for some time.

'I returned to Ireland on 13 August via a Liberator and went on a month's sick leave. I returned to flying on 19 September and to ops on 2 October being repatriated to Canada in March 1944.'

The action took place west of the Faeroes in position 6111N 1438W. The destroyer was HMS *Castleton*; the submarine U-489 captained by Obln Schmandt, the seventh out of ten 'milch cows' to be lost.[4] The RCAF official history gives 58 German survivors being picked up with six out of the Sunderland's crew of eleven.[5]

Rescue by Sunderland of a Ditched Sunderland Crew

DD861 Sunderland 'P' of 422 Sqdn was airborne at 0100 hrs on 3 September 1943 from Castle Archdale captained by F/O de le Paulle. Jacques de le Paulle, (generally known as 'De Loop'), had been detailed for an A/S patrol over the Atlantic with an ETA at base of 1425 hrs. After flying for 5½

hours the patrol area was reached in position 4700N 1350W but it was after another 2¾ hours when in position 4430N 1320W as third pilot Don Wells recalls:

'Without any warning the starboard outer engine caught fire and soon after a violent explosion occurred. The engine fell forward in its mountings, hung for a moment, and then fell free of the aircraft taking the outboard part of the wing and float with it. Power was lost in the inner engine and the port engines had to be cut to maintain stability. Barely a minute passed from the time the engine caught fire until we were in the drink.

'The hull was badly crushed and the plane started to sink; there was a lot of shouting of orders but no panic. I went aft to see if the rear gunner was all right and to release the dinghy which was stowed by the rear door. The aircraft was sinking by the nose and by the time the dinghy was pushed out of the rear door we were almost 40 foot high in the air.

'I dived feet first, came up spluttering and heard someone shouting about the DCs not being defused, but it was a false rumour. We counted heads and found that everyone was on the surface, the whole crew of twelve had survived. The only injury being to navigator Bolton who had a nasty cut on the head. One dinghy was torn and had to be repaired

The rescue of de le Paulle's crew with DD861 of 422 Sqdn by F/Lt Armstrong in Sunderland JM679 of 228 Sqdn on 6.9.43.

before we were all out of the water. The skipper was cool and confident as though this sort of thing had happened to him lots of times . . . he set about taking stock. We knew that we were about 250 miles from the northern coast of Spain and although an SOS had been sent it must have been short. Skipper calculated that our rations should be apportioned on the basis of a 14-day voyage; this worked out to ½ pint of water, 1 Horlicks tablet, ½ oz chocolate, and 1 stick of chewing gum per day, per man. We were also equipped with a couple of spray sheets, canvas pails for baling, flares, paddles and some small lines which were used to lash the two dinghies together. The portable radio transmitter had been left in the aircraft, jammed under the navigator's table. The rubber dinghy is not a comfortable place to spend time especially in rough water. With six men in each rubber ring there was little room to move; the only worthwhile occupation was talking. Considering that we had crew members from England, Scotland, France, Canada and USA, I feel we were reasonably civil.

'By mid-afternoon we were adjusted to our situation and I managed to doze off in the night despite the discomfort of having a wave break over us every little while. Time tended to drag, baling was a constant chore, the cigarettes had all disappeared, we took turns watching the horizon for ship or plane.

'The second day was quite warm but a stiff gale came up in the night and we had to hold on to avoid capsizing. Two separate aircraft flew over that day, we fired off flares but were not seen. We were somehow cheered by this and there was a general discussion about what we would do when we next got leave in London.

'Just after noon on the third day, a Liberator with USA markings flew right over us, turned and circled. Great excitement and useless shouting. After a few more laps he came over with flaps down and dropped a parachute bag with

fair accuracy. The bag hit the water about 200 yards off and our skipper dived in and struck out through the waves. After a longish swim he managed to bring the bag back and was pulled aboard. A note therein told us to hold on as help was on the way. There was also a dozen oranges and several packets of American cigarettes. A couple of long hours later a beautiful Sunderland appeared from the north and we cheered.'

This Sunderland was JM679 R/228 captained by F/Lt H.C. Armstrong who was airborne at 0855 hrs on 6 September for an A/S patrol before sighting the dinghies at 1728 hrs.

Don Wells continues:

'A wing came up and we were afraid it was too rough to attempt a landing. We tried to wave him off but the pilot found the right trough and dropped it like a real pro. We were all rather weak after three days of soaking in salt water and had to be helped into the aircraft. I was given a cup of tea and placed in the bomb bay with my back to the wall. The take-off was awesome; we were sure the aircraft would come apart but the pilot finally got it into the air and set course for home.

'The flight was not entirely uneventful as we came a bit close to Brest (it was dark at that time), and the AA gunners had a go at us. Not too long after we were landing at Pembroke Dock. The aircraft was out of fuel and the tide was out as well. After an interminable wait we were towed to the pier and managed to climb to the top of a lot of steps and walk a very long way along the pier to dry land. The day after, we met the 228 Sqdn crew briefly, and on 8 September our own CO flew to Pembroke Dock and took us back to our base at Bowmore.'

Another in the 422 Sqdn crew – Earl Hiscox – adds that the American Liberator had possibly sighted a flash from the base of the first-aid tin which Don Wells had used as a signalling mirror. From a report by 422's CO – W/Cmdr Skey – three SOS's had been transmitted and a pigeon had been released. In the dinghies sails had been erected when there was a favourable wind and they had hoped to reach Portugal. The Liberator was from No. 6 Sqdn USAAF commanded by Lt Dudock who homed the Sunderland from 228 Sqdn after sending a sighting report. F/Lt Armstrong of 228 Sqdn bounced 50 ft into the air due to the heavy swell with 45 knots IAS and just managed to remain airborne after sinking to sea level and gaining 60 knots IAS.

Armstrong crashed the following year and was lost with some of his crew. A survivor of that crash – S/Ldr J. Gilchrist – pays tribute to Howard Armstrong for 'skill and daring' in an 'epic rescue'.

Encounters with FW200 Kondors
On 22 July 1943 F/Lt Musgrave captained DD860 J/423 from Castle Archdale on a patrol in the western area of the Bay of Biscay. He had been flying for almost five hours when his rear gunner reported an enemy aircraft astern. It was a FW200 which opened fire from 1,500 yards and its first burst damaged the Sunderland's hydraulics putting the rear turret out of action. The rear gunner had been able to fire only 50 rounds and suffered splinter wounds to his face. The second pilot was wounded in the right arm and the front gunner in a knee. The Sunderland's hull was holed above and below the waterline, a trimming control was shot away and the port fuel controls were damaged. Two depth charges were reported to have been hit by rockets. Musgrave however, was able to escape into cloud and the enemy was not seen again.

An Australian captain with the Canadian squadron No. 423, F/O H.C. 'Jacko' Jackson had a similar experience. He was airborne in DP181 on 14 September detailed for a patrol 'Percussion F North 2'. Two hours after reaching the patrol area, a FW200 was sighted three miles away. The Sunderland was flying at 1000 ft, the enemy at 800 ft. The FW200 emerged from cloud 3000 yards astern and began closing

rapidly. It opened fire at 1500 yards and when the range had closed to 300 yards, the Sunderland's rear gunner responded, firing 800 rounds. The enemy broke off the engagement and disappeared before F/O Jackson had reached cloud cover.

Although some Sunderlands were later, (certainly with No. 10 Sqdn RAAF), to have an improved armament of eighteen machine-guns, the enemy retained the advantage of greater range with cannon. The hydraulic leads to the turrets on the Sunderland remained ever vulnerable.

Escort of Convoy SC143
Throughout the months of May, June, July and August, all the sinkings of U-boats by Sunderland aircraft were in the lower latitudes apart from that final one by F/O Bishop who commented that he expected the U-boat to stay on the surface to 'fight it out'. By September 1943, the U-boat tactics had changed with 'maximum submergence'.[6] In October, the Germans were again trying to gain the initiative in the U-boat war.[7] During the first eight days however, they lost eight U-boats; one of these was to Sunderland 'J' of 423 Sqdn. DD863 J/423 captained by F/O A.H. Russell was airborne from Castle Archdale on 8 October at 1027 hrs. Exceptionally, in his crew was W/Cmdr Frizzle who had been selected to become CO of 422 Sqdn. Frizzle, after a short course for conversion at Alness, had three trips with 228 Sqdn from Pembroke Dock, and was now on the first of three with 423 Sqdn.

F/O Russell had been detailed to escort convoy SC143 which was bound for the United Kingdom from Halifax and at 1734 hrs set course following an order to patrol astern of the convoy. Just two hours later on emerging from low cloud, the wake of a fully surfaced U-boat was sighted 100 yards off the port bow.

G/Capt Frizzle recalls:

'I was flying the aircraft when we flew directly over a sub at about 300 ft in pouring rain, very poor visibility and extremely rough seas. The aircraft captain – Russell – was down below having breakfast when the sub was sighted and a call went for him to come to the flight deck.

'In the interval I set up the aircraft for an attack on the sub and was well into the final run by the time Russell took over the controls. Russell continued my approach and selected four DCs, keeping the extras in reserve should we need a second attack. I stood directly behind Russell for the attack and according to the rear gunner we blew the sub out of the water and it broke in two. The U-boat made no attempt to submerge and I could see tracer bullets going just under our starboard wing.'

From three accounts given in the 423 Sqdn records, fire from the ·5-inch gun in the nose of the Sunderland must have silenced some of the German gunners, although while flying over it, the U-boat used 4·7-inch cannon to which the rear gunner responded.

One of the four DCs hung up but numbers 2 and 3 straddled the conning tower which lifted 15–20 ft following the explosions. Russell turned to make a second attack but saw only fifteen survivors with much debris and an increasing oil patch. The Sunderland had been recalled 33 minutes earlier and course was set for base.

Capt Roskill's account[8] gives this sinking of U-610 being 35 miles from convoy SC143 which comprised 39 merchant vessels and a merchant aircraft-carrier ship which had sailed from Halifax on 28 September with nine escort vessels but with a support group of four available. For this convoy he sums up the losses as being one escort vessel Orkan against U-610 sunk plus two other U-boats, U-419 and U-643, all three to aircraft of Coastal Command. Kpt. Ltn Walter Freiherr von Freyberg-Eisenberg-Allmendingen as commander of U-610 is recorded as having sunk four Allied ships and causing damage to three others.[9]

The Loss of Sunderland JM712

On 17 October Sunderland JM712 of 422 Sqdn was airborne from Castle Archdale at 0411 hrs captained by F/Lt P.T. Sargent. He had been detailed for an A/S sweep and with ETA at Bowmore of 1920 hrs. The sweep was intended to give cover to two convoys ONS 20 and ON206 outward bound for North America. The Sunderland had been flying for over eight hours when two blips were obtained on the radar screen at five miles range indicating something 20 miles south of convoy ONS 20. After emerging from rain cloud and using binoculars, two fully-surfaced U-boats were seen sailing at 16 knots. Sargent prepared to attack immediately the U-boat to port. Both vessels opened fire with cannon and guns and although Sargent took evasive action hits were scored on the Sunderland.

The Group gunnery officer F/Lt Woodward was on the forward ·5-inch Browning and F/Sgt Needham in the front turret, and after the first run their fire had cleared the decks of the U-boat's gunners. Some DCs overshot and there was a hang-up.

Sargent made a tight circuit for a second run at half mile range and approached a U-boat at 100 ft. The Sunderland suffered much AA fire, F/Lt Woodward's head was blown off and F/O Chesley Steves, the navigator, had a leg completely blown away by an explosive shell. Despite this, he insisted on giving a DR position to the second pilot F/O A.R.B. Bellis before collapsing and dying within a few minutes. Needham in the front turret was killed.

Damage to the Sunderland included the R/T shot away, front turret recuperator destroyed, auto-pilot blown out of the aircraft, W/T destroyed, radar damaged, control quadrant hit, throttle and pitch exactors destroyed, wing dinghy blown out, mid-upper turret hit and hull generally riddled.

The attack was made from 50 ft at 140 knots from the port beam and the two DCs straddled at 15–20 ft either beam. The U-boat was enveloped in explosions and lifted before disappearing. The RCAF official history[10] states that the U-boat (possibly U-470), was damaged by this attack.

The second U-boat remained on the surface firing continuously when the Sunderland was in range. Sargent set course for the convoy and reported details to HMS *Drury* by Aldis lamp and of his intention to ditch. This was achieved at 100 knots into wind touching down at 75 knots on top of the swell before the nose buried and the hull disintegrated with the whole tail assembly breaking off. The survivors were in the water for 15 minutes.

F/Lt Sargent had become entangled in the wreckage and went down with Steves, Woodward and Needham. Bellis was wounded in the shoulder and lost consciousness, it being thought that he had been thrown through the pilot's window. Despite a 20 ft swell – a rating from HMS *Drury* – Robert Leitch of Glasgow swam to Bellis, untangled him from the wreckage and swam with him back to the ship. Two others of the Sunderland crew were wounded, Rutherford and Mesney, had found themselves under the aircraft. Rutherford had concussion and lacerations; Mesney an arm temporarily paralysed and a leg fractured in four places.

They escaped from the aircraft when the tail section broke off. A boat from HMS *Drury* (K316) picked up the survivors – a total of seven. HMS *Drury* was in the 4th Escort Group which included HMS *Bentinck*; one of *Bentinck*'s crew – Bert Wells – recalls them losing only one ship from convoy ONS 20 due to it being unable to keep up to seven knots. It would have been the *Essex Lance* lost in position 5753N 2800W.

Convoys SL139 and MKS30

Two convoys homeward bound from Sierra Leone and North Africa, SL139 and MKS30, had combined on 14 November 1943 south of Cape St Vincent but on the 15th were sighted by German aircraft. A great battle was to follow involving escort vessels, U-boats, Coastal Command aircraft and long range Heinkel 177 Luftwaffe aircraft with glider bombs.

A total of 26 U-boats in three groups were ordered to attack[11] and U-333 commanded by Peter Cremer was the first to intercept

on the 16th at 1130 hrs.[12] U-333 was located by Asdic, suffered a pattern of 10 DCs and was rammed by the frigate HMS *Exe*. The starboard diesel engine was displaced, instruments were damaged and 333's periscopes were lost, but the U-boat gained a piece of a propeller from HMS *Exe*.

On the 19th, a Wellington from 179 Sqdn sank U-211 and early on the 20th, U-536 was sunk by the frigate HMS *Nene'* with the aid of the Canadian corvettes HMCS *Calgary* and HMCS *Snowberry*.

Another of the many Coastal Command aircraft involved was Sunderland W6031 of 422 Sqdn. With J.D.B. Ulrichson as captain it was airborne from Castle Archdale to take the centre patrol of a three-aircraft parallel track sweep. This was intended to cover the inbound convoy and then for the Sunderland to continue southward and land at Gibraltar. At 1740 hrs on the 20th, Ulrichson transmitted a U-boat sighting report but there was no further message until 1910 hrs when an SOS was received by Gibraltar, Malta and the Azores. The first sighting report had been from 4500N 1920W and the SOS was estimated to be from 4240N 1730W. There was an ASR attempt from the Azores but W6031 was reported lost with a crew of eleven. It was given as being shot down by U-618. Also lost about the same time was a Liberator from 53 Sqdn shot down by U-648.

A third U-boat, U-538 was sunk by HMS *Crane* and HMS *Foley* the following day. Peter Cremer, despite the serious damage to U-333, reached La Pallice on 1 December. As he gives in his own account,[13] he was the only U-boat commander to reach the merchant ships, all the other U-boats were forced to withdraw. The one merchant vessel sunk was claimed by the Luftwaffe. In the battle as charted by Capt Roskill,[14] the enemy lost three U-boats and five aircraft, L/Cmdr Morin Scott gives the final score against U-boats as one sunk, one probably sunk and three more damaged, but with one escort vessel damaged.[15]

Sighting of a Blockade Runner

In the latter half of 1943, the Admiralty was aware of a number of potential German blockade runners attempting to leave or sail for French ports. Coastal Command patrols were laid on to counter such moves. Number 423 Squadron was one of the units so involved and on 25 December their Sunderlands were on searches. Weather conditions were unfavourable on the 26th but on the 27th F/Lt H.C. Jackson was airborne at 0219 hrs in EK581 to begin a creeping-line-ahead search. At 1026 hrs the Sunderland's crew sighted the ship *Alsterufer* steaming at 15 knots on course 120°. The vessel opened fire but Jackson continued to shadow after sending a sighting report. Other aircraft were then homed to the position. At 1345 hrs Jackson broke cloud half mile from *Alsterufer* intending to attack but intense AA fire precluded any success and at 1430 hrs he set course, landing in the Scillies at 1930 hrs.

Sunderland EK581 had been one of four deployed from Castle Archdale; Liberators had also been sent and H/311 from the Czech squadron attacked with bombs and rockets setting *Alsterufer* on fire.[16] About 70 survivors took to lifeboats and were picked up by ships of the 6th Escort Group.

Canadians in Northern Ireland

Both the Canadian squadrons equipped with Sunderlands came to operate from Lough Erne in Northern Ireland, using as bases St Angelo and Castle Archdale.

Number 423 had their RAF CO –

W/Cmdr Rump – succeeded by W/Cmdr Archambault in July 1943 but a question appeared in the records for August: 'When are we going to have a Canadian crew sent to us?' A/Cmdre Rump writing in retrospect remarks: 'Sadly for me personally as part of the RCAF Canadianisation policy I handed over my command to a new RCAF commander.' W/Cmdr Rump was presented with a silver tankard inscribed: 'From 423 RCAF squadron Fog Hogs' – a reminder of the weather in which they operated. Of those on 423 Sqdn, he recalls the RCAF medical officer – Doc Sheard and a RCAF 'chiefy' – F/Sgt Wright – 'the ever willing and cheerful backbone of the ground crew'.

On 422 Sqdn, W/Cmdr Frizzle succeeded W/Cmdr Larry Skey, the latter 422's first Canadian CO in October 1943 which proved to be just prior to the unit's move from the Isle of Islay to Lough Erne to be based initially at St Angelo in November. When at Castle Archdale they suffered an infestation of rats which disposed of a rarity in WW2 – grapes – which were to be raffled. More welcome visitors included the AOC Coastal Command – Air Marshal Sir John Slessor – with the AOC No. 15 Group – AV-M Sir Leonard Slatter. Another visitor was the official RAF historian – Hilary St George Saunders – who gave a talk on the Dieppe raid in which there had been severe casualties for the Canadian troops.

3-H of No. 423 (RCAF) Sqdn on Lough Erne c. 1943–44.

A painting of DP191 when with 423 (RCAF) Sqdn 21.11.43.

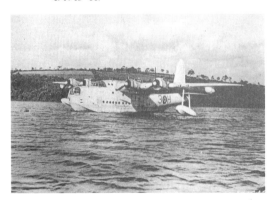

Diversions from duty included Ensa concerts and trips to Irvinestown 4½ miles distant where 'a large steak smothered with two to four fried eggs according to the diner's capacity and the whole covered with French fried potatoes . . .' was served at 'Bothwell's de luxe Dinery'.

The Canadian scribe records:

'Irish people are talkative enough but are soft spoken and their audience is limited to their immediate neighbours and consequently it is difficult for a Canadian to understand some Irish people, who, although they use the same words, and much the same pronunciation as us, have a different context in their sentences.'

When both 422 and 423 met at Castle Archdale following 422's move from St Angelo, softball took its place as the principal sport on the station. Broadcasts were given over the Tannoy at noon of the

ML814 coded WH-A while serving with No. 330 (Norwegian) Sqdn. It later operated as NZ4108 with the RNZAF but is now in the USA.

DP191 coded 3-L for No. 423 Sqdn. It later became NZ4109 with the RNZAF.

day's programme plus the previous day's scores. All ranks were represented in teams known as The Drunkards, Hell's Angels, Hoboes, etc.

An American with 423 Sqdn wished to have insignia on Sunderland W6000. A draft was made by LAC Garnier depicting a white eagle flying out of the sun onto a U-boat. Aware that the squadron was formed in Scotland, the colours used were red and yellow from the Macmillan tartan. This formed the basis for the squadron badge which was ultimately devised by the College of Heralds omitting both sun and U-boat. The eagle (a Canadian bald-headed eagle), was retained. The original sketch went to Lincoln's Inn Fields, the approved badge was presented to the squadron by AV-M W.A. Curtis, RCAF.

In January 1944 the badge of 422 RCAF Sqdn was approved by HM the King; it depicted a brave's arm in warpaint holding an upraised tomahawk and with the motto, 'This Arm Shall do it.' Its aptness becomes apparent if two lines of Bolingbroke's speech are quoted: 'And, by the glorious worth of my descent, This arm shall do it, or this life be spent.'[17]

U-625 Sunk by Sunderland U/422

Frank Morton and Sid Butler of 422 Sqdn were to exemplify that quotation on 10 March. W/O Morton was detailed for an A/S sweep from Castle Archdale. Although by then he had 1,500 hours flying, this was his first sortie as captain

The attack by F/Lt Sid Butler of 422 Sqdn which sank U-625 on 10.3.44.

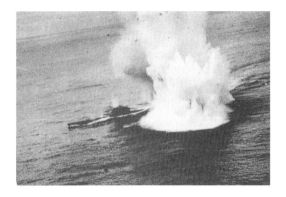

and, as was customary, was screened by a very experienced captain – F/Lt Butler.

They were airborne in EK591 'U' at 1125 hrs and set course from Eagle island at 1207 hrs. Three and a half hours later while flying at 1000 ft, Sid Butler then at the controls, sighted a U-boat at six miles on the port beam. Morton was having some tea below when the warning sounded. As he recalls:

'I returned to the 2nd pilot's seat and saw the sub surfaced and out of range and making no moves to dive. Sid offered me the wheel but I said something to the effect: "You are more experienced . . . you do it."'

'Ocean conditions were perfect for the U-boat to implement new tactics ordered by Dönitz, ie to stay on the surface and fight it out.'

The Sunderland crew had been briefed to attack on the bow thus avoiding the rapid-firing cannon aft of the U-boat. The vessel endeavoured to keep stern-on and zig-zagged before turning sharply to port and circling. After about ten minutes Butler gained a position on the U-boat's beam; he made a steep diving turn dropping from 400 ft and levelling off for a run at 50 ft.

400 yards from the vessel, the Sunderland suffered intense AA fire and as one of the gunners – Joe Nespor – recalls:

'I opened the window for a better view . . . and the aircraft shuddered as it dropped to 50 ft. Once in full view of the sub, two ·5-inch in the nose opened fire. All guns on the U-boat were immediately silenced. Just as the aircraft was approaching the U-boat, a German gunner ran towards the gun, pulled the trigger on a 20 mm cannon and the aircraft was hit on the nose. His timing was perfect as we could not depress our guns enough to reach him.'

Of this, Sid Butler states:

'I have a distinct memory of a tall figure in a grey sweater who was probably the gunner responsible for the damage our aircraft sustained in the last stages of the attack – leaving his gun at the last possible moment and diving for the conning tower as we passed overhead. A brave man indeed . . .'

The submarine was U-625 captained by ObLn Siegfried Straub which sank in position 5235N 2019W. U-625 was credited with sinking three Allied ships but with KL Hans Benker as its commander.[18]

Further Attacks on U-boats

On 24 April 1944 F/Lt Fellows of 423 Sqdn was detailed for a CLA search. He was airborne in Sunderland DD862 'A' from Lough Erne at 0708 hrs but it was to be 8½ hours later before he sighted the wake of a vessel 16 miles dead ahead. Fellows was then flying at 2000 ft and he increased speed to 140 knots and his second pilot confirmed by using binoculars, that the wake was from a U-boat steering 180° at 16 knots. When the Sunderland was at five miles on the beam of the vessel, the U-boat fired a box barrage and by turning endeavoured to keep stern to aircraft. When this turning was momentarily retarded, Fellows, with the sun behind him, commenced a run in. At 1,200 yards the Sunderland opened fire with four fixed forward guns and the twin front turret guns such that the AA from the U-boat was silenced for the last 300 yards of the approach.

The aircraft had suffered some hits from AA but six Torpex DCs set at 60 ft spacing and 25 ft depth were released from 50 ft altitude and in position 5036N 1836W.

One of the DCs must have exploded prematurely as the blast knocked out the rear gunner; the wireless operator was thrown from the astrodome stand; the port flap was made u/s; all electrical circuits were affected, and most seriously, the elevator was damaged, making trim difficult to maintain with the aircraft beginning to climb.

Control was regained, the rear-gunner recovered, and when the Sunderland flew over the attack area to release a marker, only an oil patch was seen. The aircraft returned to base becoming waterborne at 1832 hrs.

No wild claim of a 'kill' was made, rather does the squadron record suggest only 'probable damage'. However, although some post-war lists give U-311 as being sunk in this attack, it is now believed that it was U-672 which just suffered damage.

It was to be just another month before 423 Sqdn achieved another success and this when 'S' DW111 was detached to Sullom Voe. On 24 May, F/Lt Nesbitt was airborne at 0330 hrs on a special A/S sweep. After becoming airborne he was instructed to home on to Catalina V/210 Sqdn which was sighted at 1000 hrs. Nesbitt was patrolling the area for another two hours when he was instructed to transmit call signs and dashes to the Catalina. At 1419 hrs the Sunderland intercepted an SOS for position 6358N 0357E and the second pilot sighted smoke or a splash 10–15 miles to the north. The front gunner sighted a U-boat wake the same distance away with the submarine heading 35° at 12 knots. Nesbitt was then flying at 2000 ft but closed to attack. While heading for the U-boat, some wreckage was sighted to port and by then the vessel was firing heavy but inaccurate flak. Evasive action was taken but five DCs were released. The last plume from the explosions was 30–40 ft short of the hull. The U-boat had turned to starboard as the DCs exploded, and turned again later before submerging. The position of the unidentified wreckage noted earlier was confirmed as 6334N 0302E before the Sunderland returned to Sullom Voe. The U-boat is believed to have been U-921 which was damaged in this attack.

The Channel and Biscay Ports

In September 1944, the Allies took Dieppe, Rouen, Antwerp, Boulogne and Calais.[19] Coastal Command's anti-U-boat operations became directed away from the Biscay ports and by October, U-boats had begun to cover the approaches to the English Channel, to the west and north of Ireland, and round to the north of Scotland. This after a passage to Norway for refitting.[20]

Improved radar meant retraining of some aircrews particularly to counter the schnorkel-equipped U-boats. Two of the first encounters in September by Coastal Command aircraft were by Sunderlands of 423 Sqdn operating from Lough Erne.

On 3 September F/O J.K. Campbell in Sunderland NJ183 was on an A/S sweep and in less than an hour began a CLA. Within three minutes a schnorkel was sighted three miles away and on a southerly course at four knots. This was in position 5543N 0915W; Campbell attempted an attack from 50 ft when the schnorkel was only two feet above the water but the DCs failed to release. The U-boat disappeared completely before a further attack could be attempted and a marker was released. Surface vessels were homed to the area and later four lifeboats and a raft were sighted. The U-boat was U-482 operating as one of those which began an 'inshore' campaign' on this day.[21] Commanded by KL Graf von Matschkla, U-482 had sunk *Jacksonville* on 30 August, *Hurst Castle* on 1 September, *Fjordheim* on the 3rd and was to sink *Empire Heritage* on the 8th the latter in position 5527N 0801W.[22] Although all these ships were in convoy, the sinkings occurred when they were without air escort.

Three days later 423 Sqdn lost one of its Sunderlands – ML823 – which crashed into the sea off Donegal Bay. There was one survivor – W/O R.H. Voyce – who was picked up by the Navy at 0700 hrs on 7 September. The body of another from this aircraft – F/O F.W. Greenwood – was washed ashore on the 27th. Greenwood was buried at Irvinestown churchyard on 2 October.

U-boats with Schnorchels

Conditions for flying on 11 September were given as 3/10ths cloud at 1,500 ft, wind 210° 13 knots and 15 miles visibility. F/O J.E. Farren captained ML825 which was airborne at 0530 hrs. At just before 1000 hrs while on a CLA heading north, Farren sighted in position 5651N 0840W, whitish vapour or steam nine miles away. He altered course and lost height to

investigate. Using binoculars, the vapour was seen to be from a point on the surface. As the aircraft closed nearer, the vapour disappeared but a slight wake was seen extending 100 ft. It was thought to be from a U-boat on course 195°. Four minutes after the first sighting, Farren attacked with eight DCs set at 25 ft depth and spaced at 70 ft which he released from 50 ft, but the four to starboard hung up.

Three escort vessels were homed to the scene and the senior officer on the escorts confirmed over the R/T that there was a definite U-boat contact. The ships began their attacks at 1313 hrs but by the time the Sunderland had reached PLE at 1625 hrs, there was no sign of damage to a U-boat. British lists credit the frigate HMCS *Dunver* and corvette HMCS *Hespeler* with sinking U-484 in position 5630N 0740W, but an American list queries whether 423 RCAF Sqdn should share this kill.[23]

By the end of April 1944, mid-upper turrets had been installed in all of 423's Sunderlands and towards the end of the year the squadron was being provided with GEE and LORAN navigational aids. A submarine from the Royal Navy was detailed for exercises with Sunderlands intended to combat the U-boats which were fitted with schnorkels. There was training in night bombing using a low-level bomb sight Mark III in conjunction with radar and flares. By the end of the year trials with sonobuoys were in progress.

Canadians Based at Pembroke Dock

Number 422 Squadron gave a farewell party for W/Cmdr 'J. de' Frizzle at the end of October 1944 as he was posted to Canada to be succeeded by W/Cmdr J.R. Sumner. Number 422 Squadron's Sunderlands were already equipped with dorsal turrets and arrangements were made for the squadron's move to Pembroke Dock. By the end of November the unit had thirteen Mark III Sunderlands at their new base. Number 201 Squadron moved up to Lough Erne where 202 Sqdn was deployed and equipped with Catalinas.

1945 opened for the Canadian squadrons with 423 remaining at Castle

DG-V of 422 Sqdn; their last to leave Pembroke Dock 2.7.45.

Archdale commanded by W/Cmdr P.J. Grant and W/Cmdr Sumner in command of 422 at Pembroke Dock. In February 423 Sqdn lost Sunderland NJ183 when on the 11th it crashed three miles east of Irvinestown, with the entire crew of nine killed.

When the station CO of Pembroke Dock – G/Capt Bolland – was posted to Coastal Command HQ in March, he was presented with a framed copy of 422's badge. He commented that on receiving Canadians at the base where there were already the RAF Sqdn No. 228, and the Australians of 461, it had been with some apprehension and misgivings. It however, had proved a success and in the best interests of the squadrons.

Number 422 Squadron's mascot, the dog 'Straddle' evaded confinement and was alleged to have chased both chickens and sheep. A second issue of 422's paper 'Short Slip' was published in February due to the initiative of Sgt R.M. Clements and LAC Brydges who had borrowed printing apparatus from a Mrs Evans. Pembroke Dock was introduced to 'Hoe Down' square dances at St Patrick's Church Hall with about 100 people taking part. In March, 'Canada House' was officially opened. It had originally been Trinity Hall to the rear of Trinity Church in Meyrink Street.

Operationally, 422 Sqdn became geared to A/S operations against schnorkel U-boats and in March there were a number of sightings such as on the 2nd when F/O Denroche was on an armed *Loran* exercise. While flying at 1000 ft in ML884 white smoke was seen at three miles in position 5412N 0505W. When the distance was closed to one mile, the smoke disappeared. A sonobuoy pattern was dropped and when the smoke again appeared, an attack was initiated, but was aborted when again the smoke disappeared. Three destroyers arrived on the scene and when the Sunderland sighted a schnorkel and periscope, a further attack was attempted but with a hang up of the DCs. Similar sightings were made by four other crews all within a week but without evidence of any kill.

By 13 May photographs were being taken of U-boats surrendering and at the end of the month the two Canadian squadrons were aware of the intended move from Coastal to Transport Command and for them to be based at Bassingbourn. Number 422 Squadron came officially under Transport Command on 1 June; some RCAF personnel sailed for Canada in *Pasteur*. On the 15th some 228 and 461 Sqdn Sunderlands were flown from Pembroke Dock to their new bases at Castle Archdale and Mount Batten.

The 422 Sqdn scribe reported:

'P.D. is just a ghost of its former self. Empty halls and ante-rooms where one's footsteps echo back and forth between the walls as we pass through the rooms, looking for remaining bodies. A few Sunderlands tug gently at their moorings impatient to be on the way again . . . the remaining squadron 422, wanders about the camp . . . generally trying to keep busy . . .'

On 2 July, 422 Sqdn personnel saw their last Sunderland DG-V take off from Pembroke Dock for Castle Archdale. '. . . everyone felt that were losing part of ourselves when our aircraft finally left for good.' 'P/O Straddle' the squadron mascot led the parade on 24 July when 422 Sqdn departed Pembroke Dock. 'The route to the train was lined with townsfolk eager to say goodbye.'

In Northern Ireland, 423 Sqdn had a party of officers, NCOs and airmen representing the unit in lining the route taken by their Majesties the King and Queen with HRH the Princess Elizabeth visiting Londonderry on 19 July.

References

[1] JS p. 175
[2] JR p. 166
[3] SWR II p. 375
[4] SWR III pt 1 p. 31
[5] WABD II p. 584
[6] SWR III pt 1 p. 37
[7] DR III p. 61
[8] SWR III pt 1 p. 41
[9] JR pp. 126,141,160,163,173
[10] WABD II p. 584
[11] SWR III pt 1 p. 50
[12] PC p. 155
[13] PC p. 159
[14] SWR III pt 1 map 3
[15] MS p. 237
[16] JH p. 627
[17] *Richard II*, Act 1, Sc. 1
[18] JR p. 201
[19] TA WW2 p. 25
[20] SWR III pt 2 p. 173
[21] SWR III pt 2 p. 180
[22] JR p. 185
[23] USSL p. 170

Chapter 11
Other Units

Number 4 (Coastal) Operational Training Unit

Sunderland W6006 took off from the Cromarty Firth at 2055 hrs on 28 August 1943 captained by F/O Richmond. At 2156 hrs the starboard inner propeller sheared off taking with it the starboard outer propeller. Height was rapidly lost but a safe landing was made. This was my first trip in a Sunderland; I gained immediate respect for those who had served on operational Sunderlands but became disenchanted with the aircraft.

Number 4 (C) OTU then based at Alness was in sharp contrast to RAF North Front Gibraltar, my earlier station. At the latter one could walk to aircraft in a few minutes but at Alness half the day appeared to be spent reaching a flying-boat; the other half – returning.

With aircraft which had seen better days and with overworked engines, there were a number of accidents, as many as three in one night including Catalinas in addition to Sunderlands.

One such crash occurred on 27 July 1944 at 0200 hrs with Sunderland W6010. F/Lt Rodgers was detailed to give night take-off and landing instructions to two pupil captains – Ray Steed and P/O Saunders and with Steed's crew. As Ray Steed recalls: '. . . there was a complete blackout with no stars or moon – visibility zero.' He was in the galley with a rigger when P/O Saunders was starting his routine test. In a second landing approach at 600 ft the Sunderland struck four high tension cables. Twenty feet of the port wing was sheared off and the aircraft burst into flames before bouncing free for half-a-mile and sliding down a slope into a stone farmhouse. Five of the crew escaped through the astrohatch and ran down the starboard wing; the two pilots went through the windscreen and found themselves in front of the farmhouse. The only injury was a burn on the flight engineer's face which was not serious. All those in the aircraft escaped. This was at Allarton farm, Cromarty and the farm caught fire.

The farmer John Watson and his sister were seriously burned, but his nephew – Hugh Watson – who was trapped by falling masonry, fatally so. In Coastal Command it was customary for crews nearing the end of their operational training to undertake a full operational flight although 'sprog' crews were likely to be screened by experienced aviators even when reaching a squadron.

In May 1944 the flying-boat OTU achieved two successes against U-boats. The first of these occurred on the 21st when P/O E.T. King was airborne at 0550 hrs in Sunderland 'S' from the Cromarty Firth. While flying at 2000 ft at 1248 hrs a U-boat was sighted surfacing 2½ miles away. An attack was made releasing six DCs from 50 ft. Coastal Command's record gives this attack being on U-995 which was so

U-675 being successfully attacked by F/Lt Peter Frizell while 'on rest' at No. 4(C) OTU flying Sunderland 'R' on 24.5.44.

damaged that it returned to port.[1] Later, and captained by OL Hans-Georg Hess, U-995 was listed with eleven successes against Allied ships.[2]

In my own log for December 1943 appears the name – 'F/O Frizell' as captain of W3981. About 45 years later I received a letter from Capt Peter Frizell concerning his sortie in Sunderland ML736 R/4C OTU. On 24 May 1944 as he recalls:

'. . . there had been a totally restricted area off the coast of Norway as our own submarines used it frequently . . . Group decided at this time to lift the restriction, having carefully ensured that no Allied submarines were anywhere near, and being short of aircraft, asked 4 OTU to send out an experienced captain with a crew to search the area.'

Peter Frizell was airborne from the Cromarty Firth at 0739 hrs and as he continues: '. . . on a fairly bright day with some high cloud cover. After about six hours one of the gunners reported a "vessel" on the surface. I dived towards it and could not believe my eyes when I recognised it was a fully-surfaced U-boat . . . On sounding action stations, the galley reported they were unable to extend the DCs rack electrically . . . this meant some time doing it manually and I feared we might lose our chance.

'Meantime the U-boat opened fire with its 4·5-inch cannon and some machine-guns but while waiting for the racks to be extended, I had to keep within striking distance all the while expecting him to dive. I ordered the tail gunner to warn me when he saw the flash of the 4·5 figuring that if we acted promptly we could avoid being where the shell exploded. With racks extended, DCs armed, I turned for a standard quarter attack but the sub could out-turn a Sunderland . . . finally I anticipated his moves and finished up on his quarter. After I pressed the tit there was a deathly silence for a few seconds and then an unholy shout from the rear gunner . . . we had straddled the sub . . . We had a fixed rear-facing

camera and maintained our heading long enough to take a series of pictures. When we were able to turn back, I flew low over the wreckage; the last picture showed the U-boat vertical and it exploded as it sank.'

Peter Frizell had previously served with Nos 201 and 423 Sqdns completing an operational tour before becoming an instructor at the OTU. His attack on the submarine U-675 was confirmed as a 'kill' in position 6227N 0304E. He was awarded the DFC.

Recollections I have of 4 (C) OTU are of an Australian pilot convincing himself that a Sunderland with a serious mag drop on three engines would not take-off; a fitter working over an engine of a Sunderland moored out on the Cromarty Firth in extremely bitter weather, and of another Sunderland burning up rapidly in the sky.

Number 57 Maintenance Unit, RAF Wig Bay

With a few others, I was posted to 57 MU, Wig Bay in early 1944. At this station on Loch Ryan our duties were largely test flights and with some occasional ferry trips. These flights were always with a skeleton crew, one pilot, one wireless operator, and generally an engineer and rigger. Sometimes we would be without either rigger or engineer, having just three in total. This meant the wireless operator standing in for others, and for me, the nearest I could hope for to Hudson ops with a crew of four.

Most of the Sunderlands we were involved with at Wig Bay were from the factories of Shorts at Belfast or Windermere and tended to be in the 'ML' range of serial numbers. It was all fine weather flying and 'coast crawling' without a navigator, occasionally to Greenock, Windermere, Oban or Beaumaris. On 9 April we took DV964 to Windermere and collected ML764. The tranquility of Lake Windermere was hard to believe when at that time forces were being massed for the invasion of Europe. Shorts proved hospitable, and if I recall correctly, provided lunch gratis or possibly at a cost of 2/6d, (half-a-crown). Sunderland ML814 we first air-tested on 31 March. It was later to serve with 201, 330, and 422 Sqdns and to gain a New Zealand serial NZ4018 also a civil registration G-BJHS. ML778, which was air-tested on 10 June 1944 was much photographed when coded as NS-Z on the final Coastal Command sortie of WW2 and then with 201 Sqdn.

Pilots 'on rest' after a tour of operations included the Australian 'Happy' Adams and the New Zealander F/Lt Layne. The latter had served on 201 Sqdn and was able to claim a successful attack on a U-boat. 'Happy' truly justified his nickname; it was a pleasure to fly with such men.

Wig Bay in 1944 did have other types of flying-boats. There was a Coronado which seemed to be forever in a hangar, a Sea Otter with that single lethal propeller – I almost walked into it. The one Martin Mariner we 'ran up' from time to time 'on the step' at about 40 knots – but never airborne. The flight engineer's station in the Mariner allowed him much *lebensraum*, perhaps the most elegant position in the aircraft. It had an elaborate fuel system allowing rapid transference of fuel. This Mariner followed a 'self destruct' when the 30 hp APU exploded setting the aircraft on fire.

Accommodation at Wig Bay was in huts but included some American 'Quonsets' which had wooden floors and heating by oil stoves. RAF stations sometimes provided anomalies in diet; at Wig Bay, which was surrounded by herds of Ayshire cattle, there was no fresh milk; powdered milk past its 'shelf life' was used. Compensations were that such as fresh salmon could be purchased for 4/- (20 p) lb. Bicycles were issued on loan, and in easy cycling range were Stranraer and Port Patrick.

There were all-ranks dances on the station and some personnel were invited to Loch Awe castle where the atmosphere was truly Scottish and dances accordingly so. Concerts were arranged, and the two broadcasters Dobson & Young made an appearance to talk on the subject of music. A corporal on the station, no less able and entertaining, spoke on the subject of

symphonies using Beethoven's 1st as an example.

Unlike an OTU, at Wig Bay, aircrew were in the minority, with such as the senior engineer officer taking pride of place after the Station CO. There was much more contact with ground staff and on some local flights, aircrew could be outnumbered by maintenance personnel who were ostensibly checking their own work, although even the 'Queen Bee' (the senior WAAF officer), managed to get airborne.

The invasion of Europe precluded leave for most personnel, but for those who managed to reach London in the summer of 1944, the V1s, (flying bombs), were a not infrequent sight and sound. They appeared to follow a track coinciding roughly with the river Thames. From time to time, ATA aircrew arrived, some having made the Atlantic crossing. One of the ATA pilots, was such a diminutive lady that one wondered how she could possibly reach the rudder bar on a Sunderland but she had the respect of those who knew her.

In November 1944, came my posting for a second tour of ops; this was to a Wellington squadron on ten-hour night trips against E-boats. The first question asked of me at my new station was: 'Have you a car, there are so many here now unclaimed?'

Number 330 (Norwegian) Squadron

Norway was overwhelmed by the Germans in April 1940 despite support from the

The 'graveyard' at Wig Bay with the ex 201 Sqdn PP115. It was at Wig Bay on Loch Ryan that No. 57 MU received much of the output from Shorts of Belfast.

Sunderland ML824 at the RAF Museum, Hendon. After service with 201 Sqdn it went to the Norwegians and then the French. It now has the code and letter NS-Z which No. 201 Sqdn had given to ML778.

British, French and the Poles. About 200 personnel from Norway's fighting services escaped to the United Kingdom by various means and some trained pilots and mechanics were absorbed into the RAF. Others sailed in the ships ss. *Iris* and ss. *Lyra* to Canada where training was undertaken at Island Airport, Toronto Island with ss. *Iris* providing temporary accommodation. The training unit was officially opened on 10 November 1940, and came to be known as 'Little Norway'.

Men continued to escape from Norway across the North Sea or via Sweden; as late as the summer of 1942, the writer recalls seeing vessels of obvious Scandinavian origin in the harbour at Wick and of others at sea, being escorted to Britain by the Royal Navy.

Two Norwegian squadrons came to be formed in RAF Coastal Command,

WH-F of No. 330 (Norwegian) Sqdn when based at Sullom Voe.

numbers 330 and 333. The latter operated flights of Catalinas and Mosquitoes while 330 became a Sunderland equipped squadron.

Number 330 Sqdn became based initially at Reykjavik with personnel from Britain arriving on 12 April 1941 and with a further contingent reaching Iceland from Canada on the 25th to be under the command of Cmdr Hans A. Bugge. The unit was then equipped with Northrop single-engined floatplanes with eighteen of those aircraft arriving in the Norwegian ship *Fjordheim* from New York on 19 May. Their first sortie was on 23 June. Some Catalinas were received by the squadron but it was ordered to Oban on 1 December where there was conversion to Sunderlands. The first of these flying-boats – DD835, arrived at Oban on 12 February 1943 and in July became based at Sullom Voe. By the end of the year, 330 had received twenty-three Sunderlands, although the final total during the war was forty-eight.

From a Norwegian account, 330 Sqdn located fifteen U-boats[3] but it was to be in May 1944 before a positive success could be claimed. In the early part of 1944 about two dozen U-boats were based in Northern Norway.[4] Number 330 Sqdn was then operating from Sullom Voe with Mark IIIs under the command of Cmdr Torsen Diesen. During May, an ice thaw in the Baltic gave Admiral Dönitz the chance to reinforce his U-boats in Norway[5] and an opportunity presented itself to 330 Sqdn.

S/Lt C. Johnsen was airborne at 1327 hrs on the 16th from Sullom Voe as captain of JM667 V/330. His front gunner reported 2½ hours later an object at eight miles on the port bow. While flying at 500 ft in position 6305N 0310E, a U-boat was sighted on the surface heading directly north at 15 knots.

In the Sunderland's first attack the depth charges failed to release but machine-gun fire from the aircraft's front and rear turrets must have killed many of the U-boat's crew manning AA guns, although the Sunderland suffered some hits.

During the second attack, AA fire was not so heavy but the front gunner was killed and the 3rd pilot – S/Lt Buck and

Flt/mechanic Qm K. Halvorsen were slightly wounded. S/Lt Johnsen was temporarily blinded by smoke from a hit in the cockpit and flames from the front turret, but was able to release four DCs from 50 ft. Three of these exploded close to port of the U-boat whose bows rose at a very steep angle 30 seconds after the attack. After another 30 seconds the vessel went down stern first.

Both starboard engines of the Sunderland had been damaged, and 25 minutes after the attack, an engine cut and there was severe vibration. 1050 gallons of petrol were jettisoned and an SOS transmitted. This was later cancelled when the aircraft was able to gain height. At 1918 hrs, S/Lt Johnsen made a successful touch-down despite the hull being damaged in a number of places. Post-war lists give the U-boat (U-240) captained by ObLn Günther Link as being sunk in position 6305N 0310E.

The Rescue of Survivors from Canso-A 9754

On 24 June a Canso from 162 Sqdn RCAF captained by F/Lt David Hornell was airborne from Reykjavik with seven other crew members on an A/S sweep. Five hours later, Hornell attacked and sank U-1225 but the Canso was shot down and the crew took to the dinghies.[6] Two died from injuries and/or exposure. The Canso's aerial had been shot away and no signal was received, but by chance a 333 Sqdn Catalina captained by Carl Krafft sighted survivors from both the aircraft and U-boat.Lt Krafft remained circling the dinghy from the Canso for many hours until another aircraft had been homed to the area and shortage of fuel forced him to leave.

A Warwick with an airborne lifeboat reached the scene on the 25th and meanwhile an ASR launch had sailed. Although the Warwick released its lifeboat the Canso survivors were unable to reach it. Sunderland EJ133 from 330 Sqdn captained by S/Lt Ole Evensen was airborne at 1050 hrs on the 25th and reached the ASR launch three hours later in position 6318N 0053W. After exchanging signals, Evensen flew to position 6318N

The Norwegian crew of EJ133 captained by S/Lt Ole Evensen which played a part in the rescue of F/Lt David Hornell's Canso crew from 162 Sqdn RCAF on 25 to 26 June 1944.

0040W where six survivors were located. The Sunderland signalled to the ASR launch and circled the survivors' dinghy after marking the position with a smoke float. S/Lt Evensen remained on the scene until he saw the survivors picked up by the ASR launch at 1515 hrs on the 25th. The Sunderland crew located a waterlogged airborne lifeboat 1½ miles from the ASR launch before returning to base having completed a twelve-hour flight.

David Hornell, the captain of the 162 Sqdn Canso, died shortly after being picked up by the ASR launch and was

F/Lt Hornell's crew being picked up by ASR launch and watched by Sunderland W/330 on 26.6.44.

buried at Lerwick. He was awarded a posthumous VC. While with 422 (RCAF) Assn at Vancouver in 1989, the author met one of the (then) three remaining survivors – F/O Graham Campbell. He had been in the front turret of the Canso at the time of the attack on U-1225 before going to the radio to transmit an SOS which could not have been received.

The operational record of No. 162 Sqdn RCAF acknowledges the part played by both Norwegian squadrons by recording: 'The homeward bound Catalina of 333 Sqdn sighted the two sets of survivors' and, 'A Sunderland remained with our crew until the rescue launch arrived.'

There is little doubt that, but for the fortuitous sighting of the Canadian survivors by Carl Krafft's crew, none would have been rescued and the fate of both U-1225 and Canso 9754 may well have remained a mystery. The arrival of the Sunderland could well have saved further

losses from the Canadian crew due to exposure such as must have resulted in the case of the U-boat crew.

U-387 Damaged by Sunderland O/330

In a communication to Stalin dated 25 June 1944, Winston Churchill sums up the war situation in Western Europe with: (i) The opening of a Russian counter attack; (ii) The Americans about to take Cherbourg; (iii) The Allied advance in Italy towards Florence which was expected to be taken in June.[7]

In *The War at Sea*, Capt Roskill gives the prospect of an American breakthrough from Cherbourg isolating the French ports of Brest and Lorient and that a victory in Normandy during July would result in surviving U-boats being transferred from Biscay ports to Norway.[8] Such a change in the deployment of U-boats would shift the emphasis of Coastal Command patrols from 19 Group to 18 Group. This is

An attack on U-387 by Lt. Thurmann-Nielsen captain of O/330 EJ155 which damaged the U-boat

NJ172 at Sullom Voe in 1945 with 330 Sqdn and coded WH-F.

reflected by the next anti-submarine success credited to a Coastal Command Sunderland.

Operating from Sullom Voe in the Shetland Isles, Sunderland EJ155 O/330 was airborne at 1744 hrs on 19 July. Its captain – Lt Thurmann-Nielsen – had been detailed for an A/S patrol in 'Area no. 5A' and at 2310 hrs when flying at 1600 ft altitude, a radar contact was obtained. This was at 18 miles range north-west of the Sunderland and Thurmann-Nielsen lost height as he flew to investigate. Ten minutes later, when in position 6833N 0720E, a fully-surfaced U-boat was sighted from 800 ft and 3½ miles away. Nielsen made for cloud cover and when ¾ mile from the vessel, broke cloud cover at 600 ft and dived to attack on the U-boat's port beam. Six DCs were released and were thought to have straddled just aft of the conning tower with two having caused damage.

Nielsen circled at half-a-mile range and was subjected to AA fire forcing him to take evasive action. The U-boat remained on an even keel but its decks became awash. Some minutes later it disappeared in position 6829N 0719E. Low cloud and heavy rain prevented the Norwegian crew of the Sunderland sighting any possible wreckage or oil patch. Thurmann-Nielsen

returned to base the following morning at 0700 hrs after a sortie of 13½ hrs. This, the second anti-U-boat success credited to a 330 Sqdn Sunderland, was against U-387 commanded by KL Buchler which was damaged by the aircraft. The submarine was sunk by the frigate HMS *Bamborough Castle* on 9 December.[9]

In November 1944, Allied forces claimed only four U-boats and of those, just one was shared by an aircraft – a Sunderland of 330 Sqdn. By then, Norway had been reached by the U-boats from the French ports in the Bay of Biscay.[10] On the 24th S/Lt Buer captained NJ188 G/330 airborne from Sullom Voe on an A/S patrol. At 2157 hrs while flying at 1500 ft a radar contact was obtained at six miles in position 6026N 0455W west of the Shetlands. Buer lost height to attack but could see nothing due to low visibility.

Col. Alf Steffen-Olsen writing to the author about this incident says:

'S/Lt Buer got radar contact of a submarine, but in spite of his aircraft flying several times over the submarine, it could not be seen on account of heavy fog. British Naval ships, which the aircraft co-operated with were contacted on VHF and the Sunderland aircraft led one of the ships to the scene where it attacked the U-boat which was sunk.'

The U-boat was U-322 apparently making its way southwards and was one of those directed to the English Channel.[11] It was lost with all hands in position 6018N 0452W after an attack by the frigate HMS Ascension. S/Lt Buer had covered his patrol area nine times and one of his crew, now Col. E. Kruse, recalls it being a trip of 12 hrs 10 mins and mostly at night. This was 330's last A/S success recorded by Coastal Command but the squadron continued to operate from Sullom Voe until the end of the war in Europe.

On 7 May 1945 Sunderland ML827 G/330 with Cmdr Bjornbye as captain was flown from Sullom Voe to Woodhaven on the River Tay. This was to take a Military Mission to Oslo. The other Norwegian squadron, No. 333, was represented by Catalina A/333 with Cmdr Jørgensen. The three services, Army, Navy and Air Force, were represented by the passengers in the Sunderland. Both aircraft touched down at Oslo, Fornebu at 1720 hrs on 8 May. The Military Mission headed by Brigadier R. Hilton later delivered instructions to the German commander – General Bøhme.

King Haakon of Norway had left Trømso on 7 June 1940 with other members of the Norwegian Royal Family on the cruiser HMS *Devonshire*. On 10 May 1945, HMS *Devonshire* sailed from Rosyth escorted by destroyers including *Arendal* and *Stord* en route to Oslo. On board *Devonshire* was Crown Prince Olav of Norway.

References
1. CCWR p. 16
2. JR p. 301
3. TA p. 73
4. SWR III pt 1 p. 267
5. SWR III pt 1 pp. 260,1
6. AH 'FC' pp. 50–2, 103,4
7. WSC VI pp. 18,19
8. SWR III pt 2 pp. 128,9
9. SWR III pt 2 p. 172
10. SWR III pt 2 p. 178
11. SWR III pt 2 p. 183

ML824 coded WH-T for 330 Sqdn in 1945. It is now in Hendon Museum coded NS-Z for 201 Sqdn.

Chapter 12
The Battle of the Atlantic 1944–1945

AT THE beginning of 1944 of squadrons operating Sunderlands, the Norwegian unit – No. 330 – was based at Sullom Voe in the Shetlands, 201 with the two Canadian units were operating from Lough Erne; 228 was at Pembroke Dock with the Australians of 461, and No. 10 RAAF was at Mount Batten.

Overseas, flying from West African bases were 95, 204, 490 and the Free French squadron No. 343; in East Africa, based at Dar-es-Salaam was 230.

Despite the Mediterranean being 'open' and with the Italians having joined the Allies, U-boats were still successfully crossing the Bay of Biscay from French ports; running the gauntlet of the Straits of Gibraltar to enter the Mediterranean, and some were making the long trip to the Indian Ocean.

In 1944, the Battle of Britain of a few months, might have been forgotten, but not the Battle of the Atlantic which was to prevail throughout the war in Europe. Vital convoys needed constant protection which by now, following the Casablanca

Castle Archdale on Lough Erne with Sunderlands of 423 (RCAF) Sqdn coded Y1-D and of 201 Sqdn coded NS-W visible.

Conference, were at last given the priorities they deserved.[1]

The Germans had available 446 U-boats at the outset of 1944, with 168 of those on operations.[2] The first Sunderland success against these was achieved by the Australian squadron No. 10.

Sunderland EK586 U/10 captained by F/O J.P. Roberts was airborne from Mount Batten on 8 January for a 'Percussion' A/S patrol. When in position 4935N 0941W an oil slick was sighted. After investigating the area for twenty minutes, Roberts continued on course. At 1154 hrs a U-boat was sighted with its conning tower awash heading due west at twelve knots. It was then twelve miles away and Roberts radioed the position to base of 4647N 1042W and altered course preparing to attack. The U-boat, instead of submerging, surfaced fully and opened fire at two miles range with four 20 mm quadruples and 30 mm cannon. Roberts took evasive action and responded with four fixed forward guns at 1200 yards; the U-boat's AA fire ceased when the range closed to 600 yards.

The first intended depth-charge attack was abortive due to troubles with the distributor and deploying the bomb trolleys. A second run was made at 50 ft with six DCs spaced at 60 ft and set for 25 ft depth. The stern of the U-boat was straddled and it immediately slowed down, listed and began sinking at the stern. The crew of the vessel were seen leaving via the conning tower and there were dinghies and debris. At 1200 hrs the U-boat rose at the bows, there was a large explosion and it sank leaving about forty survivors. They were from U-426.

Sunderland EK577 D/461 versus U-571
At the end of January 1944, operations flown by No. 461 Sqdn were switched from

'The Bay' to west of Ireland and on the 28th three of 461's Sunderlands were so deployed. One of the three captains was F/Lt R.D. 'Dick' Lucas who was airborne from Pembroke Dock at 0836 hrs to cover convoys SC151 and ON221. Shortly before reaching his patrol area he ran out the bomb racks to check the system and found his bomb release button was u/s. F/Sgt Simmonds in the nose gun position then reported a U-boat at three miles on the starboard bow. This was confirmed by F/O Prentice in the 2nd pilot's seat. Lucas closed the range to two miles losing height at 160 knots. The navigator – Colin Bremner – took a camera to the port galley hatch and at 3000 yards range the U-boat opened fire with cannon and machine-guns. During violent evasive action Bremner fell over and was knocked out. At 1000 yards Simmonds opened fire with his two ·303 Brownings effectively knocking out the U-boat's gunners.

Lucas now attacked releasing four DCs with both pilots pressing their respective buttons. The U-boat turned sharply to port and the nearest DC fell 30 yards abeam. In a second attack two DCs released straddled the U-boat and while the Sunderland circled, Bremner recovered enough to use his camera. At the instant he released the shutter, the U-boat blew up.

A signal to base reported sinking a U-boat with 37 survivors. The Sunderland crew surveyed the scene and realising the enemy was without dinghies, released one of their own.

Another Sunderland from 461 Sqdn reached the area and also dropped a dinghy but it became for that vessel – U-571 *'Untergegangen ohne Überlebende – Total verlust'*.[3]

U-571 went down in position 5241N 1427W about 300 miles south-west of Fastnet. It had sunk (with KL H. Möhlmann as captain), nine ships, damaged four more, one of the latter by its last captain – OL Gustav Lüssow.[4]

F/Lt Lucas was awarded the DFC and later served with Qantas Airways. The RAF front gunner – F/Sgt Simmonds – was awarded the DFM.

Number 10 Squadron RAAF at Mount Batten

On 27 January the first two of six Sunderlands purchased by the Australian Government were airborne from Mount Batten for the first leg of their flight to Australia. They were ML730 (A26-1) captained by S/Ldr Egerton and ML732 (A26-3) with F/Lt Rossiter. They were crewed by those who had completed a tour of operations and represented both Nos 10 and 461 Squadrons. A message from Air Chief Marshal Sir Sholto Douglas, AOC-in-C Coastal Command, was read to mark the occasion. Two others were to be flown out the following month by F/Lt Hugall and S/Ldr Smith, ML731 (A26-2) and DP192 (A26-6). The final two, ML733 (A26-4), and ML734 (A26-5), followed in March with F/Lt Marrows and F/Lt Mainprize.

In January, No. 10's own maintenance personnel undertook a modification to defensive armament on DD865 'L'. Single, free-standing ·5 Brownings to port and starboard just to the rear of the mid-upper turret with a stand for each gunner were built into the aircraft. They were waist guns and belt fed. A further modification was to be replacing the turret in the nose with a Frazer-Nash taking two ·303 Brownings. By the end of February two extra ·5 Brownings had been installed in Sunderlands DD865 'L', JM731 'W' and JM684 'K'. They were tested to follow combat conditions and it was found that an arc from the inner engines to the tail plane could be covered, had a very small effect on flying trim and that the gunners were not thrown about in evasive action. Three-hundred rounds were carried for each gun and the total extra weight for the whole installation was 300 lb.

On 15 February however, such additions had not been applied to EK574 'Q'.

Sixteen Junkers 88s versus Sunderland Q/10

The armament on this aircraft was one ·303 VGO in the front turret, two ·303 Brownings in the mid-upper, one ·303 VGO to port and starboard of the galley, four ·303 Brownings in the rear turret, and four fixed Brownings in the nose.

EK574 captained by F/Lt J. McCulloch was airborne on an A/S patrol but diverted to an Air-Sea-Rescue operation. While flying westwards at 110 knots and 1,500 ft altitude, twelve Ju88s were sighted five miles away and then at 300 ft altitude. McCulloch turned for cloud cover seven miles distant only to sight four more Ju88s. Altogether there were twenty Ju88s in the area but only sixteen elected to attack the Sunderland.

Twelve Ju88s formed up into three formations of four aircraft each flying line abreast, each formation stepped down 100 ft and spaced 100 yds apart and on the port bow while another four Ju88s formed up line astern. McCulloch held his course and increased speed to 150 knots. There was a simultaneous attack from both formations with up to twelve of the enemy firing cannon and machine-guns. Instead of diving as the enemy probably expected, McCulloch climbed. The four on the port quarter were perhaps thwarted to some extent by the formations ahead, but in that first attack, the Sunderland's rear gunner was killed. The front gunner with his one ·303-inch VGO selected one he thought to be a leader and scored hits in the Ju88's cockpit before directing his fire to another and which was believed also to have been hit, this at a range of 400 yds. The formation of twelve passed below the Sunderland, while the other formation of four Ju88s appeared to be preparing to attack again from the starboard bow and port quarter respectively, but the Sunderland reached cloud. The action had been at 1,500 ft altitude, the front gunner had fired 100 rounds, the midships gunner 200 rounds, and two Ju88s were believed to have been damaged. There was some damage to aft of the Sunderland's hull. The action had started at 0916 hrs while McCulloch was directing vessels to a dinghy from an American aircraft C/103 of Fleet Air Wing No. 7. The crew of eight was rescued. McCulloch later went to London with his navigator to record a broadcast for Australia. The tail gunner – F/Sgt G.S. Mills – was buried in Haycombe cemetery, Bath.

Attack on a U-boat by No. 201 Squadron

A 201 Sqdn Sunderland from Castle Archdale captained by F/O D.H. Longland had been on an A/S patrol for almost nine hours on 16 February when course was set at position 54N 25W for the return trip to base.

At 1220 hrs the second pilot sighted a wake four miles away when they were above 2/10ths cloud with base 1000 ft. Height was lost from 2,300 ft and after emerging from shower cloud, a U-boat was sighted at two miles. During an attack, six DCs were released from 50 ft which straddled the vessel, four to port quarter and two to starboard beam.

For the navigator – Ray Lassiter – it was his second trip, and after hearing the warning klaxon and returning to the bridge, he saw the U-boat a mile away; as he recalls:

'The flak greeted us. Our aircraft had recently been equipped with a ·5-inch gun in the front turret replacing the ·303s and our gunner opened up at maximum range. I saw the tracer hit the target, and a short time later the U-boat's guns were silenced. As the DCs exploded I saw an enormous column of water appear close to the U-boat, and the vessel rose out of the water at an angle of about 60° pointing skywards.

'Then to our utter surprise, the U-boat reappeared, rather lower in the water, but defiantly firing Oerlikens once more. We had two DCs left but the pilot decided not to make another attack but to continue circling the slowly moving boat which we felt sure must have sustained damage due to the close proximity of the DC explosions. We thought it unable to submerge.

'Having sent an attack signal, we were instructed by base to remain to the limit of our endurance, another Sunderland was on the way.'

Longland, in W/201 EK594, passed the relief Sunderland en route to base in a sortie of 15 hrs 40 mins duration, with just 60 gallons of fuel remaining. The squadron record states that the U-boat was reported sending an SOS being unable to repair the damage, but this attack does not appear in published lists. The Sunderland's front gunner was awarded the DFM.

Air Combat and Rescue

F/O Bunce as captain of ML740 was one of three detailed by 461 Sqdn to patrol over the Bay of Biscay. There was a 35 knot wind, a 20 ft swell but the sky was clear. At 2345 hrs when flying at low altitude, the rear gunner reported two Ju88s on the port beam at two miles. Bunce gained height and the front gunner then sighted four Ju88s to starboard, which were followed then from amidships of three more Ju88s closing on the port quarter. Thus a total of nine enemy fighters.

A signal was transmitted and DCs jettisoned. The enemy made a port bow attack from 1400 yards followed by one on the port quarter; these were countered by violent evasive action. Six Junkers then formed to starboard while the other three made a feint attack to port. These were immediately followed by attacks from starboard in which shells struck both mainplane and hull with guns in the dorsal turret put out of action. The dorsal gunner managed to regain the use of one gun and scored hits on the belly of a Junkers setting it on fire as it broke away.

The Sunderland, now twenty minutes after the action had begun, was also on fire following a shell exploding in the centre port fuel tank. The flames spread over the wing; this could well have meant it breaking off in 17 seconds.

Bunce ordered ditching stations. There were eight Ju88s on his tail still firing but the Sunderland was ditched parallel to wave crests finishing up in a trough of the 20 ft swell. Bunce and the 2nd pilot – F/O Howard – were flung 20 yds through a shattered windscreen. The bows, lower deck and tail were broken up. Some of the crew were washed out of the aircraft, while others had to battle against water pressure. A dinghy broke away from three of the crew on the starboard wing but it was retrieved for all three to enter. Two more of the crew on the wing were swept away by a wave and lost. A third pilot went down with the aircraft while clinging to a propeller. Four were now in the sea trying to reach a dinghy 150 yards away. After 15 minutes, one of the four received a blow from a dinghy pack which had surfaced from the sunken aircraft. There were now seven survivors from Sunderland ML740.

Meanwhile, one of the other 461 Sqdn aircraft had picked up Bunce's radio signal but confused it with a U-boat sighting report. This second Sunderland captained by F/O H.M. Godsall then flew to the area only to be attacked by four Ju88s. The fuel line to his starboard outer engine was cut as was the hydraulic lead to the dorsal turret. There were further hits to hull and mainplane and an incendiary entered the flight deck. Despite these hits to hull and mainplane in five attacks during a fifteen minute combat, Godsall fought them off and returned to Pembroke Dock without casualties.

Bunce, meanwhile, with six survivors of his crew, was adrift for just over two days. These seven were first sighted by a Catalina and later, another Sunderland from 461 Sqdn dropped some food. Two destroyers sailed from Plymouth and one of these, HMS *Saladin*, picked them up. During the period of search for the survivors, over fifty aircraft had been routed through the area.

Operation 'Overlord'

It was realised early in World War II that Germany could not be defeated by air and sea power alone. Following the Casablanca conference, staff headed by Lt-General Sir Frederick Morgan,[6] prepared plans later submitted at the Quebec conference in 1943, for the invasion of France between Cherbourg and Le Havre.

A limiting factor was the number of landing craft which could be available; the enemy opposition comprised mines at sea and on beaches, coastal batteries in addition to air, land and sea forces to be countered.[7]

Mastery of the air was achieved by bombing of aircraft factories and bases, and at the time of the invasion, 11,000[8] first line

A U-boat with the flag of surrender to a 228 Sqdn Sunderland.

aircraft were available including almost 2,000 fighters from 171 squadrons.

To limit land opposition, a bombing campaign was directed against all enemy communications, railways, bridges and radar in advance of the landings.

The Royal Navy deployed major fleet units to counter possible intervention by surface vessels, but for the armada to be assembled, the Allies had 1,213 vessels from battleships to midget submarines including 286 escort vessels, these to cover 4,126 landing craft.[9]

The maritime aspects of 'Overlord' were coded operation 'Neptune'. The limitation imposed by landing craft decided three Army divisions on beach-heads of 30 miles; the lack of port facilities between the rivers Vire and Orne required the production and deployment of the artificial harbours 'Mulberry' proposed by Earl Mountbatten's staff. To provide fuel for up to 200,000 vehicles, the pipeline from the Isle of Wight to Normandy, 'Pluto' was devised, followed by a second from Dungeness to Calais later.

The obvious route for the armada, Dover to Calais was discounted as it was expected by the enemy, but diversions to promote that belief were maintained and a tactical surprise was achieved.

South coast ports from Milford Haven to Felixstowe were used but with a mineswept channel from the Isle of Wight to Normandy for the invading armada.

At 0130 hrs on 6 June airborne troops were descending inland of the beaches; 5,200 tons of bombs were released by heavy bombers on the enemies' gun emplacements, which were further countered by shell fire from battleships and cruisers.

Initial casualties of 10,000 were forecast and such was the case, but those clearing

U-1105 surrenders to F/O Arrighi of 201 Sqdn in NS-V ML764 on 9.5.45 in position 5655 1105W.

mines on the beaches suffered a rate of 52% losses.[10]

The task for Sunderlands and shared with other aircraft, was for their A/S patrols to cover every part of an area at least once in every half hour, both day and night. These areas were in six zones between southern Ireland and Land's End to the Brest peninsula. For this No. 19 Group deployed twenty-one squadrons in addition to those required for convoy escort and anti-shipping sorties. There were still aircraft available for Nos 15 and 18 Groups to cover the north-west transit routes from Norway. Dönitz had anticipated the invasion and ordered U-boats from Norway to Biscay ports beginning 16 May and of the seven sunk following twenty-two sightings quoted by Capt. Roskill up to 3 June, five were by 18 Group and two were sunk by 15 Group aircraft. Two of the 18 Group's five were claimed by Sunderlands.[11]

Capt Roskill gives the deployment of U-boats against the invasion forces on 6 June as being in two groups: 621, 764, 953, 275, 269 and 441 heading from Brest towards the Isle of Wight. A second group shown as eighteen in number, 993, 981, 608, 333, 270, 281, 228, 985, 260, 255, 262, 759, 437, 445, 766, 714 and 382 covering the French Biscay ports from Brest southwards, but not so positioned until the 10th.[12]

F/Lt Les Baveystock of Number 201 Squadron

The first Allied U-boat kill following the invasion was from none of those listed above; it was U-955 sunk by Sunderland ML760 captained by F/Lt Les Baveystock, DFC, DFM, of 201 Sqdn.

In May he had been asked to leave his own crew to be captained by his second pilot and to himself captain the crew of an injured pilot. Up to the 6 June he had made eleven trips with them but on 5 June he recalls:

'. . . we knew that the invasion was about to begin for while flying over the Irish sea we saw the huge armada of battle-wagons on its way south to soften up the German defences. I awoke on 6th to find the whole station alive with the news that the invasion had commenced. At the flight office I found I was scheduled to fly that night on a special trip down off Gijon in Spain, to find and attack a known U-boat which had been harried for two days without success. It had been attacked on the night of the 5th and remained submerged throughout the daylight hours.'

Baveystock's father had just died but leave was delayed as he was one of the few captains with night attack experience. Accordingly he was airborne from Pembroke Dock at 1942 hrs on 6th for a CLA patrol off the Spanish coast; his crew were those who had been with F/O Longland. Another Sunderland, but from 461 Sqdn, arrived a half hour before them.

Baveystock continues:

'Shortly before midnight we picked up a blip on our radar at nine miles range. We felt sure it was our quarry as the size of the blip was the same as we normally got from our tame sub we practised with.'

Height was reduced from 450 ft to 250 ft as the Sunderland homed but the blip disappeared at half-mile and the crew commenced dropping low level flares which revealed only a long white wake. Baveystock sent a sighting report and was ordered by Group to adopt homing procedure and as he recalls:

'Unknown to us the other Sunderland picked up our signal and turned round to join us. We were now climbing to a safe height when suddenly the whole area lit up and the 461 Sqdn Sunderland dived in to make an attack on *us*. He had picked up our blip on his radar and mistaken it for the U-boat, we were approaching it about 300 mph but they passed directly beneath us neither pilot having time to take avoiding action.'

The other Sunderland, N/461 left at its PLE – 0240 hrs. Baveystock's crew had dropped a flame float over the U-boat's crash-dive position and he continues:

'We now started baiting tactics flying for two minutes, about four miles north of the flame-float then turning south, crossing the float again, and going four miles south, back again, four miles to east, then four miles to west. Knowing his batteries would be very low, after being kept under all day, we reckoned he would only be doing a few knots. Also as it would be dawn at about 0500 hrs, we estimated he would need to resurface at the latest by 0300 hrs to get two hours necessary for a recharge.'

At 16 minutes before that hour, flying at 400 ft, the Sunderland crew obtained a radar contact at eleven miles; they homed descending to 250 ft. Five minutes later they were in position 4513N 0830W and there was AA fire from the U-boat at half mile range. As Baveystock says:

'We must have been silhouetted against the faint light of the clouds . . . we immediately started dropping flares and our U-boat was fully lit up a little to

The operations room board at Castle Archdale listing aircraft of 201, 202 and 423 Sqdns on 14.3.45.

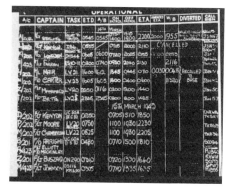

port and turning sharply to his starboard. As he came broadside on, his four 20 mm cannon opened up with tracer streams all around us. I turned the aircraft into attack and opened up with my four fixed guns as the front gunner fired with his twin Brownings; the whole area was a criss-cross of tracer bullets and shells but when 200 yards away, all return fire stopped for we had smothered the guns with continuous fire from our six Brownings.'

Six DCs and a marker were released from 75 ft straddling the U-boat at an angle of 15° abaft the vessel's port beam. Three to four seconds later a heavy thud was experienced by the Sunderland crew as though the aircraft had been hit. Of this Baveystock remarks:

'Our DCs had an underwater travel of 36 ft forward and 20 ft down so it appeared as if No. 4 DC had gone off directly under the centre of the hull but with No. 5 making a direct hit on the superstructure and exploding prematurely alongside.'

This same crew but without Baveystock, was later shot down while on another U-boat sortie; two of the crew had been awarded the DFM but were unable to receive the decoration; Les Baveystock gained a bar to his DFC.

U-955 sunk by the Sunderland crew in position 4513N 0830W was the only kill on the night of the 6/7th but there were five other U-boats, (U-415, U-963, U-256, U-989 and U-212) so damaged by Coastal Command aircraft that they returned to port.

Sunderlands of Number 228 Squadron and U-970

The next U-boat lost was again claimed by a Sunderland from Pembroke Dock but deployed No. 228 Sqdn. F/Lt C. Gordon Lancaster was airborne in ML877 on the 7th June detailed for an A/S patrol. He reached position 4550N 0413W in seven hours and as one of his crew – Tim Brown recalls:

'A radar contact was picked up at about fifteen miles crossing our path from starboard to port. In a rapid exchange of fire the Sunderland was later discovered to have been hit in fifteen places but without serious damage.'

At 2333 hrs in position 4543N 0415W after dropping flares, a fully-surfaced U-boat was sighted. An attack was made from 100 ft releasing six depth charges, although one failed to fuse, as Brown continues:

'. . . they had straddled the U-boat just aft of the conning tower, and the stern was seen to lift out of the water. A large oil slick was seen later, but there was no further contact. At the time the attack was assessed as a 'probable' kill . . . this was quite distinct from Jimmy Quinn's attack the same night.'

F/Lt J. Quinn had taken off eleven minutes before Lancaster and at 2341 hrs gained a radar contact seven miles to port. Four minutes later a fully-surfaced U-boat was sighted in position 4510N 0409W but the vessel submerged before an attack could be made. At 2349 hrs a further radar contact eight miles to port was received. Quinn circled for a down-moon position and six minutes later sighted a fully-surfaced U-boat up-moon and to starboard at five miles. An air gunner in the crew – Jim Gilchrist – remembers:

'At the moment the alarm sounded Rossiter and I opened the galley hatches and fixed up the VGOs. As we did so, heavy flak came up, we both ducked . . . I then went to the rear turret . . . Bill, (the gunner in the nose), began firing long concentrated bursts and Quinn shouted to Bill to cease firing – the tracers were dazzling his vision, then the dive to attack.'

This was from 70 ft and a straddle of the U-boat was estimated. The vessel circled gradually losing way and with the forecasing under water for 1 hr 50 mins before it disappeared leaving an oil patch.

T.E. 'Ross' Rossiter recalls this being the maiden flight of 'R' ML766; F/Lt Quinn was awarded a bar to his DFC, his front gunner – Bill Williams the DFM. Coastal Command credits R/228 with sinking U-970,[13] an American list gives 228 Sqdn sinking U-970 in position 4515N 0410W.[14] 228's operational record gives serial numbers only not aircraft letters.

U-333 and Sunderlands ML856 and ML880

At the time of the Normandy invasion there were twenty-one U-boats in south-west Norway and thirty-six in French ports.[15] At 0535 hrs on 6 June, (D-Day), the thirty-six were ordered to sail, but only nine of these were fitted with schnorkels, and one of the other twenty-seven – U-333 – was delayed in sailing.

The A/S patrols laid on by No. 19 Group, Coastal Command[16] proved so effective that according to U-333's commander Peter Cremer, a non-schnorkel U-boat could remain on the surface only thirteen minutes on average,[17] not enough to charge batteries and compressed-air bottles.

At 0639 hrs on the 10th F/Lt H.A.L. McGregor of No. 10 Sqdn RAAF was airborne in ML856. Two and a half hours later the Sunderland was west of Ile de Yeu where U-333 was just surfacing. The U-boat was unable to submerge as both air bottles and batteries needed charging. In the Sunderland, the violent manoeuvre made in positioning for an attack resulted in bomb trolleys not being run out to starboard, and the front turret not being manned as customary crew changes were then being made.

McGregor, in making his run using his four fixed forward guns, overshot when releasing his port depth charges, the nearest exploding 30 yards from the U-boat. It was to be very different the following night.

On the 11th F/Lt M.E. Slaughter of 228 Sqdn captained ML880 on an A/S patrol from Pembroke Dock and was airborne at 1810 hrs. The aircraft with eleven aircrew failed to return. In a letter, Peter Cremer U-333's commander explains what happened.

'The night 11/12 I was obliged to come to the surface because my batteries were empty. Two aircraft were in the air, but I could not identify the type . . . the height could have been 1000 ft. I had to stay on the surface and wait for the attacks. My 3·7 cm gun was damaged during the preceding fights as well as my 2 cm AA gun. I had only one twin 2 cm gun operational.'

'Suddenly one of the aircraft attacked at very low altitude, I guess it was 150 ft. The Sunderland started to shoot at a distance of roughly 500 yds with all his weapons and the situation was really disastrous and nearly hopeless for me. Having only one gun I started to shoot at 50 yds and it was impossible not to miss him. I hit the starboard engine which was immediately burning. The bullets from the aircraft were piercing the conning tower and the tanks and I was constantly losing oil. It was a real miracle that nobody was wounded. Meanwhile the Sunderland lost height and nearly hit the conning tower, it was not more than three feet . . . the aircraft crashed into the sea midst exploding depth charges. The sea was burning around.

'It was an incredibly brave and death defying attack. The second aircraft was approaching at a much greater height. Zig-zagging I tried with full speed to escape his attack. After overflying he circled round the wreck. During the rescue of the aircraft we heard low radio signals. I was seriously damaged and dived. I was anxious about the new

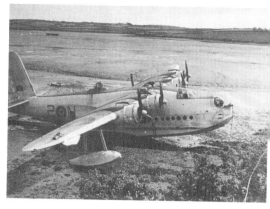

ML747 2-N of No. 461 (RAAF) Sqdn aground at Angle Bay, Pembroke Dock.

The crew of D/461 EK577 after sinking U-571; included are the captain – F/Lt Lucas and the navigator Colin Bremner.

No. 228 Sqdn aircrew c. 1945 with W/Cmdr A. Lywood, DFC as CO.

attacks. My position was south of Brest with course north to the invasion front ...'

In a 'phone call to the author, Peter Cremer stated that one of his crew thought he saw two of the Sunderland crew escape from the aircraft into a dinghy; the squadron record however, mentions no survivors. Just a few weeks earlier, the author had been on an air-test of that ill-fated aircraft.

Attacks on U-971

Although F/Lt Slaughter's attack on U-333 was the last to be officially credited to No. 228 Sqdn, there were further attacks by the squadron which some of their aircrew considered had caused probable damage. These attacks have however, been masked by those of aircraft from other squadrons and by surface vessels.

On 21 June P/O Hart captained Sunderland 'L' ML789 on an A/S patrol from Pembroke Dock. At about 1450 hrs while in position 4936N 0828W and flying at 1,350 ft altitude, a fully-surfaced U-boat was sighted. The submarine commenced

violent evasive action and opened fire. Height was lost as Hart ran in for an attack with machine-gun fire from the four fixed forward guns and the nose turret.

Depth charges were released from 50–75 ft but they overshot. A Halifax from 502 Sqdn now attacked with A/S bombs that appeared to miss. The Sunderland made a second attack with two DCs just as the U-boat submerged and they exploded slightly ahead and to port of the swirl. This U-boat may possibly have been U-971 whose sinking was credited to No. 311 Sqdn and surface vessels.

A Canadian account[18] gives a Liberator of the Czech squadron being seen by the destroyers HMCS *Haida* and *Eskimo* dropping depth charges on the night of the 23rd. HMCS *Haida* and *Eskimo* reached the marker released by the Liberator and for over two hours dropped DCs before searching with Asdic and detecting a submarine outline. With further attacks, U-971 surfaced, the destroyers opened fire and the U-boat sank but fifty-two survivors were picked up by the destroyers. U-971 is recorded as having sunk in position 4901N 0535W thus three degrees east of the Sunderland's attack and on approximately the same latitude.

A further attack by 228 Sqdn was to occur the following August but for which no credit for success was given.

Armament on the Australian Sunderlands

Number 10 Sqdn RAAF's record for June 1944 gives their Sunderlands being armed with four fixed ·303 Brownings in the nose, two ·303 Brownings in the front turret, one ·303 on each side of the galley, a mid-upper twin ·303 Browning machine-gun turret; twin ·5 belt-fed Browning guns (beam installation) on each side, and four ·303 Brownings in the tail turret. These give a total of eighteen. The forward-firing power often proved crucial during attacks on U-boats particularly when the submarines elected to remain on the surface to 'fight it out'.

Thus: F/O W.B. Tilley captained W4030 H/10 on 8 July from Mount Batten. While

U-571 photographed by navigator C. Bremner at the instant she blew up after the attack by F/Lt Lucas of 461 Sqdn on 28.1.44.

on the fifth circuit of his A/S patrol at 1435 hrs, a fully-surfaced U-boat was sighted six miles away heading northwards at 8 knots. Tilley immediately dived to attack from about 2000 ft altitude. The vessel took evasive action but opened fire at two miles range. At 2,000 yards range the Sunderland responded with the four fixed guns and at 1,250 yards with the front turret guns sweeping the U-boat's decks such that all AA fire ceased by the time the aircraft passed over the vessel.

Six 270 lb Torpex DCs were released from 75 ft altitude set for 25 ft depth and spaced at 60 ft. A straddle was achieved between stern and conning tower. While the Sunderland circled at one mile range, the U-boat was seen settling at the stern with a list to port and making no headway.

The vessel opened fire again for a few minutes but by 1500 hrs its crew had launched two large dinghies and there were many smaller ones on the forward deck.

Five minutes later, F/Lt R.E. Cargeeg also from No. 10 Sqdn attacked from Sunderland 'K' JM684 but his DCs fell short. A Liberator T/105 now attacked with eight DCs. By now however, Tilley's crew saw the U-boat sinking stern first with the bow disappearing vertically. Survivors were in dinghies, others in the water. Tilley made a further run releasing a dinghy and a food pack. The squadron record gives the radio in Tilley's Sunderland as going u/s but the squadron history[19] states him assisting in homing HMCS *Restigouche* to the area and picking up thirty-seven survivors. It gives also, the U-boat's commander – KL Hans Märtens – being killed during the attack plus another in the crew. Tilley's aircraft suffered no damage and had fired 4,300 rounds of ·303 and 175 rounds of ·5 calibre. The U-boat's armament had been estimated as two twin 20 mm and one 37 mm cannon. The squadron history gives the two 20 mm cannon being used but with a 30 mm cannon put out of action in the first attack.

Although three aircraft had released a total of twenty DCs, it appears that two from the six released by Tilley had proved

lethal – this may be contrasted with another U-boat counting 550 DCs from surface vessels and escaping after being in Spithead![20]

From photographs taken of the attacks by H/10 and K/10, the squadron was satisfied that F/O Tilley's attack had been decisive in sinking the U-boat in position 4655N 0635W. It was U-243 which had been deployed off Norway on 10 June but later sailed round Scotland and was heading for Brest when attacked.[21]

Number 201 Squadron Sunderlands and Equipment

By the end of June 1944, 201 Sqdn was equipped with fourteen Sunderlands all in the 'ML' series apart from 'W' (EJ150). Two of the fourteen were in reserve, 'S' ML772 and 'C' ML769. The forward armament alone was better than the early Sunderlands with four fixed ·303s, two ·303s in the front turret plus one ·5 Browning. These were in addition to the usual four-gun tail turret, the twin dorsal turret, and the two VGOs in the galley. Equipment included Mark III radar, GEE Mark II, a radio altimeter and a low-level bomb-sight.

One of these Sunderlands was ML881 NS-P which flew from Pembroke Dock on 11 July with an experienced captain – F/Lt 'Wally' Walters – screening F/Lt Buszard with an inexperienced crew. They were on patrol at 0700 hrs and almost four hours later the port inner engine gave trouble and they headed for base. When the engine cleared, the Sunderland returned on patrol and at 1345 hrs while flying at 2,700 ft, the second pilot sighted a wake 8½ miles on the starboard bow. Using binoculars a schnorkel and periscope were seen heading east at 3–4 knots.

As Wally Walters recalls:

'By the time we lost height to attack from 50 ft the U-boat had commenced a steep emergency dive in which the rusty stern was clearly seen above the surface.

'The aircraft was armed with Torpex 250 lb DCs which at the attack speed of 120 knots were so spaced that a U-boat caught in the straddle would be destroyed. I straddled it with the six spaced DCs . . . I think No. 3 did the damage by detonating under the U-boat a little aft of amidships. There were no survivors. I doubt it came out of the dive.'

Number 201 Squadron's line book adds that ML881 returned to the area but nothing was seen except pieces of wood and white froth. G/461 saw a freshly arisen bright red patch on the sea about 50 yards in diameter. The line book concludes: 'A classic attack in the old pre-radar style.'

The Naval historian, Capt Roskill acknowledged this as a 'rare success for an air patrol'.[22] The U-boat, U-1222 sunk in position 4631N 0529W, ie west of La Rochelle, was credited with sinking no ships, but its commander at that time, KL Heinz Biefeld claimed successes against three Allied ships including one from the ill-fated convoy PQ17 when captain of U-703.[23]

Operations Over the Bay of Biscay
In the first week of August there was a combined offensive with surface vessels and aircraft from both Coastal and Bomber Commands.[24] Number 228 Squadron's records at that time refer to their patrols being at the western end of the English Channel to prevent U-boats reaching Allied convoys supplying the Cherbourg area. The Squadron's patrols were moved to west of the Brest peninsula when that area was occupied by land forces.

When the enemy's bases at Brest, Lorient and St Nazaire were cut off, the U-boats moved down to Bordeaux. The Squadron's Sunderlands then patrolled off Lorient and in the second half of August, largely off the Gironde.

With little sign of Luftwaffe aircraft and much of the French coast controlled by the Allies, Sunderlands were able to operate closer inshore and this is confirmed by the positions given for acknowledged successes by Coastal Command's Sunderlands in that month.

On 9 August F/O George Bunting captained ML879 from Pembroke Dock at 0536 hrs. While flying at 1000 ft three hours later and in position 4757N 0527W, a U-boat was sighted 2½ miles away. It submerged almost immediately and, as Bunting now writes: 'The first two DCs were dropped ahead of the crash dive swirl.' Minutes later while circling, a periscope was sighted and a second attack was made. 'The remaining six DCs straddled just ahead of a moving periscope.'

Heavy black oil was seen to well-up forming a large patch, and at 0954 hrs there were violent air bubbles, followed by lighter oil. An escort group was homed to the area. Bunting's second pilot writes:

'I think it more than likely that Bunting's two attacks caused damage. The U-boat surfaced on the port bow just as we turned to start a new leg of our patrol. It immediately submerged again and George was able to drop two DCs just ahead of the swirl. A few minutes later he raised his periscope . . . and kept it up while we made a circuit and dropped the remaining DCs from 80 ft. A lot of oil came to the surface, and a second lot much later. We stayed on the spot for several hours of daylight until a Naval escort group arrived in response to our homing. No other aircraft was involved to the time that we set off for base.'

F/O Bunting was awarded the DFC following what was thought as a probable 'kill'.

Post-war lists do not include this attack but, for the 9 August U-608 is given as being sunk by HMS *Wren* and a Liberator of 53 Sqdn in position 4630N 0308W. The Liberator is given as having sighted a mile long oil slick from a U-boat, and Capt. Roskill gives three U-boats as having been diverted to the area, two of which were sunk, (U-608 and U-981) on the 10th and 12th respectively.[25]

A Moonlight Attack on U-385
P/O Ivan Southall, a Sunderland captain with No. 461 Sqdn had completed a sortie

on 9 August but the following night was required to fly again. This was due to land-based aircraft being grounded by fog and additional patrols were to be flown by the Pembroke Dock squadrons.[26] His aircraft had been taken by another crew and a hastily prepared ML741 'P' was made available for Southall's take-off at 2220 hrs.

Southall had climbed to 500 ft before it was realised that the radar was u/s but one of the crew, F/Sgt Stevenson managed to get it working. At about 0130 hrs the Sunderland was heading east of south and just off Brest which was clear of fog. Just under an hour later while flying at 1000 ft, a radar contact was made at 10 miles distance.

Southall had trained himself to bomb manually and had prepared his mind well in advance of this trip to use moonlight rather than flares should the occasion arise. Half-a-moon had risen and it was the second pilot – P/O Wylie – who sighted a wake; at six miles Southall saw a U-boat. It was fully surfaced and heading south at 8–9 knots.

When the Sunderland had closed to half a mile, Southall put the aircraft into a power dive, the bomb racks had already been deployed and six DCs armed. They straddled the vessel, two to port, four to starboard. An escort group was called by R/T to the area where the Sunderland crew had released a flame float to mark the position of the attack. It was learned that depth charges from the Sunderland had seriously damaged the U-boat with rudder and starboard hydroplane lost and starboard propeller damaged; a serious leak was hardly countered by the operation of pumps.

U-385 surfaced again after some hours and was attacked by HMS *Starling* which picked up many survivors from the position 4616N 0245W. U-385 was one of twelve U-boats lost in the Bay of Biscay during a three-week Allied offensive.[27] In April of that year, U-385 had attacked two ships, sinking one and damaging the other.[28]

There was a further successful night attack by another captain in 461 Sqdn. He was F/O D.A. Little who was airborne in A/461 at 2025 hrs on 12 August. Just before midnight his radar operator reported a contact at 6½ miles range. The Sunderland's crew prepared for an attack and at ¾ mile, flares were released. There was an immediate response with AA fire from a U-boat which then became visible. Fixed and turret front guns silenced the German gunners. DCs were released but with the navigator at the bomb-sight. There were six dropped and from 300 ft altitude. From Ivan Southall's account, the pressure hull of the U-boat was damaged.[29] The Sunderland crew lost sight of the vessel which was to be further harassed by a Wellington from 179 Sqdn before U-270 was abandoned by its crew. It sank on the 13th in position 4619N 0256W.

It had been carrying additional personnel and 71 out of 81 were rescued by British destroyers. On this final trip, U-270 was captained by OL Heinrich Schreiber, but during earlier voyages with KL Paul Friedrich Otto, U-270 had sunk three ships and damaged two others.[30]

Number 201 Squadron, Success and Loss

No. 201 Squadron's line book for August 1944 states that early in the month a start was made on painting squadron letters 'NS' on the aircraft. Their CO at that time (W/Cmdr K.R. Coates), is quoted as saying: 'NS means *Nulli Secundus* which being freely translated means we won't be No. 2, which we previously were, being latest arrivals at Pembroke Dock.'

On 15 August Allied landings had begun on the south of France under operation 'Anvil/Dragoon' but the area of Brest, Lorient, St Nazaire and the Gironde were still to be taken. No. 201's operational records at this time give a series of patrols by their Sunderlands south of the Brest peninsula. On the 18th the unit flew only two sorties with the weather given as 10/10ths cloud at 1000 ft with rain and visibility 1–3 miles but forecast as improving. One of the two sorties was aborted; this was in Sunderland NS-Q with Jim Wilson who returned from a patrol off

Lorient due to the rear turret becoming u/s.

The other aircraft was NS-W EJ150 captained by F/Lt Les Baveystock who reached his patrol area off St Nazaire at 1705 hrs. The weather was clear with visibility 5–10 miles and five minutes later while flying at 500 ft in position 4646N 0339W, a wake was sighted at four miles, and at three miles distance, a periscope was visible.

As Baveystock recalls:

'. . . I took over the crew of F/Lt Bent, a Canadian who had just finished his tour. My 2nd pilot was Brian Landers, my navigator F/O Ian Riddell, a New Zealander, . . . we carried a 3rd pilot – a Canadian, F/O McGregor.

'We had been briefed to look for U-boats which were being used by the Germans to ferry senior officers from the Brest peninsular which had been cut off from the main German forces by the advancing American army, and it was believed they were being taken down to Bordeaux. Our search was south-west of Belle island off the French coast.'

Baveystock was caught literally with his pants down. When the klaxon sounded he rushed to take over the controls. Landers was in the left-hand seat and Baveystock took over the second seat vacated by McGregor. Landers ran out the DCs while both he and Baveystock made the settings of the controls for an attack.

'A signal was sent by W/T and when Landers brought the aircraft round, the wake from the periscope was clearly visible. I then took over and flew the aircraft from the 2nd pilot's seat and delivered a normal attack such as we had practised many times. I had tightened the stick of six DCs before taking the 2nd pilot's seat so that the DCs would release at 50 ft intervals instead of the normal 60 ft. The stick fell with three on each side slightly ahead of the periscope which was still visible. No. 3 DC must have exploded directly alongside the hull

for the effect was devastating. A huge mass of white surging froth of air, oil and wreckage came to the surface covering an area about 100 ft in diameter. This massive eruption of air continued for about 15–20 minutes before subsiding but with bubbles coming up from two adjacent points. We believed that the U-boat had broken in half.

'We homed an escort group to the scene and they picked up a lot of charts and confirmed much Diesel oil and wreckage on the surface. In spite of its utter simplicity and lack of danger, I often wonder how many men I sent to their death, but in those days we did not think of U-boats as containing men like ourselves. We just thought of the U-boats as vicious killers of our shipping . . .'

The U-boat attacked by Baveystock, (his second kill), was U-107 captained by Lt. Karl-Heinz Fritz and sunk in position 4646N 0339W.

Flight Lieutenant D.R. Hatton of Number 201 Squadron

In November No. 201 Sqdn moved from Pembroke Dock to Castle Archdale reflecting the change in the deployment of U-boats from Norwegian rather than French ports. As the squadron's line book records: 'Back to gumboots, Nissen huts and the Larne-Stranraer crossing.'

Their first attack on the 9th is headed: 'Hatton sets the ball rolling'. F/Lt Hatton, as captain of NS-U had sighted at eight miles, smoke and a wake with a distinct bow wave. Six DCs were released but they undershot. After contacting a frigate, Hatton returned to release two more DCs on the still moving wake. No damage, was the assessment of the two attacks.

On 6 December Hatton captained Sunderland NS-Y on a CLA patrol and was airborne at 0710 hrs. Three and a half hours later he received a signal to proceed to position 5840N 0445W and co-operate with escort vessels in a U-boat search. By 1053 hrs he had reached that area to sight a sinking escort vessel which had been torpedoed. This was the frigate HMS *Bullen* claimed by U-775 in position 5842N 0412W. The Sunderland circled the liferafts on which there were survivors. For the whole of the day Hatton saw only other escort vessels throwing patterns of depth charges.

Just after sunset, in fading light, while flying at 400 ft in position 5844N 0420W, the Sunderland crew sighted white smoke at five miles distance. At one mile range a wake 1100 ft long with its source moving at 11–12 knots was observed. An attack was attempted from 50 ft but the DCs failed to release. In a second attempt with six DCs, three fell along the wake spaced at 60 ft. Both wake and smoke disappeared. Five minutes later an oil patch spread over the surface for one half mile. When PLE was reached, Hatton returned to base. The Admiralty assessment at the time was a probable kill. Post-war the credit has been given solely to HMS *Loch Insh* and HMS *Goodhall* as sinking U-297 in position 5844N 0429W.[31]

F/Lt Hatton was not to know of the assessments as on 14 March 1945 he was airborne in NS-A at 0203 hrs and 27 minutes later the Sunderland crashed in the hills northwest of Killybegs, County Donegal. The aircraft caught fire and was completely destroyed. There were no survivors.

Number 15 Group's Final Success
On 30 April an anti-submarine kill was shared with surface vessels. F/Lt K.H. Foster of 201 Sqdn captained ML783 from Pembroke Dock. At about 0800 hrs while flying at 1000 ft over the Irish Sea, the 1st pilot and front gunner sighted a cloud of white smoke issuing from the sea. It was from a grey object 1½ ft diameter and projecting about 2 ft and moving at 12–15 knots.

During an attempted attack the Sunderland's port bomb rack jammed against the bomb door and could not be freed. The aircraft's crew fired at the schnorchel which submerged. Sonobuoys were released to detect any U-boat but only water noises were heard. A nearby frigate

was informed and a square search was made. At 1133 hrs the 2nd pilot sighted spray and white smoke 2½ miles away and when the Sunderland was flying at 500 ft. The port bomb rack was wound out manually and six DCs were released from 70 ft.

Three frigates were led to the area and after obtaining a bottom contact in position 5342N 0455W, they attacked at 1900 hrs. From 201's record, 'Diesel oil, wood and German tins' surfaced. The Admiralty assessment given in 201 Sqdn's line book reads: 'U-boat known sunk. The credit for this success is awarded to Sunderland H/201 and 14th Escort Group. The U-boat was destroyed as a result of attack delivered by *Hesperus* and *Havelock*.' The post-war published record gives U-325 sunk by H/201 shared with HM ships.[32] Capt Roskill suggests U-242 being the likely victim.[33] The assessment by the Air Staff of HQ Coastal Command did not rule out the possibility of lethal damage to the U-boat by a depth charge released from the Sunderland.

The Surrender of U-boats
Admiral Dönitz on 4 May 1945 ordered U-boats to cease hostilities and return to base. There were then twelve in British waters and thirty-three in the Atlantic. The Admiralty, on the 8th, and following the signing of the German surrender on the 7th, stated that the German High Command had been directed to order all U-boats at sea to surface, report their positions and sail to directed ports.[34]

F/O E.C. Arrighi was airborne from Castle Archdale in Sunderland V/201 ML764 on an A/S patrol but at 1035 hrs on 9 May was ordered to escort a surrendered U-boat and at 1248 hrs sighted it in position 5559N 1108W when the vessel was on course 330° at 15 knots. The U-boat crew was crowded into the conning tower, waving madly and giving the thumbs-up sign. It identified itself as U-1105 and was flying a blue-and-white flag.

One of Arrighi's crew – Ron Powers – recalls: 'The skipper had ordered us to battle stations, all guns ready to fire and DCs run out ready to drop in case. We flew over her at normal attack height. I was in the galley at the time and took photographs of her.'

U-1105 was instructed to proceed to Loch Eriboll. It had been launched in 1943 but its only claim was to have damaged an escort destroyer *Redmill* in April 1945 when captained by OL Hans-Joachim Schwarz. It was later handed over to the USA as war booty.

Not all the U-boats responded to the order to surrender. On 11 May F/Lt P.E.H. Thomas captained V/201 on an A/S patrol of the entrance to the North Channel. At 1230 hrs in position 5605N 0826W white smoke was seen but with no wake. Sonobuoys were released and a U-boat detected. Four DCs were released spaced at 75 ft. Some crashes were heard followed by renewed engine noises.

Coastal Command's Final Operational Sortie

W/Cmdr J. Barrett, the CO of No. 201 Squadron was recalled from leave to take a crew selected, as the line-book states: 'More for accident of birthplace than for any degree of competence'. A second Sunderland captained by F/Lt Arrighi was flown to take photographers.

W/Cmdr Barrett was airborne at 1643 hrs in a Mark V, NS-Z ML778 on 3 June to escort convoy HX358 of fifty-one merchant and escort vessels. It was met at 2121 hrs in position 5105N 1815W and escorted until 0019 hrs on 4 June when in position 5109N 1723W. The CO's crew of thirteen included F/O J.C. Caffey, RCAF, F/O L.F. Williams, RAAF, and W/O J.K. Gunman, RNZAF.

The Battle – Data and Opinions

In his summing up of the U-boat war, Churchill states that the whole of the European campaign depended on the Atlantic convoys[35] and that 80 per cent of the 21,194,000 tons of shipping lost was in the Atlantic including British coastal waters and the North Sea. Only 5 per cent of the shipping losses were in the Pacific.[36]

Despite Allied bombing, more U-boats were built in November 1944 than in any other month of the war.[37]

John Terraine, in quoting from Richard Humble gives for the bombing of U-boat bases and yards between January and March 1943; the dropping of 7,026 tons bombs for the loss of 141 aircraft but with not one U-boat damaged.[38]

Coastal Command's last operational sortie made by ML778 NS-Z in position 5240N 1430W on 3.6.45 seen from B/201.

Of the 1,162 U-boats built and commissioned between 1939 and 1945, 632 were lost at sea.[39] Sunderlands were involved in sinking or damaging about 56 German and Italian submarines,[40] and typically releasing in their attacks four 250 lb DCs, any one of which could be lethal to a submarine. This was considered 'defensive' as opposed to bombing Germany – an 'offensive' operation. Thus were some Shorts personnel diverted from building Sunderlands to building Stirling bombers. The Sunderland over the Atlantic, whether detailed for an A/S patrol or convoy escort, served more than one purpose. It was a boost to the morale of merchant seamen crossing the Atlantic at say, seven or eleven knots; it would always serve as a reconnaissance aircraft to report shipping movements whether hostile or otherwise.

Aircraft, whether or not they sighted a U-boat, might well have been detected by such craft and serve to harass U-boat crews, and not of least importance, prevent a U-boat from reaching a convoy.

The RAF historian – Hilary St George Saunders – quotes a German analysis of U-boat losses in the decisive month of May 1943: 35 per cent occurred when the U-boats were approaching the operational area and were all due to aircraft; within the operational area, 10 per cent were claimed by aircraft with a further 13 per cent shared with surface vessels.[41] The effect on the morale of U-boat crews by aircraft is illustrated by Saunders with quotes from captured U-boat crews such as from a U-506 officer who didn't mind a cruiser or destroyer, but if an aircraft . . . 'we've had it . . .'[42]

The early Sunderlands were intended for reconnaissance and to cover the outposts of the Empire; their crews were trained accordingly. The 'built-in' disadvantages the aircraft had for A/S work, were overstretched engines, propellers which could not be fully-feathered, a lack of forward-firing power, long hydraulic leads, notably to the rear turret, and bomb gear which could not be rapidly deployed with certainty. By 1944 some of these disadvantages were overcome in the Mark Vs.

References

1. WSC IV p. 619
2. JH p. 268
3. HH pp. 289–290
4. JR pp. 87–196
5. From Air Ministry c. 1942
6. EBP p. 279
7. WSC V pp. 514–27
8. WSC VI p. 5 and SWR III pt 2 p. 24
9. SWR III pt 2 pp. 17–19
10. EBP p. 282
11. CCWR pp. 10,11 and SWR III pt 2 p. 20
12. SWR III pt 2 map 26, p. 55
13. CCWR p. 12
14. USSL p. 168
15. SWR III pt 2 p. 56
16. Ibid.
17. PC p. 181
18. JS pp. 302–3
19. KB p. 362
20. SWR III pt 2 p. 127
21. SWR III pt 2 p. 127
22. SWR III pt 2 p. 127
23. JR pp. 198–200
24. SWR III pt 2 p. 130
25. SWR III pt 2 p. 130
26. IS p. 161
27. SWR III pt 2 p. 131
28. JR p. 180
29. IS pp. 171–6
30. JR pp. 161,71,2,7
31. SWR III pt 2 p. 164
32. CCWR p. 10
33. SWR III pt 2 p. 298
34. SWR III pt 2 p. 302
35. WSC VI p. 472
36. WSC II p. 8
37. WSC VI p. 472
38. JT p. 441
39. SWR III pt 2 p. 304
40. Ibid.
41. HS RAF III p. 45
42. HS RAF III p. 57

Chapter 13
Post-War Operations

Number 230 Squadron Converts to Mark V Sunderlands

Number 230 Squadron had been operating Mark Is, IIs, and IIIs throughout World War II but in January 1945 began to receive Mark Vs, the first arriving at Koggala, the unit's base in Ceylon on the 6th. It was PP147 captained by F/Lt C. Potter and became U/230. It was fitted with P&W 1830-90B engines and was equipped with Mark III ASV. The Mark IIIs to be replaced were scheduled for Korangi Creek and 'eventual storage'. Number 230 Sqdn was then commanded by W/Cmdr C.E.L. Powell but had as Station CO G/Capt G. Francis, a former 230 Sqdn commander.

In February there was an outbreak of small-pox amongst the civilian population and all squadron personnel were vaccinated. By then the unit was preparing to operate a ferry service to Burma where the Sunderlands were scheduled to use ss. *Manela* as a base for day and night anti-shipping strikes. On 3 February the SEAC Supremo – Lord Louis Mountbatten – received a directive to liberate Burma followed by the liberation of Malaya and the opening of the Straits of Malacca.[1]

An operation as part of those objectives was 'Dracula' – the capture of Rangoon and cutting off the Japanese from their bases and communications to Siam.[2] Operation Dracula was a seaborne invasion with air support and S/Ldr Deller became a detachment commander of four Sunderlands to transport freight to the 14th Army. On 13 March W/Cmdr Powell, G/Capt Francis and S/Ldr Sheardown flew from Koggala via Coconada to Akyab in PP145 to inspect the harbour for a suitable alighting area.

Anti-shipping tactics were formed. These would involve three Sunderlands flying parallel searches and on locating a target, the sighting aircraft would home the other two and then all three would circle at 120° intervals. One would make a bombing run over the target ship while the other two Sunderlands would counter AA fire. This procedure was exercised with the help of the Royal Navy.

There was also fighter affiliation with No. 81 Squadron. A photograph of 230 Sqdn personnel was taken in front of Sunderland PP145 before their departure for Akyab where ss. *Manela* would be moored as the unit's advance base. Initially seven aircraft were at Akyab with five other Sunderlands at Koggala. Ground staff and aircrews for the first seven aircraft were inoculated against cholera and anti-malarial precautions included spraying the Sunderlands with DDT. Aircrew were issued with mepacrine and quinine tablets in case they force-landed in the jungle and were warned of the impending operation against Rangoon.

F/O Toller captained ML799 on 30 April in a series of cross-over patrols protecting invasion fleets heading for Rangoon. The first leg was from Akyab to 1105N 9247E, ten miles south of the Andaman islands. When in position 1015N 9328E the Sunderland crew sighted part of the covering force, two battleships, *Richeleau* and HMS *Queen Elizabeth* with four cruisers steaming for Port Blair. The battlecruiser HMS *Renown* sailed to bombard the Nicobar islands.

On 1 May S/Ldr H. Sheardown was airborne at 0307 hrs in PP145 to rendezvous with thirty-eight DC-3s which were carrying paratroops. A rendezvous was made in position 2008N 9253E before tracking to Calventuria Island thence to Foul Island and finally 1650N 9413E where Sheardown waited while the troops were released before escorting the formation back to base. From Capt Roskill's account[3] these troops would have been a Gurkha battalion intended to take the Japanese battery at the river mouth before the main forces arrived. An anti-climax was to find that the Japanese had withdrawn from Rangoon on 25 April.

W/Cmdr Powell flew down coast via Pagoda Point, Diamond Island and Elephant Point thence up river to Rangoon. This was on 5 May in ML799 and with him as passengers were Army medical and administration officers. Powell touched down in the northwest channel where his passengers were ferried by a Royal Marines landing craft. Fuel for the Sunderland was obtained from a beaching party.

Number 230 Squadron in Burma

The Japanese were still on the west bank of the river and there was sniping and looting in Rangoon. Due to some action near the Sunderland following a Japanese landing craft attempting to rejoin its forces, all guns on the flying-boat were manned. The following day ML799 returned to Akyab with the passengers but now including a Naval correspondent – Lt-Cmdr Villiers.

On 10 May S/Ldr Sheardown flew ML800 to Rangoon taking the AOC – Air Marshal Sir Keith Park, General Sir Oliver Leese, Air Vice-Marshal the Earl of Bandon and others. Sheardown returned to Akyab the next day with the VIPs plus two Sisters of Mercy who had been interned by the Japanese and had walked from Akyab to Rangoon.

Number 230 Sqdn now moved to Rangoon where ss. *Manela* was moored, and due to a sandbank, five miles from the Sunderlands' moorings. Some maintenance personnel were then located at Syriam. It was given as a day's work to visit an aircraft taking 2½–3 hours.

The squadron now adopted an anti-shipping role with such as F/Lt Haarscher attacking two schooners on 11 June with DCs – one schooner blew up while two sampans were subjected to machine-gun fire. On the 15th F/Lt Holstein in PP157 was on an armed recce from Rangoon across the Gulf of Siam. In four attacks with DCs and machine-guns, he blew up one

landing barge and caused another to be beached.

The capture of Rangoon was celebrated on 16 June in a fly-past before Earl Mountbatten. Number 230 Squadron was represented by Sunderland PP145 flown by S/Ldr Sheardown. During the month of June, 230 Sqdn laid on a daily sortie over the Malay peninsula to the Gulf of Siam and in ten consecutive days claimed six ships sunk, with seventeen others damaged by bombs, DCs and machine-gun fire; albeit, vessels of low tonnage. A 10,000 ton tanker reported by the Sunderlands was sunk by Liberators. After these operations the fuel situation was 3000 gallons left – enough for 30 flying hours.

Transport and Mercy Missions for Number 230 Squadron

Wing Commander Powell in T/230 with his crew, ten maintenance personnel and S/Ldr Deller, flew from Rangoon to Redhills Lake, Madras on 26 July. W/Cmdr D.E. Hawkins succeeded Powell as CO of 230 Sqdn in August, and after the Japanese surrender, the new task for 230 became the transport of people and freight. On 1 September, two Sunderlands were flown by F/Lt C.V. Brown and P/O C. Wykes from Redhills Lake to Rangoon taking War Graves Commission personnel in one aircraft and Commissions for Japanese Control and Military Services in the other.

A Victory in the Far East fly-past before Mountbatten on 12 September was led by Seletar's station commander – G/Capt G. Francis – with six Sunderlands, 230 Sqdn represented by F/Lt W.D. Hallisey in 'R'. Their aircraft were then being converted with seating for twenty passengers and bunks for twelve and with eight of the Sunderlands equipped with the navigational aid 'LORAN', for which the Americans had facilities in the operational areas.

A nostalgic flight was flown on 13 September by Sunderland U/230 to Singapore; the first for the unit since 15 February 1942. It was of 11 hrs 50 mins duration from Madras with 2,250 gallons fuel and a 3,000 lb load of Red Cross parcels. This was the beginning of a daily service;

Redhills Lake, Madras to Seletar, Singapore where crews, by reducing the average petrol consumption, increased the payload to 3,500 lbs. No. 230 Sqdn was stretched to fulfil this obligation and 240 Sqdn's CO offered to provide an aircraft if necessary.

By the end of October, 230 Sqdn had flown in to Singapore 112 passengers, largely medical personnel, together with 68,429 lbs freight, mainly Red Cross parcels. Flown out from Singapore were 315 ex POWs with 14,830 lbs baggage.

Such missions were not without loss. On 15 October F/Lt R. Levty-Haarscher captained a crew of six in Sunderland NJ277 X/230 flying out fifteen ex POWs from Singapore. A burnt-out wreck was discovered by the Army's Force 136 on the slope of a hill 2,000 ft high north-west of Johore in position 0135N 103°34'E. It was later verified as the missing Sunderland by S/Ldr Nicholson with the help of Chinese guerillas in the dense jungle. All twenty-two on board were lost.

A signal was received from SE Asia Command for 230 Sqdn to move to Seletar beginning 15 November and completing the move by the 30th. The troopship ss. *Derbyshire* embarked seventy personnel on the 26th arriving at Singapore on 1 December. A freighter, the ss. *Stancleave* at Madras on 6 December took aboard fifty tons of 230's equipment in 48 hrs largely due to the work of the unit. It arrived at

Singapore on the 27th. A full-sized hangar at Singapore enabled minor inspections on the Sunderlands to be completed in four days instead of up to seven days which prevailed at Redhills due to weather conditions.

The arrival of a 230 Sqdn Sunderland at Kuantan was apparently the first ever seen there and local boatmen charged 10 cents to visit the aircraft 'the great sea bird'. The squadron record likened it to Henley Regatta with the locals dressed in their best. Every opening of the Sunderland was used as an entry point including the front turret. No charts were available for the area but there was liaison with the Army through Col. Chapman, DSO.

In December, 748 (presumably ex POWs), and 351 Dutch women and children were evacuated from Java by the Sunderlands. The sight of the first ex POWs was enough for 230 Sqdn to be fully committed to the task. Ex POWs in the Far East suffered from malnutrition, beri-beri and leprosy plus other ailments. At the end of 1945, 230 Sqdn had twelve Sunderlands with three more in reserve. The unit returned to the United Kingdom in the following April.

Number 209 Squadron in the Far East

Number 209 Sqdn had been operating Catalinas during much of the war in Europe[4] but converted to Sunderland Vs in early 1945. As S/Ldr John G. Walker recalls:

'209 was reformed out of the three squadrons in East Africa'. John Walker became a Flight Commander under a South African CO – Lt-Col H.J.T. Sheldon – and continues: 'In July the squadron flew to Koggala in Ceylon, via the Seychelles and Diego Garcia. On 25 July a detachment flew to Rangoon, or more correctly, to Syriam on the opposite side of the Pegu river. We were billeted in houses originally occupied by oil company employees. They had been thoroughly looted, and virtually only the shell of the building remained. The climate was very hot with high humidity. Our job was to attack

A victory flypast by 240 Sqdn of Sunderlands and Catalinas at Redhills Lake.

shipping on either side of the Kra Isthmus. It was thought that the Japanese were using these vessels, mostly small fishing boats, to bring supplies to their army which had been driven back over the Sittang river. We had no night-flying facilities and had to operate by day. There were several problems with take-off from the river. Firstly we had to make sure there were no obstructions. These were usually tree trunks but on one occasion, I found a baby elephant which must have fallen in and drowned. Secondly the river was fast-flowing and on occasion, was greater than wind-speed. In that case we sometimes took off down wind if the wind and flow were in the same direction. The weather was usually good but on one occasion I had to fly at 50 ft with the radio altimeter switched on and radar. We also had the new Air Position Indicator which proved very useful.'

'We were not well-equipped to attack the comparatively small mostly wooden ships. The water was too shallow for DCs. We had no bombs and bullets merely embedded themselves in the wood. We considered the vessels were nearly all being used for fishing and it was sheer murder to shoot down the crews. We therefore adopted the policy of flying up and down the coast and firing bursts of machine-gun bullets in front of any ship we saw. This did the trick and the traffic ceased.'

John Walker flew on five of these armed recces as they were known and which averaged about 11½ hours duration. One on 27 July in Sunderland PP150 with F/Lt McKendrick, as he relates:

'On one occasion we bombed a Japanese supply train hitting an oil-tanker truck .. . in general we used to fly down the coast of Tenasserim to Victoria Point, and then cross over the Kra Isthmus to Chumphon. Then up and down the coast of Siam. We also crossed over to the west and patrolled northwards from Phuket

Island. It was on this stretch that F/Lt McKendrick spotted two heavily camouflaged Japanese ships. He attacked and one blew up. We operated until the news of the Japanese surrender.'

'The squadron then concentrated at Ceylon where we transported Allied POWs from Singapore, a most rewarding job. Number 209 then went to Hong Kong after the British Pacific Fleet had occupied it, (just beating the Chinese)!'

John Walker remained at Kai Tak, Hong Kong until April 1946 when he flew back to Wig Bay on Loch Ryan, Scotland in Sunderland NJ265. Number 209 Sqdn was to remain in the Far East and to become amalgamated with 205 Sqdn.

Number 205 Squadron at Koggala

This unit which had been equipped with Catalinas must have received its first Sunderland about 6 June 1945. The records at this time lack specific dates and serial numbers. The Sunderland was air-tested by S/Ldr Daller of 230 Sqdn and with S/Ldr Beckingsale to 'get aquainted'. The CO – W/Cmdr R.J. Freeman – had a one hour trip on the 12th in P/205 with F/O Jackson's crew and thereafter, the squadron was converting from Catalinas to Sunderland Vs.

By the end of the month, 205 had eighteen crews including four posted from 191 Sqdn which had been disbanded. The Catalinas were flown to the 'graveyard' at Korangi Creek. Initially there was a shortage of Sunderland captains and the station CO – G/Capt G. Francis – and W/Cmdr Fursman each took up a crew every morning. Later, experienced pilots such as S/Ldr Ogle-Skan and F/Lt Bellis arrived; while, by July, the flight commander – S/Ldr Dunn – had gone solo. Somewhere between 1–4 August, S/Ldr Ogle-Skan with F/O Metcalfe, flew on 205's first Sunderland sortie. This was to the Cocos Islands taking urgent freight including an 'iron lung'. A siren was sounded on 15 August marking what came to be known as 'VJ Day'. Ten days later, there was a Victory fly-past. Number

205's duties included Air-Sea-Rescue, Met. flights and transport trips to the Cocos Islands. By the end of August they had eleven Sunderland GR Vs at Koggala. Flights to the Cocos Islands included taking Red Cross parcels in loads of 4000 lbs nightly. On 13 September the unit was aware of another duty – what became known as the 'Courier Run'. This was to Singapore and included ferrying ex POWs from there. Bunks were fitted to the Sunderlands and fifteen ex POWs were expected to be evacuated on each return flight to Koggala. By November ten runs per week were being made from Koggala to Singapore and the squadron scribe suggested that the motto should be changed from *Pertama di Malaya* to *Adhuc in Lanka*. On the night of 29–30 September P/205 captained by F/Lt Harding had returned with several small children as passengers. The wardroom was used as a nursery and there was no trouble apart from some playing swings on the petrol cocks. Following a newspaper report of this trip, F/Lt Harding was called 'uncle'. On 12 November, F/O Alexander flew Lady Louis Mountbatten from Koggala to Seletar and was thanked for a pleasant journey also with a word of commendation for the way the squadron was coping.

Number 88 Squadron and the Malayan Emergency

Number 88 Squadron was formed at Kai Tak, Hong Kong from No. 1430 flight on 1 September 1946. The unit was equipped with Sunderland GR Vs for an all-up weight of 58,000 lbs.[5] Initially, as W/Cmdr D.M. Gall, a former CO of 88 Sqdn recalls:

'Our task was not the usual maritime role, but transport on the route from Hong Kong to Iwakuni in Japan, keeping the route 'warm' for BOAC. Iwakuni was administered by the RAAF, which had a fighter station hard by. We had a lot of dealings with them, and with our Navy of course, especially when we reverted to our maritime role . . .'

Iwakuni was a former Japanese Naval air station on Honshu and near the west shore of the Inland Sea.

In 1948 there began what came to be known as the 'Malayan Emergency' with communist terrorist elements promoting demonstrations followed by sabotage and assassinations. The terrorists appeared to be 'contained' for two years, but meanwhile, there was a further development – the Korean War. Both the Malayan Emergency and the Korean War involved the Sunderland squadrons.

No. 88 Sqdn with Sunderland ML882 Hong Kong 1951.

Korea and Malaya

After the defeat of Japan, Russia occupied North Korea, the Americans occupied South Korea and the 38th parallel served as a military dividing line. On 25 June 1950, eight North Korean divisions began to invade South Korea and President Truman authorised forces to support South Korea. The following day the British put some Royal Navy forces at the disposal of the American commander – General McArthur.

Number 88 Squadron moved to Iwakuni in July with S/Ldr M. Helme as CO but came under US Navy command. Patrols were over the Tsushima Strait and the Sea of Japan as far as Vladivostock.[6]

In addition to 88 Sqdn, two other units, Nos 205 and 209 also equipped with Sunderlands, came to share maritime duties in the Korean War forming the Far East Flying Boat Wing based at Seletar. Hostilities continued for three years before a truce was signed in July 1953.

Patrols were undertaken along the Malayan coast against illegal immigrants and arms smugglers. Of operations by Sunderlands over the Malayan jungle, an air gunner – J. Reilly, DFM – who flew with F/Lt Brand in 88 Sqdn recalls:

'Headquarters would receive a message from Army HQ that they had pinned down communist bandits in a particular area of the Malayan jungle and for us to assist the Army by flushing them out. We would then fully arm the Sunderland with anti-personnel bombs. These would explode at knee height by barometric pressure and the bombing was controlled by the navigator in pattern bombing. There was a lot of work in this; the bombs had to be placed in racks, fused, then the side doors of the Sunderland let down for the racks to be wound out by hand and with turbulence from the jungle rocking the aircraft like a ship in a storm.'

These operations were from Seletar of which Reilly gives as examples 2 August 1951 in NJ272 when 232 bombs were used with 3,000 rounds of ·303 and ·5 calibre.

During a trip on 4 August, again with Sunderland NJ272, 160 bombs were released and 5,500 rounds of ammunition fired. Figures given for machine-gun armament on the three squadrons, (88, 205 and 209), ranged considerably from eight up to twenty guns including ·303s and ·5s. An armourer with 88 Sqdn – John Nance – recalls three turrets with provision for four fixed Brownings in the nose and two ·5 waist guns aft of the wing roots.

The Yangtse River Incident

In April 1949 the Royal Navy's frigate HMS *Amethyst* F116, was on a routine mission to Nanking. On the 19th it anchored about 100 miles up the Yangtse river at Kiang Yin, captained by Lt-Cmdr B.M. Skinner. At that

The bombing of a supply train at Thung Song station, Southern Siam by Sunderland NJ265 Sqdn 14.8.45.

two weeks . . . F/Lt Letford was duly 'redecorated'; the AFC this time, as far as I can remember.

'Some time later, the *Amethyst* was repaired and ready to make a dash to escape from the Yangtse. We had only two Sunderlands available, and we were ordered to prepare to go to her rescue if she was so damaged again or even sunk. I remember at the briefing, the AOC asked how many survivors each Sunderland could carry if necessary. As there were 88 men on board, it was not a difficult sum!'

time Communist armies had reached the northern bank of the Yangtse and were about to achieve a series of crossings of the river in hostilities against Chiang-Kai-shek's Nationalist forces.

While heading towards Nanking the following morning, HMS *Amethyst* was bombarded by a Comminist battery on the north shore at San-Chiang-ying. The ship was hit fifty-three times and out of a crew of 183, were twenty-three dead or dying and thirty-one wounded. The captain was fatally wounded, and the ship ran aground near Rose Island, still in range of a Communist battery. After the radio was repaired, a signal was received by the RAF at Kai Tak 750 miles away for an aircraft to take medical supplies to *Amethyst*

Number 88 Sqdn was at that time based at Kai Tak with Sunderlands commanded by S/Ldr D. Gall, DFC and, as he recalls:

'I was in London on the first of a few days leave, when I read in the morning paper that HMS *Amethyst* had been attacked by the Chinese on the Yangtse River, and that my Flight Commander, F/Lt Ken Letford (who had won the DSO, DFC & Bar on Bomber Command), had flown to the scene and delivered our doctor, F/O Fearnley to the *Amethyst*. The Sunderland was subjected to some fire, but fortunately was not badly damaged, and none was injured. I cut short our leave and we returned as fast as we could, doing the round trip in the unprecedented time of

The Sunderland, captained by F/Lt Letford was airborne from Kai Tak at 0730 hrs on the 21st taking additionally, another doctor but from the Royal Navy also two Army parachute-droppers in case a touchdown could not be made. The cruiser, HMS *London*, which attempted a rescue, was contacted by the Sunderland which was advised to land at Shanghai. At Shanghai, the aircraft was refuelled, and Letford received a signal from *Amethyst* emphasising the need for medical supplies. Despite Communist guns, the Sunderland touched down near *Amethyst* at 1730 hrs and long enough for the RAF MO – F/O Fearnley – to take some medical supplies and for him to be left on board *Amethyst*.

With the loss of *Amethyst*'s captain, a Naval Attaché at Nanking, Lt-Cmdr J.S. Kerans, was able by a circuitous route to

PP118 J/201 at Castle Archdale, Lough Erne, July 1945.

A flypast with SZ560 on one engine by S/Ldr F. Weaver of the Wig Bay Test Flight, seen here over West Freugh 18.9.54.

DP198 W/209 over Seletar, May 1959.

U/209 captained by S/Ldr J. G. Walker over paddy fields south of Rangoon, July 1945.

A 209 Sqdn flypast over Singapore in 1951, seen from SZ566.

NZ4117 of the RNZAF over Suva. It was formerly RN286.

reach *Amethyst* but which remained pinned down by Communist batteries which were ever threatening. Limitations caused by food, but specifically lack of fuel, prompted Kerans to make a dash to escape under cover of darkness and follow the river when it was in spate. This dash began at 2209 hrs on 30 July[7] after many meetings with the Communists who had just adopted stalling tactics. *Amethyst* escaped despite the hazards created by the Communists and the natural hazards of navigating such a river.

Air-Sea-Rescue by Number 88 Squadron
On 15 January 1951 F/Lt Houtheusen was airborne from Iwakuni in C/88 RN282 on an A/S patrol of the Sea of Japan, but at 1025 hrs was diverted to an Air-Sea-Rescue mission. A US Navy fighter pilot, Ensign Edward J. Hosstra, had been strafing at low altitude the enemy-held harbour of Wonsan on the North Korean coast. His Corsair aircraft was damaged and he plunged into the sea 200 yards off the coast and in flames. He was able to use his dinghy and was circled by other American fighters who radioed for help. Sunderland RN282 landed near the hostile harbour to pick up Ensign Hosstra who was from Leavenworth, Kansas. Meanwhile the fighter screen was short of fuel but two others arrived to take over protection. For the 88 Sqdn crew it was a trip of 11 hrs 10 mins. Despite going down in flames, Hosstra suffered only singed hair.

The Far East Flying Boat Wing
During the Korean War, the three squadrons, Nos 88, 205 and 209 formed the Far East Flying Boat Wing commanded by W/Cmdr D.H. Burnside with the main base of Seletar, Singapore but with a monthly rotation of the three units to Iwakuni.

The Korean War ended in 1953 and the Malayan Emergency was effectively over in 1954. Number 88 Sqdn was disbanded at Seletar in October 1954, its aircraft passing to Nos 205 and 209 Sqdns. On 1 January 1955, 209 amalgamated with 205 under S/Ldr D.J.G. Norton. With independence

being gained by some territories in the Far East, there was a need for the United Kingdom to obtain a base free of political considerations. Addu Atoll in the Maldives lying just south of the equator was selected with two islands – Hittadu and Gan – of those ringing the lagoon, as possible land bases. Sunderlands of 205 and 209 provided a transport service for personnel, food and mail but by August 1957 the flying boats were being phased out in favour of land-based aircraft.[8] In May 1958 Shackletons were coming into service with 205 Sqdn based at Changi, Singapore.

The last operational flight of a Sunderland was on 14 May 1959 when DP198 W/205 was airborne from Seletar at 0800 hrs. It undertook an exercise with HMS *Caprice* and was captained by W/Cmdr R.A.N. McCreedy and with navigator Eric Tait.

On 15 May F/Lt J. Poyser as OC of the No. 205 Sqdn detachment, captained Sunderland ML797 in farewell formation flying for 1½ hours around Singapore Island. There was a last flight by ML797 P/205 on behalf of the C-in-C Far East Air Force, Air Marshal the Earl of Bandon.

The Berlin Airlift
Following the capitulation of Germany in 1945, Berlin remained in the zone controlled by the USSR but with provision for the Western Allies to have access by road, rail and air to West Berlin which was placed under control of the Western Allies. On 24 June 1948 the Russians cut the road and rail links to Berlin from the west.

Operation 'Plainfare' – an airlift to Berlin – was put into effect; this was to supply West Berlin with essentials of food and fuel. Part of the RAF's operations in supplying Berlin was undertaken by Sunderlands of Nos 201 and 230 Squadrons when they were based at Calshot. The Sunderlands provided a shuttle service between Hamburg and Berlin, the flying for each crew being from one to three return trips per day and with a flying time from Hamburg to Berlin of about one hour.

One of 230's Sunderlands was 'Y' SZ581 captained by F/Lt Bailey with Fred Weaver

The RAF camp at Young Sound, Greenland at 7428N 2035W with 230 Sqdn 6 to 9 August 1954.

Off-loading Sunderland SZ581 of 230 Sqdn on Britannia Lake, Greenland 12.8.52 posn. 7707N 2340W, captained by F/Lt Cassells.

as second pilot, which was flown from Calshot to Hamburg on 4 July. S/Ldr Weaver gives this account:

The crew of PP115 of No. 201 Sqdn at Young Sound 13.8.52.

'We were based at Finkenwerder, at the former Blohm und Voss works where we took off and landed on the river Elbe. Our moorings were in a fairly large relatively shallow area adjacent to but separated from the main river by a line of sunken vessels, whose masts and superstructure projected above the water.

'We were not under any specific control, flying up and down the corridor at a height of 1,000 ft and lower; underneath the controlled traffic above us. We called out our own seaplane tender when taking off and landing at Hamburg, and at Gatow tower whenever we were in its vicinity. We flew along the left hand side of the corridor mainly over open countryside

230 Sqdn Sunderlands at Milford Haven on 14.8.54 returning from Greenland.

or along the river Elbe in poor weather. At first the work load was immense, flying three round trips into Berlin a day which amounted to about 6½ hours airborne time, but to this adding loading and unloading, refuelling every time we returned to Hamburg, to say nothing of mooring up, taxying etc. making long and tiring days. Everyone gave his all; there was a blackboard ashore on which the identity of the crew which achieved the shortest elapsed time for the three round trips was displayed. Loads were taken to the aircraft by Army amphibious DUKWs; crews were ferried by German launches.'

Loads included powdered eggs, yeast, potatoes and – notably – salt, as the Sunderlands were treated against corrosion. Sometimes car engines were added to the loads. Return loads to Hamburg included electric-light bulbs and passengers, and as S/Ldr Weaver continues:

'With the onset of winter we flew out from Berlin poor children, some suffering from malnutrition. On the first occasion, the very first child was a baby in arms which I promptly passed on to the signaller. The others were of both sexes up to about 15 years. Some had their belongings in brown paper parcels tied with string, others carried small battered cases. Some had their toes protruding from their shoes. The crew plugged in headsets so the children could talk to each other and gave them sweets. We could not understand their language and on the second or third day, a German male nurse was allocated to each crew.

'Whenever we arrived in Hamburg with a load of these children, we all stood on the wing to watch them leave in Army DUKWs. They waved to us with happy faces and it's difficult to describe one's feelings at the time. I suppose it was a mixture of pity and sorrow, for those children who were in our care for just an hour or two but with whom we established a kind of bond

and trust, coupled with a feeling of elation, having fulfilled a rather difficult task.'

In the early stages, the RAF had been joined by aircraft from 'Aquila Airways' which provided Short 'Hythe' flying-boats. Fred Weaver's last round trip was on 10 December 1948 before he returned to Calshot with F/Lt Bailey on the 17th.

By then operations from Finkenwerder to Havel See, Berlin had ceased due to the danger of ice both on the river Elbe and Havel See.

The Russian blockade of Berlin was lifted on 12 May 1949, but the airlift which had continued after the withdrawal of the Sunderlands, was maintained until September 1949.

The Greenland Expedition

In 1951 an expedition to explore Queen Louise Land in Greenland was organised by Cmdr C.J.W. Simpson, DSC, RN. On 23 July the expedition party was flown by a 201 Sqdn Sunderland from Pembroke Dock to Reykjavik. Two days later a flight was made to King Oscar's fjord on the east coast of Greenland where the Sunderland touched down. On the 28th, a point was reached 700 miles from the north pole to recce Seal Lake and the Storstrommen glacier. On 29 August a 201 Sqdn Sunderland was able to land on what came to be known as Britannia Lake to recover the first expedition party.

There was a further expedition in 1952 with 230 Sqdn providing the airlift but with a ship, the MV *Tottan* taking stores and equipment to Young Sound. From Young Sound, Sunderlands would ferry what was required to position 7707N 2340W on Britannia Lake, with 230's CO – S/Ldr J.G. Higgins, DFC – leading a detachment from Pembroke Dock. The airlift began on 7 August when an advance party of the expedition was flown to Britannia Lake together with freight. About this time, aircrew in the RAFVR were given the opportunity of doing their compulsory fortnight's training with a squadron. Brian Lort who had served with 210 and 270

Squadrons, but then in the VR, became attached to 201 Sqdn at Pembroke Dock. As he recalls:

'Towards the end of my first week the CO came into the Mess to say that he had just received an urgent signal requesting, if possible, that an aircraft fly to Young Sound carrying a replacement dinghy and spare engine to assist in ferrying duties, otherwise the ice might beat them before all the equipment had been flown north . . . F/Lt Dickins and his crew were selected for the job, and F/O Harris (another RAFVR visitor) and myself were offered the opportunity of joining the crew as additional pilots.'

They were airborne on 10 August in PP115 for a seven-hour flight to Reykjavik. On the 12th, PP115 captained by F/Lt Dickins, flew to Young Sound position 7428N 2039W. F/Lt Cassells captained SZ581 from Young Sound to Britannia Lake, 7707N 2340W with the RAFVR pilots in the crew. While helping to unload the Sunderland, Brian Lort met the 2nd in command of the expedition, – a Met. man whom he'd last seen at Lagos while serving on 270 Sqdn Catalinas. By 23 August the five Sunderlands involved returned to Pembroke Dock.

Number 201 Sqdn served the expedition the following year when the detachment was led by S/Ldr McCready who flew from Pembroke Dock to Reykjavik on 30 July. While on Britannia Lake on 17

Sunderlands of the SAAF coded RB and not to be confused with No. 10 Sqdn RAAF. In the foreground is RN296 M-RB.

August, Sunderland C/201 during an attempted take-off, was thwarted by ice. The hazards of ice with a strong wind resulted in the Sunderland running aground with consequent damage to the hull. This was ultimately sealed with cement after the aircraft had been removed from the rocks using blocks and tackle. C/201 was airborne from Britannia Lake on the 19th and flown to Wig Bay for repairs.

One of the last Sunderlands used to support the Greenland expedition was ML763 captained by F/Lt Donaghue and navigated by Eric Tait of 230 Sqdn. They left Pembroke Dock at 0845 hrs on 5 August 1954 and flew to Reykjavik via the Mull of Kintyre. The following morning after a flight of 5 hrs 40 mins they reached the RAF base at Zachenborg, position 7428N 2035W on Young Sound. On 7 August they touched down on Britannia Lake for just over four hours before returning to Young Sound that evening. F/Lt Donaghue in ML763 arrived back at Pembroke Dock on 13 August at 1430 hrs having been delayed at Reykjavik for four days.

Number 40 Squadron RAAF

Sunderland aircraft had been flown out to Australia in early 1944 by RAAF crews, the last two arriving on 1 March.[9] Number 40 Sqdn RAAF was formed at Townsville on 31 March. There were not enough moorings at Townsville in the small, man-made harbour, and aircraft were kept at Rathmines pending a move to Port Moresby. Also at Rathmines, were the CO, W/Cmdr Vic Hodgkinson, the Flight Commander, S/Ldr Tom Egerton, and the Engineering Officer, F/O Bill Sykes.

Initially there was a daily return service from Port Moresby to Townsville, and once a week, after a night stop at Townsville, the Sunderland proceeded to Darwin via Karumba, also making a stop at Groote Island if required, and with a night stop at Darwin. The service was for American forces and aircraft were loaded at Townsville with 10,000 lb of fresh fruit and vegetables, and with some off-load for the

RAAF at Karumba. On the return trip, the crew picked up either a slaughtered pig or a large grouper fish to supplement 40 Sqdn's diet of corned beef, tinned herring and baked beans.

There were odd flights to Madang, Milne Bay and places in unoccupied New Guinea. Flights between Port Moresby and Townsville took Service personnel, mail, fresh food and supplies for the bar which included Australian whiskey at 5/- bottle (25p). There were two crews for each aircraft, later reduced to one, and Qantas at Rose Bay, Sydney undertook major overhauls with Qantas having available spares, although the holding base for Sunderland spares was Dubbo.

Number 40 Sqdn personnel built their own HQ and workshops at Port Moresby with scrounged material, although much of the timber for frames was flown in from Brisbane by Sunderlands. The unit was allocated an area known as 'Tin City' but W/Cmdr Hodgkinson arranged to take over an abandoned hospital for accommodation and private houses for Officers' and Sergeants' Messes. After he was succeeded by another CO, he understood that the unit was ordered back to 'Tin City' with a lowering of morale and an increase in medical problems.

An unusual mission for 40 Sqdn was, as Vic Hodgkinson recalls:

'. . . to transport eighty WAACs from Brisbane to Hollandia, General MacArthur's new forward base at that time. The "girls" were to be HQ staff. They were a well-worn lot and pretty tough. The aircraft were laid on and I

A-A SZ576 of 201 Sqdn on the River Thames with F/O Halliday 13.9.54.

skippered one of them. Having loaded at Brisbane with this lot plus twenty chickens we set off for Port Moresby via Townsville. The night stop was at Port Moresby. The next day took us to Hollandia. Our lot were very friendly and apart from the chickens escaping and laying eggs, both sectors were uneventful. On arrival at Hollandia (the landing area was in the crater of an extinct volcano), we warped sternwards back into the shore. Word had got around of this influx of females and the area was alive with Yanks. As each WAAC came ashore she was swamped by a mob and disappeared into the jungle. One can only imagine what happened to them.'

During 1945, six Martin Mariners with their aircrews and some maintenance personnel were transferred to No. 40 from 41 Sqdn.

Number 40's last flight was with A26-2 (ML731) captained by F/Lt Griffith and with Bill Vout as flight engineer. This was on 12 March 1946 from Cairns to Rathmines. The final move of 40 Sqdn RAAF had been to Rathmines and there on 19 July 1946, F/O Bill Vout recalls:

NZ4116 a Mk V with No. 5 Sqdn RNZAF off Lauthala Bay, Fiji 1960.

A/201 DP198 moored near the Tower of London captained by F/Lt Nicholl in 1956.

The last Sunderland at Seletar ML797 P/205 May 1959.

'I was the sole remaining member and had the duty of presiding over the demise of the squadron . . . nailing up two crates of documents . . . and consigning them to Records, Melbourne . . . and despatching the final signal . . .'

In 1613 flights the squadron had transported over 12 million pounds of freight and passengers. Of the six Mark III Sunderlands it had been allocated, five were purchased by Trans-Oceanic Airways and three of these, ML731, ML733 and ML734 were used on flights from Sydney to Lord Howe Island and New Guinea. By 1952 all were scrapped.

Sunderlands with the South African Air Force

The RAF squadron No. 262 based at Congella, Durban, was taken over by the SAAF on 15 February 1945 to become No. 35 SAAF. The South African – W/Cmdr

Servicing a Mk III of No. 40 Sqdn RAAF at Rathmines.

E.S.S. Nash DFC, RAF – remained in command pending the arrival of a SAAF officer. Number 262 had been equipped with Catalinas[10] but by March No. 35 Sqdn began to receive Sunderland Mark Vs.

An American pilot – Ray Steed – who served with No. 422 (RCAF) Sqdn flew Sunderland PP153 from Oban to Gibraltar and was then routed Kasfaret, Khartoum, and Kisumu to Dar-es-Salaam where he arrived on 9 March. He delivered it to W/Cmdr Smith of 35 Sqdn and before returning to the United Kingdom, the RAF crew familiarised the South Africans with the Sunderland.

For his second delivery flight, Ray Steed ferried RN281 to Lake Umzingazi 100 miles north of Durban where 35 Sqdn had its training facility. Steed, with his crew, remained at Umzingazi until VE day converting Catalina pilots and crews to Sunderlands. While there, Ray Steed heard that PP153, the first Sunderland he had delivered, had struck a hippo while landing on Lake Umzingazi. The pilot had then flown to Congella to make a crash landing with damage to the port wing. PP153 became a 'Christmas tree' for spare parts. From South African records the accident occurred on 26 April.

Lt-Col D.A. du Toit took over command of 35 Sqdn from W/Cmdr Nash on 13 April about the time when a further seven Sunderlands were being received. The Catalinas were then being dismantled and conversion of the squadron was progressing.

ML814 at Chatham dockyard Sept. 1987. It was damaged by the hurricane in the following month. It is now in the USA.

There was a need for the repatriation of South African troops from the Middle East and Lt-Col du Toit suggested that the Sunderlands might be so employed. With initially fifteen trained crews, a single daily service was made to Kasfaret on the Great Bitter Lake in the Suez Canal. The route chosen was from Durban via Dar-es-Salaam, Kisumu and Khartoum, the route used by BOAC. The service began on 2 November and with the intention of taking up to forty passengers on each flight. Within six weeks, 1,022 personnel were flown to Durban while 34,338 kg of Christmas parcels were delivered to the Middle East.[11] From a newspaper report, 101,756 passengers were ultimately transported and the total casualties were fifty-five passengers with twelve aircrew. The service ceased on 2 March 1946 for the repatriation of troops.

The South African Air Force received sixteen Mark V Sunderlands, fifteen of these received SAAF serial numbers from 1701 to 1715 and these gained the code letters 'RB' (the same as No. 10 RAAF); PP153 received only the letter 'M'. Their last Sunderland flight was by RN281 1710 coded D-RB and dubbed *Dynamite Daisy*. The flight was on 8 October 1957. The *Cape Argus* had reported in 1955 that 35 Sqdn would re-equip with Shackletons and would move from Durban to Cape Town, but it was to be in 1957 when the unit received eight Mark III Shackletons.

Short Flying Boats with the Royal New Zealand Air Force

Some Short 'Empire' flying boats were delivered to New Zealand in 1940 and were operated on the Trans-Tasman route by a civil airline. They were the only long range aircraft available to New Zealand at that time and they were seconded with their civilian crews to the RNZAF for reconnaissance against possible German raiders.

In 1941 the RNZAF received four Short Singapore III flying boats from No. 205 Sqdn RAF. The Singapores came to operate with No. 5 GR Sqdn RNZAF from Fiji. Both No. 5 and No. 6 Sqdns were in 1943 equipped with Catalinas but in the following year, the RNZAF received its first Sunderlands.

They were four Mark IIIs intended for transport service and had been given RAF serial numbers ML792-ML795 but were to become NZ4101-NZ4104. All four left Britain in October and were routed via West Africa, South America, the Caribbean, the USA and across the Pacific to Fiji. They arrived at Auckland on 4 December 1944.

Some personnel from 490 (RNZAF) Sqdn were involved in the ferrying. These Sunderlands were operated by a Transport Flight at Hobsonville for personnel and freight between New Zealand and Fiji, New Caledonia and Espiritu Santo in the New Hebrides.

The four Mark IIIs were loaned to the civil airline, New Zealand National Airways Corporation in November 1947 before being returned to the RNZAF in 1951 and later to be scrapped in 1954.

Sixteen re-conditioned Sunderlands brought up to Mark V standard were purchased by New Zealand. The first to arrive were PP110 and ML814 on 13 June 1953, at Hobsonville to become NZ4105 and NZ4108 respectively. They were allotted to No. 5 Sqdn at Lautala Bay in August replacing the unit's last two Catalinas. No. 5 Sqdn had an establishment of six aircraft but other Sunderlands were operated by No. 6 Sqdn based at Hobsonville and by the Operational Conversion Unit which was formed in May 1955.

The final delivery was of RN286 (NZ4117) which arrived on 9 May 1955. In that same month, two of the New Zealand Sunderlands flew to Singapore and took part in exercises with No. 205 Sqdn RAF. The general use of the Sunderlands however, was reconnaissance and mercy missions across the South Pacific area.

When the Territorial Air Force was disbanded, No. 6 Sqdn was replaced by the Maritime Conversion Unit. In 1964 approval was given to replace the Sunderlands with Orion P3B aircraft, the first of these arriving 27 September 1966, and coming into service during 1967.

There had been a maximum of sixteen

Sunderlands in service during the years 1955–59 but by April 1967 the number had been reduced to six. SZ584 (NZ4115) was acquired by the Museum of Transport and Technology at Auckland; ML814 (NZ4108) was sold to a civil airline Ansett but later returned to Britain and in 1991 was reported to be at Calshot – and still airworthy.

References

1   GO p. 427
2   WSC VI p. 588
3   SWR III pt 2 p. 317
4   AH 'FC' pp. 22,35,84
5   DL p. 80
6   DL pp. 114–16
7   LE *Yangtse Incident*
8   DL p. 169
9   Ibid.
10 AH 'FC' pp. 84–87
11 HJM and NDO p. 345

Acknowledgements

Although in preparing this script I referred to official operational records, much help was provided by official bodies and many ex-service personnel from the Royal Navy, RAAF, RCAF, RNAF, RNZAF, RYAF and the SAAF. The historical sections of the Australian, British, Canadian, French, Italian and New Zealand Ministries provided material or answered questions.

Of the many ex-Service personnel who helped me, some maintained contact throughout this project namely, Vic Hodgkinson, Don Wells, Jack Bruce, Bob Wardner; and from the RAF, Geoffrey Bartlett, Eric Harrison, Tom Harvey and Fred Mock. Egil Johansen kept me informed on Norwegian aspects.

Editors of *Air Mail*, *RAF News*, *Navy News*, *Air Force*, *Intercom* and *The Turret*, were kind enough to publish requests on my behalf. John Espie read the script, but to him no errors may be attributed. May I now express my thanks to those listed hereunder:

Alington, W/Cmdr P.H. DFC, RAF, 230, 210 Sqdns; Bailey H.L.; Balderson, Bill 210 Sqdn RAF; Bartlett, W/Cmdr, G.C.C. AFC, RAF, 224, 59 Sqdns; Barton, Roy 204 Sqdn RAF; Baveystock, F/Lt L. DSO, DFC, DFM, 201 Sqdn RAF; Bednall, W/Cmdr Dundas RAF 230 Sqdn; Beesley, F/Lt Glyn 228 Sqdn RAF; Belcher, N.; Bevan-John, G/Capt D. OBE, JP, RAF 228 Sqdn; Bishop, S/Ldr A.A. DFC, RCAF 423 Sqdn; Bremner, G/Capt C.D. RAAF 461 Sqdn; Bruce, Cmdr Jack, USN; Brown, F/Lt Tim 228 Sqdn; Bush, Trevor; Busson, Jean-Pierre, French Ministry; Butler, J.G. SAAF Museum; Butler, F/Lt Sid, DFC. 422 (RCAF) Sqdn; Butt, R.D. Capt. RN HMS *Birmingham*; Cleaver, W. 53 Sqdn RAF; Conacher, Don 10 Sqdn RAAF; Cook, Arthur C. 230 Sqdn; Coy, F/O John 228, 240 Sqdns RAF;

Craven, Air Marshal Sir Robert, KBE, CB, OBE, DFC, RAF; 201, 210 & 228 Sqdns; Cremer, Lt-Cmdr, Peter (of U-333); Cunningham, S/Ldr C.A. RCAF, 202, 423 Sqdns; Curwen, Reg 210 Sqdn RAF; Davies, Ed.; Diss, Roy 230 Sqdn RAF; Drummond, E. (HMS *Serene*); Duncan, Don. J. 240 Sqdn RAF; Eden, Mrs Mary (35 Sqdn SAAF); Edwards, H.W.F. AFC 209 Sqdn RAF; Ellis, W/Cmdr L.E. DFC, RAF 228 Sqdn; Espie, John L. S/Ldr RAF; Evans, John; Fantozzi, Cav. Delio (ex *Rubino*); Flanagan, G/Capt T.C. MSc, RAF; Francis, G/Capt G. DSO, DFC, RAF 230 Sqdn; Franzitta, C.te Eugenio (ex *Torelli*); Freebody, Edward F.; Frizell, Capt Peter, DFC, RAAF 201, 423 Sqdns; Frizzle, G/Capt J.R. RCAF 422, 423 Sqdns; Gall, W/Cmdr DFC, RAF 201, 88 Sqdns; Gibson, Simon 210, 95 Sqdns; Gilchrist, S/Ldr J.K. 228 Sqdn; Hadley, Ken 205 Sqdn; Harland, Denis V. 4(C) OTU RAF; Harrison F/Lt Eric 228 Sqdn RAF; Harrison, S/Ldr P.A. RNZAF; Harvey, P.H. 201 Sqdn RAF; Harvey, G/Capt Tom RAF 201, 490 Sqdns; Haslam, Sam; Hicks, Dean 10, 461 Sqdns RAAF; Hodgkinson, Capt Vic. DFC, RAAF, 10, 40 Sqdns RAAF; Hotson, Fred, W. 201 Sqdn; Holroyd, F/Lt W.H. RCAF 422 Sqdn; Hughes, B.A. BEM, 230 Sqdn; Jackson, S/Ldr F. 228 Sqdn RAF; Jackson, Capt. H.C. 423 Sqdn RCAF, 40 Sqdn RAAF; Jennings F/O J.A.; Johansen, Lt-Col Egil RNAF, 333, 330 Sqdns; Jones, Mrs Evva ('Slim' 201 Sqdn); Kelly, F/Lt R.A.N. BEM, RAAF 6 Sqdn RAAF; Kernahan, J.K. 228, 270 Sqdns RAF; Kingsland, G/Capt Sir Richard, DFC, 10 Sqdn RAAF; Kneale, W/O 228 Sqdn RAF; Kruse, Col. E. RNAF 330 Sqdn; Lacy, F/Lt Alan 228 Sqdn; Lamb, Alan; Lamond, W/Cmdr H.W. 210, 228 Sqdns RAF; Landers, Brian 201 Sqdn RAF; Lane, Capt Sydney, 201 Sqdn RAF; Lassister, F/Lt Ray, 201 Sqdn RAF; Laughlin, Frank R. 423 Sqdn

RCAF; Lee, P.D. 490 Sqdn RNZAF; Leese, Dick 95 Sqdn RAF; Lindsay, G/Capt Don. OBE, DFC, RAF 201, 228, 230 Sqdns; Loader, John E. RAF; Lobley, W/O K.A. 205 Sqdn RAF; Loite, Jean-Jacques (Free French); Lort, Brian, 210, 270, 201 Sqdns RAF; Lord, Geoffrey 205 Sqdn RAF; Lucas, Stan 10 Sqdn RAAF; Lywood, W/Cmdr Alan, DFC, RAF, 230, 228 Sqdns; McKinley, Air Vice-Marshal D. CB, CBE, DFC, AFC, RAF 228 Sqdn; McLean, W/O L.N. 204, 95 Sqdns RAF; McMillan, F. 88 Sqdn RAF; Maroni, Lt-Cmdr W. (*Rubino*); Marrows, F/Lt D. DSO, DFC, RAAF 461, 40 Sqdns; Martin, W/Cmdr D. OBE, BSc, 10, 210 Sqdns RAF; Martyn, B.A. 201 Sqdn RAF; Mock, Fred 230 Sqdn RAF; Morton, Frank 422 Sqdn RCAF; Mountford, A.E. 423 Sqdn RCAF; Nance, John M. 88 Sqdn RAF; Nespor, Joe. E. 422 Sqdn RCAF; Nortje, Brig. J.F. 35 Sqdn SAAF; Orriss, A.W. HMS *Brocklesby*; Outen, E. (HMS *Wild Swan*); Ovens, Harry S. 461 Sqdn RAAF; Pearce, A/Cmdre F.A. 210, 95 Sqdns RAF; Pendry, B. Lough Erne Museum; Pocknell, D. 423 Sqdn RCAF; Powers, Ron 201 Sqdn RAF; Quantrill, David; Ragnarsson, Ragnar; Redshaw, Eric 230 Sqdn RAF; Reilly, J.M. DFM 88 Sqdn RAF; Robinson, S/Ldr L.K. CBE, DL, SSC, LlB, 201 Sqdn RAF; Rossiter, T.E. 228 Sqdn RAF; Rushmer, Don R. 205 Sqdn RAF; Rump, A/Cmdre F.J.W. 210, 423 Sqdns RAF; Savage, James, JP, 10 Sqdn RAAF; Scott, Lt-Cmdr Morin, RNR (HMS *Auricula*); Severi, Capt Antonio ITN, Ufficio Storico; Sheardown, S/Ldr H.R. 230 Sqdn; Short Bros plc, Belfast; Smith, Bernard 228, 270 Sqdns RAF; Southall, Ivan DFC. 461 Sqdn RAAF; Stanic, D. No. 2 (Yugoslav) Sqdn; Stanojlovic, Mrs Vera; Steed, Ray 422 Sqdn RCAF; Steffen-Olsen Col. Alf 330 Sqdn RNAF; Stephens, F/Lt G. 270, 230 Sqdns RAF; Stiebler, Capt Wolf (of U-461); Tait, Eric DFM, 201, 88, 230, 205/209 Sqdns RAF; Taylor, G/Capt C.R. OBE, 230 Sqdn; Taylor, Mike 230 Sqdn; Terlinden, S/Ldr Leon, DFC, 201 Sqdn RAF; Thompson, Dudley RAF; Tomislav, Prince of Yugoslavia; Troughton, Fred, HMS *Brocklesby*; Vout, E.W. 10, 40 Sqdns RAAF; Vracaric, M.J. No. 2 (Yugoslav) Sqdn; Walker, S/Ldr J.G. DFC, 210, 190, 165 Sqdns RAF; Walters, F/Lt I.F.B. DFC, 201 Sqdn RAF; Wardner, Lt-Col Robert, DFC, USAF; Waite, Vic. S. 228 Sqdn RAF; Warrener, F/Sgt Paul, 201 Sqdn RAF; Wells, C. Bryan 228 Sqdn RAF; Wells, Don 422, 413 Sqdns RCAF; Wells, F. (HMS *Bentinck*); Wells, Jack 228 Sqdn RAF; Wheaton, Reg. 461 Sqdn RAAF; White, F/Lt Stan DFC, 228, 201 Sqdns RAF; Williams, Ron 204 Sqdn RAF; Wright, Jim H. 423 Sqdn RCAF; Wright, J.F. 88 Sqdn RAF; Wight-Boycott, W/Cmdr, A. CO, No. 201 Sqdn RAF.

Bibliography

Air 27- 151, 152, 153, 161, 910, 1178, 1179, 1209, 1210, 1216, 1298, 1299, 1412, 1413, 1414, 1415, 1416, 1422, 1423, 1483, 1571. *Operational Records* Public Record Office. C-12295, C-12296 *Operational Records R.C.A.F.*

Air Publication 1566C *Pilot's Notes Sunderland III*, HMSO.

Air Publication 1566E *Pilot's Notes Sunderland V* HMSO.

Alexandra, Queen of Yugoslavia (1959) *Prince Philip – A Family Portrait*, H&S.

Arheim, Tom (1984) *Fra Spitfire Til F-16*, Sem & Stenersen A/S.

Baff, Kevin (1983) *Maritime is No. 10; A History of No. 10 Squadron RAAF*, K. Baff.

Barnes, Chris (1979) *Shorts Aircraft Since 1900*, Putnam.

Bednall, Dundas (1989) *Sun on my Wings*, Paterchurch Publications.

Bertini, Capt. Vasc. Marcello (1972) *I Sommergibili in Mediterraneo* Vols 1 & 2, Ufficio Storico M.M. Rome.

Bowyer, M.J.F. & Rawlings J.D.R. (1979) *Squadron Codes 1937–56*, Patrick Stephens.

Churchill, Winston S. *The Second World War*, Vols I–VI, Cassell, London.

Cremer, Peter (1984) *'U-333'* (English Version) Bodley Head.

Crowther J.G. & Whiddington R. (1947) *Science at War*, HMSO.

Cunningham, Admiral of the Fleet, Viscount (1951) *A Sailor's Odyssey*, Hutchinson.

Darby, Charles (1978) *RNZAF; The First Decade 1937–46*, Kookaburra Tech.

Douglas, W.A.B. (1986) *The Official History of the R.C.A.F.*, Vol. II, Toronto Press.

Earl, Lawrence (1950) *Yangtse Incident*, Harrop.

Eller, R/Adml E.M. (1963) *U.S. Submarine Losses in World War II.*

Fioravanzo, Giuseppe (1976) *Le Azioni Navali in Mediterraneo*, 3rd Edn, Ufficio Storico M.M. Rome.

Franks, Norman L.R. (1986) *Conflict Over the Bay*, William Kimber.

Franks, Norman L.R. (1990) *Search, Find and Kill*, Aston Pub.

Frederica, Queen of the Hellenes (1971) *A Measure of Understanding*, MacMillan.

Halley, James (1988) *The Squadrons of the RAF & Commonwealth 1918–1988*, Air Britain.

Hannah, Donald (1983) *Shorts*, Flypast Reference Library.

Hendrie, Andrew (1983) *Seek and Strike – The Lockheed Hudson in WW2*, W. Kimber.

Hendrie, Andrew (1988) *Flying Cats – The Consolidated Catalina in WW2*, Airlife.

Herington, John (1954) *Air War Against Germany and Italy 1939–43* AVM.

Herington, John (1963) *Air Power Over Europe 1944–45* AV-M.

Herlin, Hans *Verdammter Atlantik*, Wilhelm Heyne Verlag, München 1985.

Hodgkinson, Vic. (1989) *Beachcomber – The Story of a Sandringham*

Jackson, Robert (1988) *The Berlin Airlift*, Patrick Stephens.

Jenks, C.F.L. (1980) *New Zealand Military Aircraft & Serial Nos.*, AV.His.Soc.

Keegan, John (1989) *The Times Atlas of the Second World War.*

Lee, Sir David (1984) *Eastward, A History of the RAF in the Far East 1945–1972*, HMSO.

Masters, David (1941) *So Few* Ayre & Spottiswoode.

Martin, Lt-Gen H.J. & Col. Neil D. Orpen (1979) *South Africa at War 1939–45*, Vol. VII, Purnell.

Middlebrook, Martin (1976) *Convoy – The Battle for the Convoys SC122 & HX229*, A. Lane.

Norris, Geoffrey, *The Sunderland Profile*, Profile Publications.

Odgers, George (1968) *Air War Against Japan 1943–45*, AWM.

Peter II, King of Yugoslavia (1955) *A King's Heritage*, Cassell.

Pentland, Geoffrey, *Aircraft of the RAAF 1921–78*, Kookaburra Pub.

Poolman, Kenneth (1962) *Flying Boat – The Story of the Sunderland*, W. Kimber.

Potgieter, Herman (1981) *Aircraft of the SAAF* Janes.

Potter, E.B. (Ed) (1981) *Sea Power – A Naval History*, Naval Inst. Press.

Preston, J.M. (1978) *A Short History*, North Kent Books.

Rawlings J.D.R. (1982) *Coastal Support and Special Squadrons of the RAF and Their Aircraft*, Janes.

Roberts, Nicholas (1977) *Short Sunderland Crash Log*, Roberts.

Rohwer, Jürgen (1983) *Axis Submarine Successes 1939–45*, US Naval Inst.

Roskill, Capt S.W. (1954–1961) *The War at Sea 1939–45*, Vols I–III, HMSO.

Robertson, Bruce, *British Military Aircraft Serials 1911–1979*, Patrick Stephens.

Richards, Denis & Saunders, Hilary St George (1953–54) *Royal Air Force 1939–1945*, Vols I–III, HMSO.

Schull, Joseph (1987) *Far Distant Ships, An Official Account of Canadian Naval Operations in WW2*, Stoddart & US Naval Inst.

Shorrick, N. (1968) *Lion in the Sky*, Federal Publications, Singapore.

Southall, Ivan (1956) *They Shall Not Pass Unseen*, Angus & Robertson.

Terraine, John (1985) *The Right of the Line*, H&S.

Ubaldini, Ubaldino (1976) *I Sommergibili Negli Oceani*, Ufficio Storico, M. M., Rome.

Barnett, Correlli (1991) *Engage the Enemy More Closely*, H&S.

Aeromilitaria No. 3 Air Britain 1979.

Coastal Command's War Record 1939–1945.

Scott, Morin *War is a Funny Business.*

Glossary and Abbreviations

AA	Anti-Aircraft
ABC	Admiral Sir Andrew Cunningham
AAC	Army Air Corps
AAF	Army Air Force
A/Cmdre	Air Commodore
A/F/Lt	Acting Flight Lieutenant
AH	Andrew Hendrie
AHQ	Air Headquarters
Aldis Lamp	A lamp used to transmit messages in Morse code by operating a mirror and sighting through a fixed telescopic sight
AOC	Air Officer Commanding
AOC-in-C	Air Officer Commanding-in-Chief
APU	Auxiliary Power Unit
A/S	Anti-Submarine
ASR	Air-Sea-Rescue
ASV	Aircraft-to-Surface-Vessel Equipment which transmitted electromagnetic waves which would be reflected back by vessels to produce a 'blip' on the screen of a cathode-ray-tube (CRT)
BEF	British Expeditionary Force
BOAC	British Overseas Airways Corporation
CB	Correlli Barnett
CCWR	Coastal Command's War Record 1939–1945
C-in-C	Commander-in-Chief
CLA	Creeping-Line-Ahead. A navigational search method
CO	Commanding Officer
Cross-Over-Patrol	A navigational search method
DC	Depth Charge
DD	Destroyer
D/F	Direction Finding
DG	Douglas Gillison (RAAF historian)
DL	David Lee (RAF historian)
DR	Denis Richards (RAF historian)
DR	Dead Reckoning (navigation)
E/A	Enemy Aircraft
EBP	E.B. Potter (historian)

FAA	Fleet Air Arm
FC	*Flying Cats*
F/Cmdr	Flight Commander
F/Lt	Flight Lieutenant
F/O	Flying Officer
F/Sgt	Flight Sergeant
GEE	Code name for a navigational system using electro-magnetic wave pulses from ground stations giving blips on a CRT which were used in conjunction with a special chart
GF	Guiseppe Fioravanzo (Italian historian)
GO	George Odgers (RAAF historian)
GOC-in-C	General Officer Commanding-in-Chief
HE	High explosive
HH	Hans Herlin (German historian)
HJM	H. J. Martin, Lt-Gen. (South African historian)
HMS	His Majesty's Ship
HMAS	His Majesty's Australian Ship
HMCS	His Majesty's Canadian Ship
HS	Hilary St George Saunders (RAF historian)
HP	Herman Potgieter
IFF	Identification Friend or Foe. An automatic transmitter in aircraft for its identification but which could be used for homing others.
IS	Ivan Southall
JR	Jürgen Rohwer (German historian)
JS	Joseph Schull, Lt-Cmdr RCNVR
JT	John Terraine
KB	Kevin Baff
KIA	Killed in Action
LE	Lawrence Earl
LORAN	Long-Range-Navigation. A system using signals from four ground Stations
MAD	Magnetic Anomaly Detection
Mae West	A lifejacket which could be inflated by mouth or a CO_2 bottle
MB	Marcello Bertini (Italian historian)
ML	Motor Launch

MM	Martin Middlebrook
MU	Maintenance Unit
NDO	Col. Neil D. Orpen (with Lt-Gen H.J. Martin)
OTU	Operational Training Unit
PC	Peter Cremer Lt-Cmdr (Capt of U-333)
PLE	Prudent Limit of Endurance
P/O	Pilot Officer
PRU	Photo-Reconnaisance-Unit
RAAF	Royal Australian Air Force
RAF	Royal Air Force
Radar	American term applied to equipment such as the British ASV
RCAF	Royal Canadian Air Force
RNAF	Royal Norwegian Air Force
RNZAF	Royal New Zealand Air Force
RYAF	Royal Yugoslav Air Force
SAAF	South African Air Force
Schnorkel	A tube extending above the surface from a U-boat enabling it to run on Diesel engines.
SEM	Samuel E. Morison
Sgt	Sergeant
S/Ldr	Squadron Leader
Sonobuoy	A device released from aircraft to locate U-boats which converted sound waves to an electro-magnetic signal received in the aircraft
'S&S'	'Seek and Strike'
Sqdn	Squadron
ss	steamship
SSS	Alternative to 'SOS'
SWR	S.W. Roskill, Capt RN.
TA	*Times Atlas, of World War II*
U/S	Unserviceable
USN	United States Navy
USSL	United States Submarine Losses in WW2
UMU	Ubaldino Mori Ubaldini (Italian historian)
VP	USN code for a squadron with heavier-than-air patrol planes
WABD	W.A.B. Douglas (RCAF historian)
W/Cmdr	Wing Commander
W/Op	Wireless Operator
WSC	Winston Spencer Churchill

Appendix A

German and Italian Submarines Sunk or Damaged by Sunderland Aircraft

Date	Sub.	Capt	Pilot	Sqdn	Position		Remarks
30.1.40	U-55	KL Heidel	F/Lt Brooks	228	4837N 0746W	S	Shared with HMS *Fowey & Whitshed* OA80G
28.6.40	*Anfitrite*		W/C Nicholetts	228	3718N 1954E	D	
28.6.40	*Argonauta*			230	off Alexandria	D	
29.6.40	*Rubino*	T.v. Trebbi	F/L Campbell	230	3910N 1849E	S	Sunderland L5804 picked up 3 survivors
1.7.40	U-26	KK Scheringer	F/L Campbell	10	4803N 1130W	S	Shared with HMS *Gladiolus* OA175
16.8.40	U-51	KL Knorr	F/L Gibson	210	c.4706N 1400W	D	Airborne DCs just entering service OA198
30.9.40	*Gondar*	T.v. Brunetti	F/O Baker	230	3202N 2754E	S	Shared with HMAS *Stuart*
10.2.41?	*Marcello*	C.C. Teppati	F/L Alington	210	5900N 1700W	S	*Marcello* left Bordeaux 5.2.41
1.8.41	*Delfino*	C.C. d'Cerrione	F/L Baker?	230	3212N 1446E	D	Sunderland crew shot down, some made POW
9.1.42	U-577	KL Schauenburg	F/L Brand	230	3222N 2654E	D	3×DCs+4×250 lb A/S bombs
28.5.42	*Argo*	T.v. Gigli	S/L Garside	10	40 m NW C.Caxine	D	W3983 'R' & Hudsons
5.6.42	U-71	KL Flachsenberg	F/L Pockley	10	W. of Bordeaux	D	W3986 'U'; U-71 returned to La Pallice
7.6.42	*Torelli*	C.C. Migliorini	F/L Wood	10	C.St Vincent	D	W3994, W4019 & 172 Sqdn
			F/L Egerton				
			P/O Yeoman				
11.6.42	U-105	KL Nissen	F/L Martin	10		D	W3993 6×DCs & 2×250 lb A/S bombs
1.9.42	*Giuliani*	T.v. Cazigna	F/L Wood	10	170 m off Gironde	D	W3983, W3986 & 304 Sqdn
			Fl/Lt.Pockley				
14.9.42	*Alabastro*	T.v. Bonadies	F/O Walshe	202	3728N 0434E	S	W6002 'R' 4×DCs
19.3.43	U-608	KL Struckmeier	F/L Church	228	c.5500N 2400W	D	DD837 'V' 4×DCs SC122 & HX229
20.3.43	U-384	OL von Rosenberg-Gruszazynski	F/O Robertson	201	5418N 2615W	S	W6501 'T'
20.3.43	U-527	KL Uhlig	F/L Hewitt	201		D	DD829 'Z' 6×DCs SC122 & HX229
1.5.43	U-415	KL Werner	F/L E.C. Smith	461	4448N 0858W	D	DV868 'M'; E/612 & N/172
2.5.43	U-332	OL Hüttemann	F/L E.C. Smith	461	4706N 1058W	S	DV968 'M' 8×DCs
7.5.43	U-465	KL Wolf	F/L Rossiter	10	4837N 2239W	S	W3993 'W' 8×DCs
13.5.43	U-456	KL Teichert	F/L Musgrave	423	4538N 1304W	D	W6006 'G' 2×DCs & HMS *Lagan* & HMCS *Drumheller*
24.5.43	U-441	KL Hartmann	F/O Debnam	228	4700N 0940W	D	EJ139 'L' failed to return
31.5.43	U-440	OL Schwaff	F/L Gall	201		S	DD835 'R' 4×DCs
31.5.43	U-563	OL Borchardt	F/L French	228		S	DD838 'X' & R/58
			F/L Mainprize	10			DV969 'E'
13.6.43	U-564	OL Fiedler	F/L Lee	228	4430N 1500W	S	DV967 'U' which FTR; 2nd attack by G/10 OTU
27.6.43	U-518	OL Offermann	F/L Layne	201		D	W6005 'P'
13.7.43	U-607	OL Jeschonnek	F/O Hanbury	228	4502N 0914W	S	JM708 'N' 7×DCs
30.7.43	U-461	KK Stiebler	F/L Marrows	461	4542N 1100W	S	W6077 'U'; 7×DCs; Sunderland dropped dinghy
1.8.43	U-383	KL Kremser	F/L White	228	4724N 1210W	S	JM678 'V' 7×DCs
1.8.43	U-454	KL Hackländer	F/L Fry	10	4536N 1023W	S	W4020 'B' 6×DCs; W4020 shot down
2.8.43	U-106	OL Damerow	F/O Hanbury	228	4635N 1155W	S	JM708 'N' 6×DCs
			F/L Clarke	461			DV968 'M' 6×DCs
4.8.43	U-489	OL Schmandt	F/O Bishop	423	6111N 1438W	S	DD859 'G' 6×250 lb DCs; DD859 shot down

Appendix A (contd.)

Date	Sub.	Capt	Sqdn	Pilot	Position		Remarks
8.10.43	U-610	KL von Freyberg	423	F/O Russell	5545N 2433W	S	DD863 'J' 3×DCs SC143
17.10.43	U-470?	OL Grave	422	F/L Sargent	4647N 1042W	D	JM712 'S' shot down
8.1.44	U-426	KL Reich	10	F/O Roberts	5241N 1427W	S	EK586 'U' 6×DCs & 4×Fwd fixed guns
28.1.44	U-571	OL Lüssow	461	F/L Lucas	5300N 2300W	D	EK577 'D' SC151 ON221
16.2.44	U-?		201	F/O Longland	5235N 2019W	D	EK594 'W' 6×DCs
10.3.44	U-625	OL Straub	422	F/L Butler	5036N 1836W	D	EK591 'U' 6×250 lb DCs
24.4.44	U-672	OL Lawätz	423	F/L Fellows	6305N 0310E	S	DD862 'A' 6×DCs
16.5.44	U-240	OL Link	330	S/L Johnsen	6355N 0224E	D	JM667 'V' 3×DCs
21.5.44	U-995	KL Kohntopp	40TU	P/O King	6227N 0304E	D	'S' 6×DCs
24.5.44	U-675	OL Sammler	40TU	F/O Frizell		S	ML736 'R'
24.5.44	U-921	OL Werner	423	F/L Nesbitt		D	DW111 'S' 5×DCs
7.6.44	U-995	OL Baden	201	F/L Baveystock	4513N 0830W	S	ML760 'S' flares, fwd guns & 6×DCs
7.6.44	U-970	OL Ketels	228	F/L Quinn	4515N 0410W	S	ML766 'R' 6×DCs, moonlight
11.6.44	U-333	FK Cremer	228	F/L Slaughter	4824N 0431W	D	ML880 'U' shot down by U-333
8.7.44	U-243	KL Märtens	10	F/O Tilley	4706N 0640W	S	W4030 'H' 6×DCs; HMCS *Restigouche* homed to rescue
11.7.44	U-1222	KL Bielfeld	201	F/L Walters	4631N 0529W	S	ML881 'P' schnorkel sighting; 5×DCs
20.7.44	U-387	KL Buchler	330	Lt T-Nielsen	6833N 0720E	D	EJ155 'O' 6×DCs
11.8.44	U-385	KL Valentiner	461	P/O Southall	4616N 0245W	S	ML741 'P' & HMS *Starling*
12.8.44	U-270	OL Schreiber	461	F/O Little	4619N 0256W	S	ML735 'A' 6×DCs
18.8.44	U-107	L. Fritz	201	F/L Baveystock	4646N 0339W	S	EJ150 'W' 6×DCs
25.11.44	U-322	OL Wysk	330	S/Lt Bauer	6018N 0452W	D?	NJ188 'C' & HMS *Ascension*
6.12.44	U-2977	OL Aldegarmann	201	F/L Hatton	5844N 0420W	S	'Y' U-297 credited to HMS *Loch Insh* & HMS *Goodall*
30.4.45	U-242	OL Riedel	201	F/L Foster	5342N 0455W	S	ML783 'H' schnorkel sighting, 6×DCs & HMS *Hesperus* & HMS *Hazelock*

S=Sunk
D=Damaged
FTR=Failed to return

Appendix B

Short Sunderland – Marks

Mark	First Flown	Engines	h.p.	Span	Length	Wing Area	Wt.(lb)	All-up wt.	Max. Speed	Range	Wing ldg.
I	16.10.37	Pegasus X	950	112'9"	85'4"	1487 sq.ft	28,290	50,100	210 mph	2880 mls	34 lbs/sq.ft
	7.3.38	Pegasus XXII	1010								
II	Nov. 41?	Pegasus XVIII	1030								
III	28.6.41	Pegasus XVIII	1030	112'9"	85'4"	1487	33,000	58,000	205 mph	2880 mls	39
IV	30.8.44	Hercules XIX	1770	112'9"	88'7"	1487	45,000	75,000	242 mph	2800 mls	50
V	Mar. 44	P&W R-1830	1200	112'4"	85'4"	1487	37,000	65,000	213 mph	1880 mls	44

Appendix C

Short Sunderlands with No. 330 (Norwegian) Squadron 1943–1945

Mark	Serial	On charge	Code	Off charge	Remarks
II	T9083	4.5.43	O	21.12.43	To No. 4 C OTU Alness
II	T9112	25.4.43			Not received
III	W6027	27.5.44	N	8.7.44	To No. 4 C OTU Alness
III	W6030	18.6.43	M	15.6.44	Damaged; write off 10.7.44
II	W6052	6.5.43	D	5.6.43	Missing from operation
II	W6053	5.5.43	E	10.4.44	To No. 57 MU, Wig Bay
II	W6059	30.4.43	P	13.2.44	To No. 57 MU, Wig Bay
II	W6061	5.5.43	X	15.2.44	To No. 57 MU, Wig Bay
II	W6064	5.3.43	R	26.2.44	To No. 4(C) OTU Alness
III	W6067	22.3.43	T	6.8.44	To Calshot
III	W6068	4.4.43	W	6.5.43	To No. 423 (RCAF) Sqdn
III	W6075	3.4.43	Z	12.5.43	Damaged; write off 8.6.43
III	DD835	12.2.43	P	6.5.43	To No. 201 Sqdn
III	DD843	11.3.43	S	30.4.43	To No. 423 (RCAF) Sqdn
III	DD844	13.4.43	Y	14.7.44	To No. 4(C) OTU Alness
III	DD851	18.5.43	Z	19.7.44	To No. 4(C) OTU Alness
III	DD856	6.6.43	G	14.7.44	To No. 4(C) OTU Alness
III	DP178	7.6.43	L	6.7.44	To No. 4(C) OTU Alness
III	DP181	22.3.44	U	3.5.44	To No. 423 (RCAF) Sqdn
III	DP183	8.6.43	W	20.3.44	Missing on operations
III	DP184	8.6.43	F	6.7.44	To No. 4(C) OTU Alness
III	DV992	10.10.43	H	16.7.44	To Calshot
III	EJ133	16.4.44	W	8.7.44	To No. 4(C) OTU Alness
III	EJ137	1.5.43	K	3.5.43	To No. 201 Sqdn
V	EJ138	2.5.45	WH-Y	3.11.45	Damaged at Trondheim
III	EJ155	11.7.44	O	26.4.45	To Short & Harland
III	JM666	26.2.43	Q	17.5.43	To No. 201 Sqdn
III	JM667	25.2.43	V	6.7.44	Damaged by U-boat; To Short Bros
V	ML758	2.5.45	WH-O	2.11.45	To Calshot
III	ML780	6.7.44	A	14.4.45	To Short & Harland
V	ML814	18.4.45	WH-A	6.2.46	To No. 272 MU
V	ML817	18.4.45	WH-X	25.11.45	To Calshot
III	ML818	11.7.44	X	26.4.45	To Short & Harland
III	ML819	30.7.44	V	14.11.44	Damaged at Woodhaven
V	ML824	19.4.45	WH-T	19.9.45	To Calshot
V	ML827	18.4.45	WH-G	12.5.45	Damaged
V	ML878	6.5.45	WH-R	2.46	To Calshot
V	NJ170	19.5.45	WH-L	15.12.45	To No. 272 MU
V	NJ172	3.5.45	WH-F	2.11.45	To Calshot
III	NJ177	6.7.44	F	3.5.45	To Short & Harland
III	NJ178	18.7.44	H	19.3.45	To Short & Harland
III	NJ179	18.7.44	Y	26.4.45	To Short & Harland
III	NJ180	18.7.44	R	5.5.45	To Short & Harland
III	NJ181	19.7.44	Z	4.10.44	Missing on operations
III	NJ188	13.10.44	G	14.4.45	To Short & Harland
V	NJ190	19.4.45	WH-H	16.11.45	To Calshot
III	PP140	23.1.45	V	5.4.45	Damaged
V	RN267	18.7.45	WH-B	25.2.46	To No. 272 MU

Appendix D

Short Sunderland Aircraft with the RNZAF 1944–1967

NZ Serial	RAF No.	Mark	Letter or Name	Arrived	Remarks
NZ4101	ML792	III	*Tainui*	4.12.44	Sold as scrap 3.11.54
NZ4102	ML793	III	*Tokomaru*	4.12.44	" " "
NZ4103	ML794	III	*Mataatua*	4.12.44	" " "
NZ4104	ML795	III	*Takitimu*	4.12.44	" " "
NZ4105	PP110	V	A	13.6.53	Sold 2.8.66. Broken up 1967
NZ4106	RN280	V	B	24.4.54	Reduced to spares 2.10.62
NZ4107	VB883	V	D	22.9.54	Sold August 1967
NZ4108	ML814	V	G	13.6.53	Sold to Ansett 12.12.63
NZ4109	DP191	V	H	21.7.53	Sold as scrap Feb. 1965
NZ4110	PP129	V	J	5.10.53	Scrapped 14.4.64
NZ4111	VB880	V	K	6.9.53	Scrapped at Chatham Is. 4.11.59
NZ4112	VB881	V	L	2.11.53	Off charge 2.4.66
NZ4113	PP124	V	M,P	7.8.54	Sold August 1967
NZ4114	SZ561	V	P	2.8.54	Sold 6.2.67; broken up 1972
NZ4115	SZ584	V	Q	17.11.53	To MOTAT 9.12.66
NZ4116	EJ167	V	S	27.7.53	Sold 6.2.67
NZ4117	RN286	V	T	9.5.54	Crashed 15.4.61; spares 10.8.61
NZ4118	RN306	V	V	13.5.54	Sold as scrap 1965
NZ4119	PP143	V	W	22.4.54	As spares 2.10.63
NZ4120	RN291	V	Z	6.5.54	Sold 2.8.66

Codes: KN No. 5 Sqdn 1949–59
XX MOCU 1955–59

Appendix E

Short S.25 Sunderland GR Mark V's with the SAAF

SAAF Serial	RAF Serial	Code	Remarks
1701	NJ262	Q-RB	Sold 24.3.55 J. Newark & Co
1702	PP125	K-RB	Sold 24.3.55 J. Newark & Co
1703	PP109	H-RB	
1704	RN279	F-RB	Sold 24.3.55 Non-Ferrous Metals
1705	RN296	M-RB	Sold 24.3.55 Non-Ferrous Metals
1706	RN305	O-RB	Sold 12.1.57
1707	NJ258	A-RB	Sold 24.3.55 Non-Ferrous Metals
1708	NJ263	B-RB	Sold 24.3.55 J. Newark & Co
1709	ML798	C-RB	Sold 24.3.55 Non-Ferrous Metals
1710	RN281	D-RB	Made last Sunderland flight 8.10.57
1711	NJ266	G-RB	Sold 24.3.55 Non-Ferrous Metals
1712	PP156	J-RB	Sold 10.3.55
1713	NJ259	L-RB	Sold 24.3.55 J. Newark & Co
1714	RN295	N-RB	Crashed 1.11.56. Sold 8.4.58
1715	PP104	P-RB	Sold 24.3.55 J. Newark & Co
—-	PP153	M	Crashed 26.4.45

Appendix F

RAF Sunderlands – Individual Aircraft

Serial	Units	Remarks
L2158	MAEE-204	KG-M Lost on C/E ex Bathurst 17.8.42
L2159	MAEE-209-230	Damaged at Greenock 7.5.41
L2160	209-230-4COTU	
L2161	210-230	Sunk at Scaramanga in air attack 23.4.41
L2162	210	Crashed during night landing Angle Bay 20.9.38
L2163	210-240-10-228	Driven ashore in gale, Stranraer 15.1.42
L2164	210-230	Set on fire in air raid, St Paul's Bay 10.3.41
L2165	210	Stalled in attempted landing Pembroke Dock 18.9.39
L2166	210-230	Shot down by *Delfino* 3212N 1446E 1.8.41
L2167	210	Shot down 9.4.40 during Oslo fjord recce. DA-H
L2168	210-201-228-4COTU	Crashed 21.11.43 near Nigg, Cromarty Firth
L5798	210-201-204	KG-B Damaged gale, Gibraltar; S.O.C.
L5799	204	KG-D Shot down off Shetlands 8.4.40
L5800	210-201-204-4COTU	Struck off charge (SOC) 2.7.44
L5801	210-230	Dived into sea, Johore Straits 5.6.39
L5802	210-204-201-95-461-4COTU	Crashed, Alness 16.1.43
L5803	210-230-228-95-204-95	Caught fire during refuelling, Jui 22.8.42
L5804	210-230	Broke from moorings in gale, Scaramanga 25.2.41
L5805	228-201-95	Crashed in South Atlantic 8.10.42
L5806	228-210-228-230	Failed to return (FTR) 25.7.42
L5807	228	Fired by Me-109s Kalafrana 27.4.41
N6133	228-201	FTR 9.7.40
N6135	228-210-228	Sank at Angle Bay, Pembroke Dock 10.9.39
N6138	228-201-4COTU	Float lost on landing at Alness, sank 17.7.43
N9020	228	FTR from Ionian Sea 1.11.40
N9021	MAEE-204-201	Crashed on landing, Cromarty Firth 15.12.40
N9022	210-204-210	Crashed on landing, Oban 27.12.40
N9023	228-204	Crashed into Fragjadalsfjall, SE of Reykjavik 24.4.41
N9024	210-204-210-204-95-204-4COTU	SOC 16.8.44
N9025	228-210-228	Shot down by CR42s 6.8.40
N9026	210	FTR from Atlantic 29.6.40
N9027	228-210-95	Sank in gale 11.4.41. Gibraltar
N9028	204	FTR 21.7.40
N9029	230	NM-V crashed 3145N 3228E 1.1.43
N9030	204	Crashed Plymouth Sound 16.10.39
N9044	204-4COTU	SOC 24.7.44
N9045	204	Ditched off Scillies 13.10.39
N9046	204	KG-F Caught fire on moorings, Sullom Voe 11.12.40
N9047	204	KG-B Caught fire at moorings, 10.6.41. Reykjavik
N9048	210-10 RAAF	Burnt out in air raid, Mount Batten 28.11.40
N9049	10 RAAF	Sunk by Me-109s, Malta 10.5.41
N9050	210-10-95-202-95-4COTU	SOC 29.7.44
P9600	210-10-228-4COTU	Scuttled in Loch Ryan 11.12.46
P9601	10 RAAF	Burnt out in air raid, Mount Batten 28.11.40
P9602	210-10	Crashed Lismore Island, Oban 2.9.40
P9603	10 RAAF	Hit rocks, Milford Haven 25.6.41
P9604	10-MAEE-4COTU	Crashed into hangar, Wig Bay 11.6.42
P9605	10-4 COTU	Damaged at Alness 20.10.43; for spares 5.44
P9606	10-201-4COTU	SOC 10.5.44
P9620	204	Ditched in Atlantic 29.10.40
P9621	228-201	Crashed at Scalasaig, Colonsay 9.10.40
P9622	228-201	Crashed into hill, Dunnet Head, 29.10.40
P9623	210-95	Interned Portugal 14.2.41
P9624	210	Crashed on landing, Oban 15.3.41
T9040	204-95-202-95-4COTU	Starboard inner caught fire, Alness 2.7.44
T9041	210-95-201-204-201-204	All engines failed, ditched 28.6.42
T9042	MAEE-4COTU	Mk III prototype; SOC 20.2.45
T9043	210	FTR 2.9.40
T9044	210	Sank during gale at Pembroke Dock 12.11.40

Appendix F (*contd.*)

Serial	Units	Remarks
T9045	204	Ditched 5 mls off Strathy Point, Sutherland 29.10.40
T9046	201-228-95	Damaged by Me-109s at Kalafrana 21.2.42
T9047	10 RAAF	Damaged in ASR 9.7.41, sunk 4815N 0845W by DD
T9048	204-228	Crashed at Kalamata 26.4.41
T9049	204-201-4COTU	Scuttled in Loch Ryan 11.12.46
T9050	230	Crashed at Aboukir 30.9.42
T9070	204	KG-E exploded at moorings Half Die 16.8.42
T9071	10-230	Attacked by E/A, crash-landed Ras Amr 22.12.41
T9072	204-10	Dived into sea off Holyhead 5.12.41
T9073	210-95	Caught fire off Wig Bay 22.6.44
T9074	201-204-95-204	SOC 25.10.43
T9075	210-10	Crashed 5249N 0501W 29.4.41
T9076	210-201-4COTU	SOC 11.7.44
T9077	201-228-4COTU	SOC 29.7.44
T9078	95-4COTU	SOC 24.7.44
T9083	MAEE-201-330-4COTU	Damaged in heavy landing, Alness 19.5.44
T9084	201-202-228	Stalled on landing, Bowmore, May 1942
T9085	202-228-461	FTR. 21.1.43
T9086	228-10-228	SOC 28.2.43
T9087	201	ZM-O SOC 4.2.44
T9088	228-461-228-4COTU	FTR 17.2.44
T9089	228	Struck water on landing, Oban 29.5.42
T9090	461	Crashed during ASR, Biscay 12.8.42
T9109	461-228	Damaged by JM720 in gale, Wig Bay 25.1.44
T9110	10 RAAF	Heavy landing, Plymouth Sound 5.1.44
T9111	461	Crashed after take-off, Hamworthy 21.3.43
T9112	228-330-228	SOC 12.4.44
T9113	461	Shot down in Biscay 1.9.42
T9114	461	Crashed during take-off, Angle Bay 29.5.43
T9115	461-4COTU	SOC 16.8.44
W3976	MAEE	Crashed off Helensburgh 28.11.41
W3977	201	Crashed off Donegal 5.2.42
W3978	204-201	Crashed on landing, Sullom Voe 11.8.41
W3979	10 RAAF	Force-landed off St Govans Head, 2.3.42
W3980	201-4COTU	Became 4908M, 4.11.44
W3981	204-201-240-4COTU	SOC 1.7.44
W3982	201	FTR 21.8.41
W3983	10-202-10	Became 4603M, 16.6.44
W3984	10 RAAF	SOC 20.6.44
W3985	10 RAAF	FTR 18.8.43
W3986	110-228-10	RB-U Crashed 4 mls NW Eddystone Light 20.5.43
W3987	201-230	Crashed on take-off, Aboukir 7.9.42
W3988	201	Crashed at Doonbeg, Co. Clare 3.12.41
W3989	202-228-202-228-4OTU-302FTU	SOC 23.2.45
W3990	228-202-4COTU	Sank during gale, Alness 15.2.43
W3991	228	To 5016M, Jan. 1945
W3992	228-4COTU	Sank during gale, Alness 13.2.43
W3993	10 RAAF	Struck by W4024, 7.10.43
W3994	10-202-10	FTR 30.7.42
W3995	228	Ran aground Lough Erne 10.1.43. Sank 11.1.43
W3996	228	Bombed at Kalafrana 2.2.42
W3997	201-10-2011-4COTU	Crashed 4 mls N. of Portsoy, Banff 12.10.43
W3998	201	Crashed 200 yds from Breakwater Fort, 21.12.41
W3999	10 RAAF	RB-Y Shot down by Ar.196 over Biscay 21.6.42
W4000	201	Ditched and blew up 5 mls from convoy 1.8.42
W4001	201	Hit rock in Lough Erne 4.10.42
W4002	201-302FTU	SOC 22.2.45
W4003	10-201-302FTU-272	Damaged during storm, Killadeas 21.9.45
W4004	10-202-10	FTR from Biscay 17.5.43, RB-Z
W4017	228-302FTU	SOC 19.1.45
W4018	201	Scrapped May 1945
W4019	10 RAAF	FTR from Biscay 9.8.42
W4020	10 RAAF	Shot down by U-454, Biscay 2.8.43
W4021	230	Sank 7/8.11.43
W4022	230	SOC 3.1.45

Appendix F (*contd.*)

Serial	Units	Remarks
W4023	230	SOC 29.8.46
W4024	202-119-10	Scrapped March 1947
W4025	201	Shot down by convoy WS21 31.7.42
W4026	228	Crashed at Dunbeath, 25.8.42
W4027	4COTU	Caught fire during take-off, sank Alness, 5.3.44
W4028	202-119-4COTU	SOC 12.7.45
W4029	202	Crashed during landing Gibraltar, 22.8.42
W4030	202-119-10	Struck boat during take-off, Mount Batten 16.9.44
W4031	4COTU	SOC 12.7.45
W4032	228	Ditched 5 mls off Tiree 4.9.42
W4033	4COTU	SOC 28.2.45
W4034	4COTU	Scrapped Feb. 1947
W4035	4COTU	Crashed on landing, Cromarty Firth 11.8.42
W4036	201	Crashed on landing, Lough Erne 18.11.43
W4037	202-4COTU	Converted to Sandringham
W6000	423	Sank during gale, Wig Bay 13.12.42
W6001	423-119-4COTU	Sank during gale, Alness April 1943
W6002	202-119-4COTU	SOC 14.7.44
W6003	202	Float lost Gibraltar 12.8.42. Sank
W6004	228	Struck Catalina, Loch Ryan 29.12.42. Sank
W6005	201-4COTU	SOC 27.3.45
W6006	423-4COTU-423-4COTU	Crashed at Alness 13.8.44
W6007	423-131 OCU	Scrapped Feb. 1947
W6008	423	Ditched 5300N 1400W 12.3.44
W6009	423-4COTU	Crashed Dornoch Firth 14.1.45
W6010	201-4COTU	Crashed Allarton Farm, Cromarty 27.7.44
W6011	423-131 OTU	Scrapped Feb. 1947
W6012	204-4 COTU	SOC 12.7.45
W6013	423	Crashed on Knocklayd Mountain, Antrim 5.12.43
W6014	201-4COTU	SOC 12.7.45
W6015	204-95-4COTU	Scrapped Sept 1947
W6016	95 or 204	Missing en route to Gibraltar 28.11.42
W6026	422-4COTU	Port wing broken on landing, Alness 22.3.45
W6027	422-330-4COTU	SOC 28.4.45
W6028	422	Crashed at St Angelo 19.2.44
W6029	422	Crashed on landing, Oban 19.12.42
W6030	422-330	SOC 10.7.44
W6031	422	FTR 20.11.43
W6032	422-131 OTU	Scrapped Feb. 1947
W6033	422	Crashed in Hvalfjord, Iceland 28.9.43
W6050	MAEE-461	Damaged in gale, Pembroke Dock 24.1.44
W6051	MAEE-201-4COTU	SOC 10.7.44
W6052	423-330	FTR 5.6.43
W6053	423-330	SOC 30.4.45
W6054	10 RAAF	Crashed Plymouth Sound 13.11.42
W6055	201	Scuttled in Loch Ryan 11.12.46
W6056	246-4COTU-131 OTU	To 4782M May 1944
W6057	246	Scuttled in Loch Ryan 16.3.45
W6058	246	To 4798M June 1944
W6059	201-330	SOC 5.4.44
W6060	246-4COTU	Broke back on landing, Alness 27.11.43
W6061	423-330	SOC 16.2.44
W6062	95	SOC 11.11.43
W6063	204-95	Crashed on ASR 0430N 1712W 30.3.43
W6064	423-330-4COTU	SOC 13.11.44
W6065	95	Force-landed off Oporto 5.3.43
W6066	246-422-131 OTU	Scrapped Feb. 1947
W6067	330	SOC 5.2.45
W6068	330-423-131 OTU	Scrapped Feb. 1947
W6075	330	Crashed in Lough Neagh 12.5.43
W6076	95	SOC 21.6.45
W6077	461	SOC 20.12.45
W6078	230	SOC 16.8.45
W6079	204	Crashed on take-off, Port Etienne 2.10.43
W6080	308FTU	SOC 3.9.43

Appendix F (*contd.*)

Serial	Units	Remarks
DD828	423-201-4COTU	SOC 25.3.45
DD829	201-131 OTU	Scrapped March 1947
DD830	228	Crashed 2 mls W of Ailsa Craig 3.2.43
DD831	422	Broke adrift in gale Loch Indaal, Islay 25.1.44
DD832	MAEE-4COTU	Scrapped March 1947
DD833	204-F1.7E-1FBSU	Float collapsed, Wig Bay 10.9.43
DD834	204-228	Sold June 1945
DD835	330-201-228-131 OTU-228 -131 OTU-228	SOC 12.7.45
DD836	228	Sank in gale, St. Mary's, Scillies 24.1.44
DD837	228	FTR from Biscay 15.5.43
DD838	228-423-422-4COTU	SOC June 1945
DD839	4COTU	Undershot at Alness and overturned 27.11.43
DD840	4COTU	SOC 26.3.47
DD841	4COTU	Sold 30.6.44
DD842	4COTU	SOC 12.7.45
DD843	330-423-131 OTU-4OTU	SOC 12.7.45
DD844	330-4COTU	SOC 28.4.45
DD845	246-422-131 OTU	Scrapped Feb. 1947
DD846	246-422	Crashed 5347N 1060W off Clare Is. 25.5.43
DD847	228-131 OTU	Scrapped Feb. 1947
DD848	201	Struck hill, Brandon Head, Kerry 22.8.43
DD849	423-131 OTU	Scrapped Feb. 1947
DD850	422-4COTU	Scrapped Feb. 1947
DD851	330-4COTU	Crashed on rly 2 mls NE Invergordon 26.11.44
DD852	10 RAAF	Struck by ship, Plymouth Sound 2.9.44
DD853	423-131 OTU-461	SOC 21.6.45
DD854	422-131 OTU	SOC 23.5.45
DD855	201-422-4COTU	Caught fire on take-off, landed and sank Alness 20.4.45
DD856	330-4COTU	Cylinder blew off, landed 3.5.45
DD857	201	Crashed on landing, Lough Erne 30.6.43
DD858	201-423	Hull split on landing, Lough Neagh 23.10.43
DD859	423	Shot down by U-489 6111N 1438W 4.8.43
DD860	423	To G-AHEP 19.3.45
DD861	422	Ditched 4405N 1030W 3.9.43
DD862	423	Caught fire 10 mls W of base, sank 31.5.45
DD863	423	Ditched 5430N 0930W 13.11.43
DD864	228	FTR from Biscay 14.12.43
DD865	10 RAAF	SOC 5.6.45
DD866	461-302FTU-FE	SOC 16.8.45
DD867	10-423-131 OTU	SOC 5.3.45
DP176	119	Ditched in Bay of Biscay 15.4.43
DP177	10 RAAF	FTR from Biscay 11.8.43
DP178	422-330-4COTU	Missing from night exercise, Alness 14.3.45
DP179	119-10	Ditched 20 mls SW of Scillies? 3.10.43
DP180	230	SOC 31.1.46
DP181	330-423	Bow split open in landing, Lough Erne 11.11.43
DP182	302-343	Ditched in South Atlantic 2.2.44
DP183	330	FTR 20.3.44
DP184	330-4COTU	SOC 12.7.45
DP185	201-4COTU	SOC 25.3.45
DP186	95	Scrapped Feb. 1947
DP187	308FTU-343	Retained by Aéronavale June 1945
DP188	204	Scrapped Feb. 1947
DP189	230	SOC 16.8.45
DP190	270	SOC 21.6.45
DP191	423-131 OTU	To NZ4109 19.6.53
DP192	10 RAAF	To RAAF 15.2.44
DP193	201-423-131 OTU	SOC 26.3.47
DP194	302FTU-95	SOC 21.6.45
DP195	- - -	Sold 22.1.48
DP196	461-201	SOC 26.3.47
DP197	4COTU	Crashed at Lothbeg, Sutherland 15.8.44
DP198	423-209-205-201-209	SOC 1.6.59
DP199	461-88	SOC 30.6.51

Appendix F (*contd.*)

Serial	Units	Remarks
DP200	461-4COTU-230	Scrapped Oct. 1957
DV956	95-302FTU-95	Ditched 1251N 2156W 30.4.45
DV957	95	Crashed W. of Wellington, Sierra Leone 3.9.42
DV958	202-119-228-10	SOC 26.4.46
DV959	204	Scuttled June 1945
DV960	461-131 OTU	SOC 31.5.45
DV961	461-4COTU	To 4666, March 1944
DV962	202-119-461	Caught fire at moorings, Pembroke Dock 7.6.43
DV963	95	SOC 13.7.45
DV964	95	Sold 21.6.45
DV965	204-F1.7E-343	Damaged in gale, Wig Bay 21.9.45
DV966	204	Damaged in gale, Wig Bay 21.9.45
DV967	MAEE-228	FTR 13.6.43. Shot down by U-564
DV968	461	Shot down by Ju-88s, Biscay 13.8.43
DV969	10 RAAF	FTR 21.9.43. Shot down by Ju-88s
DV970	228-422-4COTU	SOC 25.4.45
DV971	119	FTR from 4750N 0840W 15.12.42
DV972	119	Damaged by own DC; ditched in Bristol Channel 25.11.42
DV973	95	Crashed at Bathurst, 13.4.44
DV974	204-95-204	Crashed at Bathurst, 1.10.43
DV975	95	Crashed at Jui, Sierra Leone 3.11.42
DV976	MAEE	Ditched off Southend 21.10.47
DV977	228	FTR from Biscay 12.7.43; shot down by Ju-88s
DV978	246-228-423-131 OTU	Float damaged, Lough Erne 3.12.44
DV979	246	Crashed on landing, Loch Indaal, Islay 24.1.43
DV980	246-228-423-131 OTU	SOC 14.6.45
DV985	461-308FTU-343	Crashed off Goree Is. West Africa 26.4.44
DV986	461-308FTU-343	Crashed off Port Etienne 19.9.43
DV987	308FTU-343	SOC 21.6.45
DV988	228-422-4COTU	SOC 26.3.47
DV989	461-131 OTU	SOC 28.6.45
DV990	422	FTR 24.5.44. Shot down by U-boat 6334N 0302E
DV991	204	Lost float, DCs exploded, Jui 13.7.44
DV992	330-4COTU	Struck buoy and sank, Alness 6.11.44
DV993	10 RAAF	FTR from Biscay 17.11.43
DV994	422-4COTU	SOC 26.3.47
DW104	204	SOC 26.3.47
DW105	95	Crashed at Port Etienne 5.1.44
DW106	270	Missing en route to Gibraltar 18.12.43
DW107	95	Sank at Bathurst 15.10.44
DW108	270	Crashed at Jui 27.9.44
DW109	270	Scrapped March 1947
DW110	228	Crashed into Blue Stack Mountain, Donegal 31.1.44
DW111	270-228-423-4COTU	Scrapped March 1947
DW112	423-302FTU-230	SOC 29.8.46
DW113	10 RAAF	SOC 28.12.45
EJ131	230	Missing 20.8.43; crashed in Mozambique
EJ132	461-230	SOC 29.5.45
EJ133	119-461	SOC December 1944
EJ134	461	Combat with 8x Ju-88s; beached at Marazion 2.6.43
EJ135	230-302FTU-490	To Aéronavale June 1945
EJ136	230	SOC 15.4.45
EJ137	246-330-201-4COTU	SOC 28.6.45
EJ138	119-208FTU-461-330	Ran onto rocks, Trondheim 2.11.45
EJ139	246-228	FTR 24.5.43; shot down by U-441
EJ140	230	Struck hill in Kenya 29.12.43
EJ141	230-205	Force-landed Maldive Is. 31.3.45
EJ142	119-461-4COTU	SOC 12.7.45
EJ143	230	SOC 12.3.45
EJ144	95	Sank at Bathurst 15.10.44
EJ145	204	Ditched 100 mls NW of Port Etienne 17.7.43
EJ149	4COTU	SOC 26.3.47
EJ150	201	SOC 23.3.47
EJ151	201-228-422	SOC 28.6.45
EJ152	4COTU	To Min. of Supply 9.9.48

Appendix F (*contd.*)

Serial	Units	Remarks
EJ153	461-235 OCU-230	SOC 1.11.56
EJ154	461	Struck marine craft Pembroke Dock 13.12.44
EJ155	230-4COTU-88-209-205	Scrapped Oct. 1957
EJ156	423	Sold 13.5.47
EJ157	423	Engine on fire Castle Archdale 12.5.45. SOC
EJ158	423	SOC 26.3.47
EJ163	302FTU-95-343	To Aéronavale June 1945
EJ164	308FTU-270	Ditched 0457N 0335W 3.10.44
EJ165	302FTU-490	Scrapped March 1947
EJ166	-	
EJ167	-	To RNZAF 4.6.53 (NZ4116)
EJ168	302FTU-343	To Aéronavale June '45
EJ169	302FTU-95	Scrapped March 1947
EJ170	- -	Sold 13.5.47
EJ171	302FTU	Sold 22.1.48
EJ172	302FTU	Sold 2.6.47
EK572	228	FTR from Biscay 11.11.43
EK573	10 RAAF-4COTU	SOC 23.3.47
EK574	10 RAAF	Struck buoy, sank, Plymouth Sound 1.6.44
EK575	461-228-423-10	SOC 30.11.45
EK576	422-4COTU	SOC 12.7.45
EK577	461-4COTU	SOC 15.7.45
EK578	461	Shot down by six Ju-88s, Biscay 16.9.43
EK579	201-131 OTU	Sold 22.1.48
EK580	204	Crashed in night landing, Bathurst 9.10.44
EK581	423	SOC 26.3.47
EK582	204	Scuttled 21.6.45
EK583	423-131 OTU	SOC March 1947
EK584	270	SOC 2.6.45
EK585	270	Caught fire at moorings, Apapa 7.6.44
EK586	10 RAAF	SOC 31.12.45
EK587	95	To Aéronavale June 1945
EK588	270	Crashed en route to W. Africa 8.1.44
EK589	170	SOC 9.7.45
EK590	201-461-4COTU	SOC 26.3.47
EK591	422-4COTU	SOC 2.11.45
EK592	270	Scrapped March 1947
EK593	302FTU-270	Scrapped March 1947
EK594	201-422-10 RAAF	SOC 12.8.45
EK595	302FTU-201-422-Iraq Flt	Damaged in collision, Basra 5.3.46; scuttled 1.4.46
EK596	302FTU	Scrapped March 1947
JM659	230	Struck by whirlwind, Brahmaputra river, 4.7.44
JM660	- -	To BOAC 8.1.43
JM661	- -	To BOAC 15.1.43
JM662	- -	To BOAC 16.1.43
JM663	- -	To BOAC 21.1.43
JM664	- -	To BOAC 29.1.43
JM665	- -	To BOAC 29.1.43
JM666	330-201-423-131 OTU	Scrapped March 1947
JM667	330-302FTU-209-205	SOC 8.10.54
JM668	4COTU	Scrapped 10.3.47
JM669	204	Ditched S. of Port Etienne 14.4.43
JM670	95-343	SOC 21.6.45
JM671	95	SOC 21.6.45
JM672	204	Crashed after take-off, Jui, 28.8.44
JM673	230	Recalled in bad weather; FTR. 28.11.44
JM674	204-343	To 1 F11; SOC 21.6.45
JM675	461	Nosed in during Biscay ASR; 28.5.43
JM676	119-461	Shot down over Biscay 29.11.43
JM677	95	SOC 21.6.45
JM678	228-461-228-10 RAAF	Caught fire at moorings, sank Mount Batten 19.6.44
JM679	228-422-4COTU	SOC 6.7.45
JM680	204	Struck W6062 at take-off, sank Half Die 31.5.43
JM681	MAEE	Sold 8.5.47
JM682	204	Scrapped Feb. 1947

Appendix F (*contd.*)

Serial	Units	Remarks
JM683	461-4COTU	SOC 12.7.45
JM684	10 RAAF	SOC 12.7.45
JM685	461-228-10 RAAF	SOC 7.12.45
JM686	461-4COTU	SOC 28.6.45
JM687	204	FTR 18.7.43
JM688	30FTU-343	SOC 21.6.45
JM689	308FTU-343	To Aéronavale 6.45.(1 F 8)
JM704	308FTU-343	(1 F 2) Crashed Dakar 5.2.44
JM705	308FTU	(1 F 1) Crashed Dakar 22.10.43
JM706	308FTU	(1 F 6) SOC 21.6.45
JM707	461	Shot down by E/A over Biscay 30.8.43
JM708	228	Ditched after engine fire, Biscay 17.1.44
JM709	228	FTR from Biscay 6.1.44
JM710	204	Crashed into sea, Half Die 22.9.43
JM711	308FTU-230-Iraq Flt	SOC 29.8.46
JM712	422	Shot down by U-470 17.10.43, 5900N 2900W
JM713	MAEE-4COTU	Sold 25.8.47
JM714	MAEE-302FTU	Sold 22.1.48
JM715		Sold 30.4.47, now at Southampton Museum.
JM716		To BOAC 7.3.45
JM717	302FTU-490	SOC 21.6.45
JM718	4COTU-230-235 OCU-FBTS230	Scrapped 4.10.57
JM719	302FTU	Sold May 1947
JM720	228-302FTU	Sold 1.10.46
JM721	10 RAAF-57MU	Sunk in Loch Ryan 17.11.44
JM722		To BOAC 21.8.43
ML725		To BOAC 27.8.43
ML726		To BOAC 2.9.43
ML727		To BOAC 3.9.43
ML728		To BOAC 8.9.43
ML729		To BOAC 15.9.43
ML730		To RAAF 11.11.43 (A26-1)
ML731		To RAAF 11.11.43 (A26-2)
ML732		To RAAF 11.11.43 (A26-3)
ML733		To RAAF 11.11.43 (A26-4)
ML734		To RAAF 11.11.43 (A26-5)
ML735	MAEE-461	FTR 2.10.44
ML736	4COTU	SOC 26.3.47
ML737	4COTU	Crashed in Cromarty Firth 3.2.45
ML738	4COTU	Crashed on take-off, Cromarty Firth 3.1.45
ML739	201-461-4COTU-302FTU	To Aéronavale 19.2.52
ML740	461	Attacked by nine Ju-88s; ditched Biscay 23.3.44
ML741	461-4COTU-CCIS-4COTU -302FTU	Scrapped 12.4.50
ML742	201	Scrapped 26.3.47
ML743	461-201	Struck mountain nr Killybegs, Co Donegal 14.3.45
ML744	461	SOC 26.3.47
ML745	228-88-205	SOC 24.5.57
ML746	461-423	SOC 26.3.47
ML747	461-4COTU	SOC 31.7.46
ML748	461	Damaged by heavy seas, sank Scillies 11.6.44
ML749	201-228-4COTU	Scrapped March 1947
ML750	422	To Aéronavale 26.7.47
ML751		To BOAC 13.1.44
ML752		To BOAC 21.1.44
ML753		To BOAC 23.1.44
ML754		To BOAC 2.2.44
ML755		To BOAC 3.2.44
ML756		To BOAC 3.2.44
ML757	461-4COTU-302FTU	To Aéronavale 19.6.51
ML758	461-330	Scrapped March 1947
ML759	201-422	Scrapped 26.3.47
ML760	201	Shot down by U-boat? 4815N 0545W 12.6.44
ML761		Sold 18.3.46
ML762	228	FTR from Biscay 10.6.44

Appendix F (*contd.*)

Serial	Units	Remarks
ML763	228-ASWDU-230	SOC 30.9.57
ML764	201	To Aéronavale 29.7.51
ML765	MAEE	SOC 6.11.47
ML766	228	Lost float, capsized, sank Pembroke Dock 14.11.44
ML767	228-4COTU	Scrapped March 1947
ML768	201	Scrapped 31.5.55
ML769	201-228-422	Sold 25.8.47
ML770	228	Struck rock, Scillies, sank 21.2.45
ML771	461	Scrapped March 1947
ML772	201-88	SOC 30.6.55
ML773	422	SOC 26.3.47
ML774	228-461	Struck by ship in gale, sank Pembroke Dock 18.1.45
ML777	422-423	Scrapped 24.1.47
ML778	422-461-201-4COTU	To Aéronavale 12.5.51
ML779	4COTU	To Aéronavale 27.4.51
ML780	330-4COTU-235OCU	Scrapped 11.8.48
ML781	422-461-4COTU-CCIS	To Aéronavale 14.4.51
ML782	201-228	Crash-landed Mount Batten 11.12.44
ML783	201-423-201	Sold 15.4.46
ML784	423-201	Sold 12.4.46
ML785	ASWDU	Sold 22.8.47
ML786		To BOAC 12.7.44
ML787		To BOAC 25.7.44
ML788		To BOAC 28.7.44
ML789		To BOAC 28.7.44
ML790		To BOAC 3.8.44
ML791		to BOAC 11.8.44
ML792	302 FTU	To RNZAF 18.10.44 (NZ4101)
ML793	302 FTU	To RNZAF 23.10.44 (NZ4102)
ML794	302 FTU	To RNZAF 18.10.44 (NZ4103)
ML795	302 FTU	To RNZAF 27.10.44 (NZ4104)
ML796	4COTU	To Aéronavale 4.8.51; now at Duxford
ML797	308 FTU-230-205	SOC 30.6.59
ML798		To SAAF 31.5.45 (1709 C)
ML799	302 FTU-FE	To Aéronavale 4.6.51
ML800	302 FTU-230	To Aéronavale 28.7.57
ML801	4COTU-302FTU	Scrapped March 1947
ML807		Sold 19.9.46
ML808	131 OTU	Sold 22.8.47
ML809	302 FTU	Sold 7.9.46
ML810	302 FTU-490	SOC 21.6.45
ML811	302 FTU	Missing en route to E. Africa 3.6.44; wrecked in Congo
ML812	228-201-4COTU-302FTU	SOC 30.6.55
ML813	10 RAAF-201	Scrapped 26.3.47
ML814	201-422-330	To RNZAF 26.5.53 (NZ4108). Airworthy 1991
ML815	228	SOC 30.9.45
ML816	422-4COTU	To Aéronavale 10.8.51
ML817	MAEE-201-423-330-235 OCU-230	SOC 16.10.57
ML818	330	Sold 30.5.46
ML819	330	To Aéronavale 30.8.51
ML820	4COTU	To Aéronavale 23.11.51
ML821	422	To Aéronavale 26.9.51
ML822	10 RAAF	SOC 12.7.45
ML823	423	Crashed NW of Donegal Bay 6.9.44
ML824	201-330	To Aéronavale 26.10.51; now at Hendon
ML825	423	Scrapped 26.3.47
ML826	4COTU	To 6100M July 1946
ML827	461-330	Ditched 6109N 0914W 12.5.45; crew rescued
ML828	10 RAAF	Transferred to civil use 15.7.46
ML829	10 RAAF	Crashed on take-off Mount Batten 9.2.45
ML830	10 RAAF	Scrapped March 1947
ML831	10 RAAF-461	Hit by ship in gale Pembroke Dock 18.1.45
ML835	302 FTU-490	To Aéronavale June 1945
ML836	422-131 OTU	SOC 31.5.45
ML837	302 FTU-95	SOC 21.6.45

Appendix F (contd.)

Serial	Units	Remarks
ML838		To BOAC 5.4.46
ML839	10 RAAF	Sank in Plymouth Sound during gale 12.10.44
ML840		Sold 2.6.47
ML841	4COTU-302FTU-343	To Aéronavale June 1945
ML842	131 OTU	SOC 6.9.45
ML843		Sold 23.5.46
ML844	270	SOC 21.6.45
ML845	302 FTU	Ditched on ferry trip; towed, sunk 2758N 1251W by gunfire 23.7.44
ML846	302 FTU-230	SOC 13.9.45
ML847	302 FTU-95	SOC 21.6.45
ML848	10 RAAF	SOC 26.3.47
ML849	302 FTU-270	Scrapped March 1947
ML850	302 FTU-490	Scrapped March 1947
ML851	302 FTU-343	SOC 21.6.45
ML852	302 FTU-490	Ditched off Cape St Mary, West Africa 14.7.44
ML853	302 FTU-270	Scrapped March 1947
ML854	302 FTU-204-343	To Aéronavale June 1945
ML855	302 FTU	Crashed 30 mls N of St Louis, Senegal 17.7.44
ML856	10 RAAF	SOC 30.11.45
ML857	302 FTU-490-270	SOC 21.6.45
ML858	302 FTU	Crashed on SW of St Kilda 8.6.44
ML859	302 FTU-490	SOC 21.6.45
ML860	302 FTU	Ditched 2725N 1320W 23.7.44
ML861	302 FTU-230	SOC 28.6.45
ML862	302 FTU-490-204	SOC 21.6.45
ML863	302 FTU-490	SOC 21.6.45
ML864	302 FTU-490	SOC 16.5.45
ML865	302 FTU-230-SF	SOC 28.6.45
ML866	4COTU	To Aéronavale 19.11.51
ML867	302 FTU	SOC 21.6.45
ML868	302 FTU-230	SOC 31.1.46
ML869	302 FTU-490	Scrapped March 1947
ML870	302 FTU-343	SOC 21.6.45
ML871	302 FTU-343	SOC 21.6.45
ML872	302 FTU-204	To Aéronavale 14.12.51
ML873	4 COTU	Scrapped 31.8.55
ML874	302FTU-270	SOC 21.6.45
ML875	201-4COTU	SOC 6.11.47
ML876	201	Sold 29.3.46
ML877	228	To Aéronavale 8.1.51
ML878	228-330	SOC 25.9.47
ML879	228-461-422	Sold 17.11.47
ML880	228	Shot down in flames by U-333, 11.6.44
ML881	201-209	SOC 30.9.57
ML882	201-4COTU-88-209	SOC 31.10.56
ML883	422-423	Struck by surface craft, sank Calshot, 17.12.44
ML884	422	SOC 26.3.47
NJ170	422-330	To Aéronavale 25.5.51
NJ171	228	To BOAC 8.5.46
NJ172	422-330	SOC 30.9.47
NJ173	422	SOC 26.3.47
NJ174	422	SOC 26.3.47
NJ175	422	Prop. lost after take-off, crashed at Belleek, Fermanagh 12.8.44
NJ176	422-88	Crashed on take-off, Seletar 21.11.49
NJ177	330-209	Damaged 19.8.54
NJ178	330	SOC 26.3.47
NJ179	330	Sold 10.4.46
NJ180	330-FBTS	Damaged 23.2.54; to 7146M
NJ181	330	FTR 4.10.44
NJ182	423-ASWDU	To Aéronavale 8.1.52
NJ183	423	Caught fire after take-off; crashed 3 mls E of Irvinestown 11.2.45
NJ184	423	Overshot at Lough Erne, ran aground 8.5.45
NJ185	423	SOC 26.3.47
NJ186	423	Crash-landed Jurby 20.5.45
NJ187	423	SOC 30.4.57

Appendix F (*contd.*)

Serial	Units	Remarks
NJ188	330	Sold 20.5.46
NJ189	422	SOC 26.3.47
NJ190	201-330	To Aéronavale 19.2.52
NJ191	228-4COTU-209-205	SOC 30.11.56
NJ192	228-201-4COTU	SOC 20.2.46
NJ193	461-10-201-205	SOC 28.2.57
NJ194	201	Scrapped 31.8.53
NJ253	10 RAAF	To BOAC 1.11.45
NJ254	10 RAAF-209	SOC 31.8.55
NJ255	10 RAAF	Sold 9.4.46
NJ256	10 RAAF	SOC 12.7.45
NJ257	4 COTU	Sold 29.4.46
NJ258	302 FTU-4COTU-302FTU	To SAAF 5.45 (1707 A)
NJ259	302 FTU	To SAAF 26.4.45 (1713 L-RB)
NJ260	302 FTU-209	Struck hill 20 m SW Mombasa 14.5.45
NJ261	302 FTU-209	SOC 30.5.46
NJ262	302 FTU	To SAAF 31.5.45 (1701 Q-RB)
NJ263	302 FTU	To SAAF 4.45 (1708 B-RB)
NJ264	461-10-201-230	SOC 28.10.48
NJ265	302 FTU-209-235 OCU	SOC 31.8.55
NJ266	302 FTU	To SAAF 13.6.45 (1711 G-RB)
NJ267	461-10-201-209-201	Crashed on take-off Pembroke Dock 3.3.54
NJ268	461-10-201-CCIS-205	Sank at Wig Bay? 17.9.50
NJ269	4 COTU	To 5753M Dec. 1945
NJ270	302 FTU-205	Scrapped March 1947
NJ271	302 FTU	SOC 20.9.45
NJ272	302 FTU-240-205-209-88-205	SOC 31.5.57
NJ273	302 FTU-240	SOC 6.11.47
NJ274	302 FTU-205	SOC 6.11.47
NJ275	302 FTU-240-209	SOC 30.9.57
NJ276	302 FTU-240-209	Crashed at Seletar 14.7.48
NJ277	302 FTU-230	Crashed into hill 0136N 103°33E, 15.10.45
PP103	302 FTU-209	Crashed Seletar 27.3.46; engine failure at 200 ft
PP104	302 FTU	To SAAF 31.5.45 (1715 P-RB)
PP105	302FTU-209	SOC 10.3.47
PP106	302 FTU-209	SOC 10.3.47
PP107	302 FTU-209-205	Struck Mt. Morrison, Taiwan 28.1.51
PP108	302 FTU-209	Scrapped 10.3.47
PP109	MAEE-302 FTU	To SAAF 13.6.45 (1703 H-RB)
PP110		To RNZAF 15.1.45 (NZ4105)
PP111	4 COTU	Airframe strained at 1,800 ft, 5.12.45 SOC
PP112	4 COTU-201-209	SOC 30.6.58
PP113	4 COTU-461-10-201	Dived into sea 20 m N of Inishtrahull Is. 5.7.47
PP114	461-10-201-209-88	SOC 31.8.55
PP115	461-10-230-201-230-201	SOC 30.6.55
PP116	461	Crashed on take-off Pembroke Dock 16.5.45
PP117	228-201-230-201	SOC 4.10.57
PP118	228-201-230-235 OCU	Damaged 8.2.50
PP119	461-10-201	SOC 6.11.47
PP120	228-201	SOC 27.3.47
PP121	228-201-57MU	Dragged moorings in gale, Wig Bay 19.2.46
PP122	461-10-201-ASWDU-201	SOC 15.9.54
PP123	302 FTU-205	Sank during gale, Wig Bay 2.12.48
PP124	302 FTU-205	To RNZAF (NZ4113) 7.8.54
PP125	302 FTU	To SAAF 9.6.45 (1702 K-RB)
PP126	302 FTU-240	SOC 11.8.47
PP127	205	SOC 1.6.57
PP128	302 FTU-205	SOC 10.3.47
PP129	302 FTU-205	To RNZAF 1.7.53 (NZ4110)
PP130	302 FTU-240-235 OCU	SOC 30.6.55
PP131	302 FTU-240	SOC 1.9.53
PP132	302 FTU-209	Overshot on to beach, Kai Tak 21.4.46
PP135	10 RAAF	SOC 12.7.45
PP136	228	Struck by ship in gale, Pembroke Dock 18.1.45
PP137	4 COTU-205	SOC 11.2.57

Appendix F (*contd.*)

Serial	Units	Remarks
PP138	10 RAAF	Lost prop in flight, ditched 4.3.45; SOC 10.3.47
PP139	10 RAAF	SOC 10.3.47
PP140	330	Crashed 6312N 0912N off Faeroes 5.4.45
PP141	4COTU-235 OCU	SOC 31.8.55
PP142	10 RAAF	To BOAC 22.6.49
PP143		To RNZAF 19.1.54 (NZ4119)
PP144	228-201-205	SOC 30.6.55
PP145	302 FTU-230	Struck by PP117 29.4.46
PP146	302 FTU-230	SOC 6.11.47
PP147	302 FTU-230	SOC 16.10.57
PP148	302 FTU-209-205-88	Crashed during storm Iwakuni 25.3.53
PP149	302 FTU-230	SOC 21.5.54
PP150	302 FTU-209	SOC 26.9.46
PP151	302 FTU-209-MAEE	SOC 31.10.56
PP152	302 FTU-209-230	SOC 26.9.46
PP153	302 FTU	To SAAF 25.4.45 'M' (Crashed after delivery)
PP154	302 FTU-205-209	SOC 30.9.57
PP155	302 FTU-230-88-230	Crashed off Faeroes 23.10.54
PP156	302 FTU	To SAAF 31.5.45 (1712 J-RB)
PP157	302 FTU	SOC 25.4.46
PP158	302 FTU-230	Struck object in Kuantan river 3.10.45
PP159	302 FTU-209	SOC 6.11.47
PP160	4 COTU	SOC 24.4.47
PP161	4 COTU-230	SOC 6.11.47
PP162	461-10-201-MAEE	Sold 18.6.53
PP163	228-201-235 OCU	SOC 16.10.57
PP164	228-201-230-209	Damaged 19.7.50
RN264	302 FTU-209	Dragged moorings in typhoon, Kai Tak 19.7.46
RN265	302FTU-209	Struck buoy at Seletar 23.1.46; beached
RN266	302 FTU-209201-235 OCU-FBTS	SOC 30.9.57
RN267	330	SOC 6.11.47
RN268	302 FTU-230	SOC 4.5.53
RN269	302 FTU-230-201-205	SOC 28.6.53
RN270	201-230-205	SOC 25.9.58
RN271	235 OCU-201	Struck rock near St Peter Port 15.9.54, scrapped 30.9.57
RN272	201-4 COTU-235 OCU	To 6534M April 1948
RN273	201-205	SOC 12.3.57
RN277	228-201-88	SOC 14.10.51
RN278	228-201-230-205	SOC 27.8.56
RN279	461-302 FTU	To SAAF 13.6.45 (1704 F-RB)
RN280	461-302 FTU	To RNZAF 21.12.53 (NZ4106)
RN281	302 FTU	To SAAF 1.6.45 (1710 D-RB)
RN282	461-10-201-88-209-205	SOC 13.5.58
RN283	228	Tail blown off by own DCs 5222N 0550W 27.4.45
RN284	201-235 OCU-201	To Aéronavale 18.12.57
RN285	228-201-4 COTU	SOC 4.5.53
RN286	4 COTU	To RNZAF 3.10.53 (NZ4117)
RN287	4 COTU	SOC 31.7.46
RN288	302 FTU-205-235 OCU-201	Crashed off Eastbourne 4.6.55
RN289	302 FTU	SOC 6.11.47
RN290	302 FTU-205-230	SOC 30.1.54
RN291	302 FTU-240	To RNZAF 15.2.54 (NZ1120)
RN292	302 FTU-240	Caught fire, Wig Bay 14.10.48
RN293	302 FTU-205-209-88-209-205	SOC 17.8.56
RN294	302 FTU-205	SOC 13.6.52
RN295	302 FTU	To SAAF 31.7.45 (1714 N-RB)
RN296	302 FTU	To SAAF 27.7.45 (1705 M-RB)
RN297	302 FTU-240-MAEE	Sold 18.6.53
RN298	302 FTU-240-209	Scrapped 5.7.50
RN299	302 FTU-230-201	SOC 4.10.57
RN300	10-201-205-209-205	SOC 30.4.57
RN301	302 FTU	SOC 30.6.51
RN302	302FTU-235 OCU-209-88	SOC 26.12.53
RN303	302FTU-230-209-230-205	SOC 24.1.59
RN304	302FTU-230-FBTS	SOC 20.9.57

Appendix F (*contd.*)

Serial	Units	Remarks
RN305	302 FTU	To SAAF 12.10.45 (1706 O-RB)
RN306	302 FTU-205	To RNZAF 15.12.53 (NZ4118)
SZ559	302 FTU-209	Dragged mooring in typhoon, Hong Kong 18.7.46
SZ560	302 FTU-205-209-230	SOC 15.10.57
SZ561	302 FTU	To RNZAF 18.19.53 (NZ4114)
SZ562	302 FTU-209	SOC 15.8.46
SZ563	302 FTU	SOC 25.4.46
SZ564	302 FTU-240	Slipped off trolley 26.9.46 Kai Tak
SZ565	302 FTU-209-201-235 OCU	Crashed off Hillhead, Hants 16.11.51
SZ566	302 FTU-205-209-205-88	SOC 20.9.57
SZ567	302 FTU-230-201-230	SOC 15.10.57
SZ568	302 FTU-4COTU-235 OCU	SOC 19.10.56
SZ569	302 FTU-4COTU-235 OCU-205	Sank Trincomalee, SOC 3.10.50
SZ570	302 FTU-88	Broke from moorings, Kalafrana 28.2.48
SZ571	302 FTU-4COTU-201-209-88-201	To Aéronavale 14.11.57
SZ572	230-88-205	SOC 19.7.57
SZ573	BOAC-230-209	Bomb exploded, sank at moorings, Seletar 26.3.50
SZ574	201	Struck obstruction, Lough Erne, beached 31.5.48
SZ575	302 FTU-4COTU-235 OCU-230 -201	SOC 15.10.57
SZ576	235 OCU-201	To Aéronavale 4.7.57
SZ577	230-88-209-205	SOC 21.5.57
SZ578	201-209-205-88-205	SOC 16.10.57
SZ579	- -	Wrecked before delivery
SZ580	235 OCU	SOC 12.4.50
SZ581	230	Sank at moorings, Wig Bay 2.11.55
SZ582	230	SOC 30.9.57
SZ583	- -	SOC 18.8.49
SZ584	BOAC	To RNZAF 4.9.53 (NZ4115)
SZ598	- -	Crashed en route to Far East 16.2.51
SZ599	MAEE-209-88-209	SOC 21.6.54
TX293	MAEE	Damaged in gale, Wig Bay 9.2.48
VB880	302 FTU-88	To RNZAF 6.7.53 (NZ4111)
VB881	201	To RNZAF 10.8.53 (NZ4112)
VB882	302 FTU-230-209	SOC 5.6.50
VB883	302 FTU-88	To RNZAF 3.11.53 (NZ4107)
VB884	302 FTU	SOC 26.8.52
VB885	302 FTU	Crashed into sea 13.2.46
VB886	4 OTU	Sank 16.3.47, Pembroke Dock
VB887	230-88	SOC 18.7.54
VB888	302 FTU-4COTU-235 OCU-88 -209	SOC 16.8.56
VB889	201	SOC 8.8.56

Appendix G

Sunderland Flying Boats Allocated to the Free French

Serial No.	Received	Designation	Unit
DP182	c.Feb 1943	4E-5	4th GR Sqdn
JM674	c.Feb 1943	4E-6	4th GR Sqdn
JM688	24.7.43	4E-3	343 Sqdn RAF
JM706	25.7.43	4E-1	343 ,, ,,
JM704	7.8.43	4E-1	343 ,, ,,
DV985	9.8.43	3E-4	343 ,, ,,
JM689	8.43	3E-5	343 ,, ,,
DV986	27.8.43	3E-5	343 ,, ,,
DP187	20.9.43	3E-7	343 ,, ,,
DV987	1.9.43	3E-3	343 ,, ,,
W6080	7.8.43	7F-7	—

Appendix H

Squadron Codes

10 Sqdn RAAF	RB
88 Sqdn	RH
95 Sqdn	SE, DQ
201 Sqdn	ZM, NS, A
202 Sqdn	TQ, AX
204 Sqdn	RF (Londons), KG
209 Sqdn	WQ (Catalinas)
210 Sqdn	DA
228 Sqdn	UE, DQ
230 Sqdn	4X, B, NM
240 Sqdn	BN (Catalinas)
330 (Norge) Sqdn	WH
422 (RCAF) Sqdn	DG (Catalinas), 2, Y1
423 (RCAF) Sqdn	AB, 3
461 (RAAF) Sqdn	UT
35 Sqdn SAAF	RB

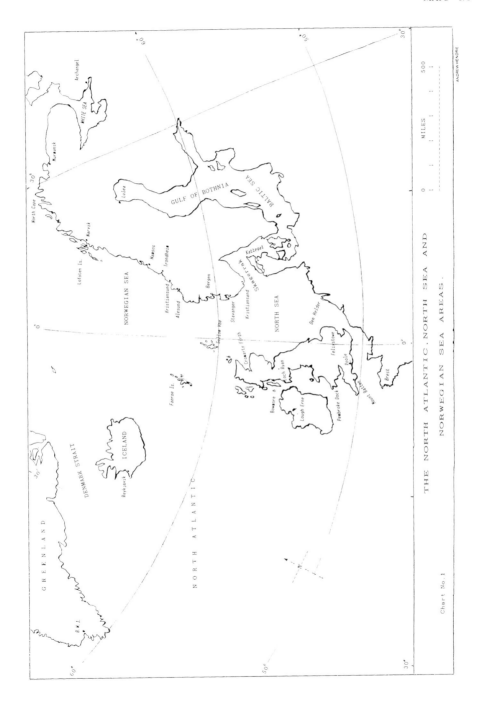

THE NORTH ATLANTIC, NORTH SEA AND
NORWEGIAN SEA AREAS.

Chart No. 1

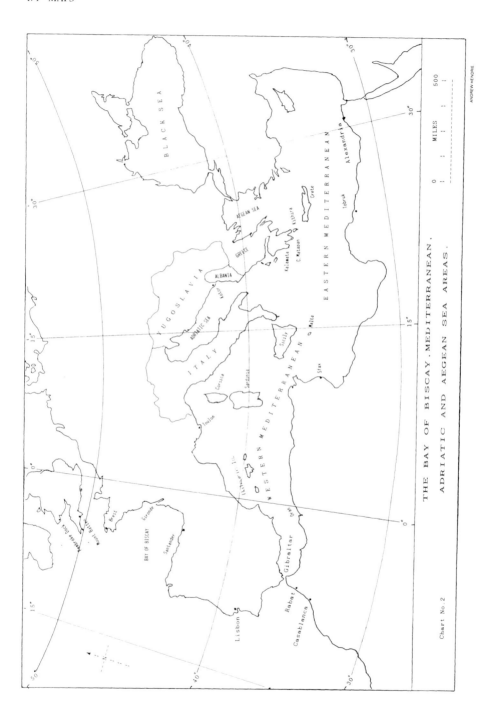

THE BAY OF BISCAY. MEDITERRANEAN.

ADRIATIC AND AEGEAN SEA AREAS.

Chart No. 2

Index